WOMEN'S LACROSSE

WOMEN'S LACROSSE

A Guide for Advanced Players and Coaches

UPDATED EDITION

JANINE TUCKER

AND

MARYALICE YAKUTCHIK

Photographs by Will Kirk and James T. Van Rensselaer

Johns Hopkins University Press
Baltimore

In Association with US Lacrosse

To Lovey, Coach, Diane, John, Ryan, and Devin—you are my inspiration.
—Janine Tucker

To Team Wensel—Brian, Caroline, and Bri—who coach me every day.
—Maryalice Yakutchik

This book was brought to publication with the generous assistance of
US Lacrosse, Inc.

Johns Hopkins University Press
2715 North Charles Street
Baltimore, Maryland 21218-4363
www.press.jhu.edu

The Library of Congress has cataloged the earlier edition as follows:

Tucker, Janine.
  Women's lacrosse : a guide for advanced players and coaches / Janine
  Tucker and Maryalice Yakutchik.
      p. cm.
  Includes index.
  ISBN-13: 978-0-8018-8846-5 (hardcover : alk. paper)
  ISBN-13: 978-0-8018-8847-2 (pbk. : alk. paper)
  ISBN-10: 0-8018-8846-8 (hardcover : alk. paper)
  ISBN-10: 0-8018-8847-6 (pbk. : alk. paper)
  1. Lacrosse for women—United States. 2. Lacrosse for women—Training—
United States. I. Yakutchik, Maryalice. II. Title.
  GV989.15.T834 2008
  796.34'7082—dc22   2007042294

A catalog record for this book is available from the British Library.

ISBN 13: 978-1-4214-1398-3
ISBN 10: 1-4214-1398-1

*Special discounts are available for bulk purchases of this book. For more informa-
tion, please contact Special Sales at 410-516-6936 or specialsales@press.jhu.edu.*

Johns Hopkins University Press uses environmentally friendly book materials,
including recycled text paper that is composed of at least 30 percent post-
consumer waste, whenever possible.

Contents

Introduction

Women's lacrosse is popular across the country and around the world. Photo courtesy US Lacrosse.

WOMEN'S LACROSSE —THE CUTTING EDGE

Worldwide, women from a dozen nations play lacrosse at the World Cup level—and their numbers are on the rise. Unlike basketball and soccer, the game of lacrosse is gender specific. Women's lacrosse is unique, not simply a variation of the men's game. Although both men and women play with sticks and balls and use some similar lexicon, the two games are, in fact, two separate games—always have been, always will be. That's why this isn't a one-size-fits-all book. *Women's Lacrosse* is specifically designed to take the women's game—rich as it is in traditions, skills, and techniques—to the next level.

Women's lacrosse is growing so rapidly that it's imperative to teach and learn the most contemporary skills and techniques as early and as consistently as possible in a player's development, avoiding a later need to break bad habits. This book is both practical and philosophical. It breaks through the mundane by boldly promoting the most innovative, creative, and contemporary approach to teaching and playing the game.

So for whom is this book written? Women in high school and college who play lacrosse or want to play. Men and women who coach high school, club, and college lacrosse. Men and women who watch women's lacrosse. Physical education teachers and athletic directors who may be stuck in the lacrosse of yesterday and are interested in the game of today. Any athletic administrator interested in incorporating this fast-growing and popular sport into their programs.

Coaching and playing lacrosse in high school and college have never before been addressed in one book in such a comprehensive and progressive way, one that embraces the radical and rapid changes that have characterized the sport and continue to redefine it. This book offers a positive and energetic approach to coaching and playing. Its contemporary focus, tone, and philosophy—as well as its everyday practicality—set it apart. It'll be a fun and motivational read that will compel players to put the book down, midchapter, and pick up their sticks to go out and try what they just learned. For coaches, it'll be as important to have on the sidelines as a first-aid kit.

In this book we progress from the quirky origins of women's lacrosse to the modern-day game, logically taking players and coaches through the critical development of basic skills to team concepts and play. Drills and practice plans bring it all together. Especially eye-opening are chapters about the college recruiting process and off-season conditioning—issues never before addressed in any women's lacrosse book.

Women's Lacrosse speaks personally and directly to players and coaches at every level, from high school through international play. It will give them "the cutting edge" throughout their careers.

For the NCAA website dealing with women's lacrosse rules, including the latest information on any current changes, as well as related memoranda, interpretations, and so forth, see www.ncaa.org/wps/wcm/connect/public/ncaa/playing+rules+administration/ncaa+rules+sports/lacrosse/womens/playing+rules/index.

And use this URL to learn how to order current rule books or download them as PDF documents: www.ncaapublications.com.

Key to Symbols in Diagrams

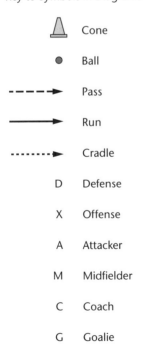

Cone

Ball

Pass

Run

Cradle

D   Defense

X   Offense

A   Attacker

M   Midfielder

C   Coach

G   Goalie

WOMEN'S LACROSSE

1

The Creator's Game, Re-created

Rosabelle Sinclair (back row, far right) introduced women's lacrosse to the United States after playing on her school team at St. Leonard's, Scotland. Photo by Feffie Barnhill, © 2001–2006 St. Leonard's School and Sixth Form College.

The oldest sport in North America, lacrosse has its roots in Native American legends and spiritual practices. Referred to as the "Creator's Game," lacrosse was played to resolve conflicts and heal the sick.

Women's lacrosse was born in Scotland after Miss Louisa Lumsden, the first headmistress of St. Leonard's School, returned home from a trip abroad, where she had witnessed a lacrosse game between the Canghuwaya Indians and the Montreal Club. Of this experience, she wrote: "It is a wonderful game, beautiful and graceful. (I was so charmed with it that I introduced it at St. Leonard's)."

One of Lumsden's students, senior Rosabelle Sinclair, brought the game to the United States. After leaving St. Leonard's, she attended Madame Osterberg's College of Physical Education in Dartford, England, and subsequently was appointed athletic director at Bryn Mawr School in Baltimore, Maryland. She not only introduced the game there in 1926 but, according to the *Baltimore Sun*, "succeeded in injecting her enthusiasm into her pupils with the result that they, in their turn, went to spread the gospel among the colleges in the East."

Here's how Sinclair described the sport with which she was smitten: "Lacrosse, as girls play it, is an orderly pastime that has little in common with the men's tribal-warfare version except the long-handled racket or crosse that gives the sport its name. It's true that the object in both men's and women's lacrosse is to send a ball through a goal by means of the racket, but whereas the men resort to brute strength the women depend solely on skill." All these many years later, skill still defines women's lacrosse, along with strength, athleticism, and speed.

A WOMEN'S LACROSSE TIME LINE

1890—The first women's lacrosse game is played at St. Leonard's School in Scotland. The June issue of the *St. Leonard's Gazette* reports this about the house matches: "Whether the game on the whole has proved successful may be doubted but at least we have advanced so far in its mysteries as to get a good and exciting game in the field with teams of eight and they lasted one hour not including a ten minute interval in the middle, after which goals were changed . . . the game was close and fast but the play rather wild and far too much on the ground."

1926—Rosabelle Sinclair, formerly of St. Leonard's School in Scotland, establishes the first women's lacrosse team in the United States at the Bryn Mawr School in Baltimore, Maryland.

1931—The United States Women's Lacrosse Association (USWLA) is founded as the rule-making body for women's lacrosse. The USWLA governs the sport on the collegiate and club levels until 1981.

1933—The USWLA holds its first national tournament in Greenwich, Connecticut.

1969—The Women's Lacrosse World Championship is inaugurated (later to be replaced, in 1982, by the World Cup tournament).

1971—The AIAW is founded. For the next decade, it will govern collegiate women's lacrosse in the United States and administer national championships.

1981—The number of colleges offering scholarships to women's lacrosse players: 13.

1981—The W. H. Brine Company offers a plastic stick head designed exclusively for women. Plastic sticks are first allowed and most women's teams retire traditional wooden sticks.

1981—Women appear for the first time on the cover of *Lacrosse* magazine in the November/December edition.

1981—The last Association for Intercollegiate Athletics for Women (AIAW) championship takes place, before giving way to the NCAA. The Division 1 champions are (1) University of Maryland, (2) Ursinus College, (3) Temple University.

1982—The first International Federation of Women's Lacrosse Associations World Cup takes place in Nottingham, England. Team USA wins.

1982—In the inaugural NCAA women's championship, the University of Massachusetts beats Trenton State University 9–6 at Trenton.

1984—Tina Sloan Green, Temple University, becomes the first African American female head coach to win an NCAA national championship.

1991—Cindy Timchal becomes the first coach to take two different Division I teams to the NCAA championship tournament (Northwestern in 1983, 1984, 1986, 1987, and 1988 and Maryland from 1991 to 2005).

1994—The first televised women's lacrosse championship takes place at the University of Maryland.

1997—Tina Sloan Green is the first black woman inducted into the National Lacrosse Hall of Fame. As the first African American head coach in the history of women's intercollegiate lacrosse, she elevated Temple University's intercollegiate lacrosse program from the club level to NCAA champion in 1984 and 1988.

1997—The University of Maryland sets a record with the most consecutive matches won: 50, from 1995 to 1997.

1998—The size of the goalie stick increases from 7 to 12 inches.

1998—US Lacrosse forms as the national governing body of men's and women's lacrosse.

2000—Most caused turnovers: Dartmouth—419 in 16 games.

2000—The restraining line is implemented 18 years after having been first proposed to the USWLA Rules Committee in 1982.

2000—University of Maryland junior Jen Adams sets two national scoring records with five goals and five assists in the second half of her team's NCAA championship win; she finishes the season with 136 points.

2001—The University of Maryland women's lacrosse team wins its seventh straight NCAA championship (ninth overall) during a 23–0 season.

2004—Julie Myers becomes the first individual to have won Division I national championships as both student-athlete and coach: in 1991 as student-athlete, and in 2004 as head coach at the University of Virginia.

2005—US Lacrosse mandates protective eyewear.

2005—Australia's 14–7 win over the United States is the biggest winning margin in World Cup history.

2005—In the largest women's lacrosse event ever on American soil, a record 10 teams participated in a 10-day World Cup event, including first-timer New Zealand and a Czech Republic team that had not played internationally since 1993. The US Lacrosse–hosted event took place at the U.S. Naval Academy in Annapolis.

2005—The number of institutions to have won the championship title over a 24-year period is 10: Delaware, 1; Harvard, 1; Maryland, 9; Massachusetts, 1; New Hampshire, 1; Northwestern, 1; Penn State, 2; Princeton, 3; Temple, 2; and Virginia, 3.

2005—Cindy Timchal becomes the second individual to have won Division I national championships as both student-athlete and coach: in 1995/96 as student-athlete and in 2005 as head coach.

2005—Northwestern wins the national championship, becoming the first school located outside the Eastern Time Zone to capture an NCAA lacrosse title at any level, male or female.

2006—US Lacrosse negotiates the largest sponsorship ever for a women's lacrosse team through deBeer for the U.S. Women's National Team.

2006—First year ever for a national media ranking in women's lacrosse; Northwestern University, two-time defending national champion, ranks first.

2006—The number of NCAA Division I member institutions to sponsor women's lacrosse reaches 80. This is more than double the number (39) in 1982, the year of the first NCAA championship.

2006—Hard boundaries are instituted for competition fields.

2007—The NCAA begins writing rules for women's lacrosse. Formerly, the USWLA and US Lacrosse maintained the rules of the women's game.

2007—*Lacrosse* magazine, the flagship publication of US Lacrosse and first feature publication devoted to lacrosse, celebrates its 30th year of production.

2007—At its first induction ceremony, the Black Lacrosse Hall of Fame honors pioneers Cherie Greer (U.S. Elite Team member) and Tina Sloan Green (former coach at Temple University and founder of the Black Women in Sport Foundation, who also played lacrosse internationally from 1966 to 1970).

2007—The Division I championships at the University of Pennsylvania in Philadelphia break all previous attendance records with a total of 12,614.

2008—A woman runs 5.1 miles in an average lacrosse game.

2009—Team Australia is the defending champion at the eighth IFWLA World Cup, hosted in Prague in the Czech Republic.

2010—The annual US Lacrosse Participation Survey reports that more than 500,000 people played organized lacrosse in 2009.

2011—A MedStar study finds that female lacrosse players suffered fewer eye and face injuries after US Lacrosse's 2004 protective eyewear mandate.

2012—More than 680,000 players participated in lacrosse on organized teams in 2011, according to the 2011 US Lacrosse Participation Survey. That figure resulted from an increase of roughly 60,000 players from 2010, the largest one-year increase in the total number of players since USL began tracking national data in 2001.

2013—The NCAA Women's Lacrosse Division I National Championship is won by the University of North Carolina, which defeated the University of Maryland 13–12 in triple overtime.

2

The Complete Player

Good is respectable. Good is admirable.
Good is enough. But good is not great.
   —Nike

Women's lacrosse players aspire to be proficient at both offense and defense.

If you're reading this book, chances are you're not satisfied with being a good lacrosse player. Greatness is within reach.

For every woman who picks up a lacrosse stick, her goal, ideally, is to develop as a complete player with a solid understanding of offensive and defensive skills, concepts, and techniques. To be an effective team player at the highest levels, a woman needs to be solid and consistent both offensively and defensively. This chapter provides detailed descriptions of attack, defense, midfield, and goalie positions in terms of the strengths and skills required to master each, such as speed, stick skills, aggressive play, conceptual understanding of the game, decision-making ability, and the ability to be ambidextrous.

TEAM PLAYER

Lacrosse is a team sport played by 12 individuals who ideally work as a cohesive unit. However, camaraderie is not innate; TEAM chemistry happens only with a conscientious mixing of talents, personalities, styles, and energies. As respect is developed and tolerance for each other's differences is embraced, a TEAM starts to take shape.

One of the biggest distinctions between a good athlete and a great athlete is that her physical skill is complemented by mental toughness. Mental toughness can be developed, learned, and practiced. How? Simply by simulating high-pressure situations. For instance, the Work-the-Middie, the Pressure Box, and the Early Slide drills all create intense situations where stick skills and decision making are paramount. If players are

---

Characteristics of a Complete Player

Athletic: speedy and quick

Tough: mentally and physically

Ambidextrous: equally strong with both hands

Balanced: balance equals body control

Coachable: respectful and eager to try new things

Student of the game: learns every day

Ambitious: never satisfied and always looking to improve

Fearless: an aggressive decision maker who's not afraid to make mistakes

Healthy: conscientious about health and nutrition, respects her body, and understands what it takes to perform at a physical peak on a consistent basis

Humble: values team success over individual accolades

Vocal: not afraid to express herself and get her teammates fired up; understands the importance of communication on and off the field.

Confident and self-assured: recognizes when she's good, but knows that there's always work to do

Fundamentally sound: understands the importance of being able to execute the fundamental skills—all the little things—well and consistently

Responsive: uses criticism, comments, and feedback constructively; makes changes rather than excuses

Courageous: not only has physical courage but the moral courage to do the right things under challenging circumstances

Complete: a team player who has the ability to play both offense and defense

able to play well under pressure in practice, they will play well under pressure in games.

Each of the field positions is important individually but means nothing individually. Each position will be mastered only within the scope of team play. The beauty of women's lacrosse is the ability of each player to recognize and use her teammates' strengths for the good of the whole. Remember, it takes 12 people on the field working together to function as a team. Coach Tucker emphasizes that her players are personally responsible for improving their abilities, not so much for individual gain, but for the benefit of teammates.

Ask yourself this question: What is my job on this lacrosse team? At Hopkins, Coach Tucker looks for this answer: "To make my teammates look good."

> We recognized the importance of this philosophy in 2000, during our second year of Division I play. We had a couple of individual players who tried to take the game into their own hands. The result was that individuals felt the weight of winning on their shoulders, and one can't beat twelve. That's when we adjusted our focus, taking it off of our players as individuals. Everybody started working with, and complementing each other, instead of watching one star. That's when "making my teammates look good" became everyone's job. It became our philosophy. It has stuck to this day.

Embrace this concept—my job is to make my teammates look good—and you'll be on your way to developing as a complete team player.

WHAT'S A FIRST HOME, AND WHERE IS THE COVER POINT?

In the past, there were great first homes and there were great cover points who never ventured far from the crease on their respective sides of the field. The positions now are known as *attack, midfield, defense,* and *goalie.* The modern game has moved away from the more traditional, confusing, and strict "first home, second home . . . cover point, point" terminology to the more contemporary, clear, and interchangeable "attack, midfield, and defense." To be great—in fact, even to compete on a high collegiate level—you must be a complete player: one who can hold her own at the offensive as well as the defensive end of the field.

At a Division I program such as Hopkins, the team embraces a "first-seven-down" concept. "First-seven-down" refers to those seven players who, out of transition, are first to make it inside the restraining line. If that turns out to be four attackers and three middies offensively, that's fine; that's a "normal" setup. However, a team could easily end up with four attackers, a middie, and two defenders who beat their midfield teammates down the field and now can take part in the offense. The philosophy is to develop the players on both ends of the field so they won't be at a disadvantage if they find themselves on the other end. When there's a turnover, the seven players who can get into the defensive end the fastest to force the ball carrier to slow down, or "settle" the ball, have the green light to go over the restraining line and defend their goal. "We want the closest and fastest seven players to be able to get down and hold their own on either end of the field," says Coach Tucker.

Back in the day, an overwhelming majority of players were more proficient with either their left *or* right hand. Now, strong players are extremely skilled with both hands. True ambidexterity involves not only two proficient hands but also the mindset of being an attacking defender as well as a defensive attacker. This is the mental toughness that an elite athlete brings to the field every day.

As contemporary as the techniques and skills in this book are, the mindset that still works today can be traced back for centuries, to the origins of the game. When Native Americans played lacrosse, it was to prepare for war; theirs was a true warrior mentality. Their game essentially was battle. Today, that battle continues as you develop your ability to stay strong and aggressive and tough, no matter what happens, both on and off the field.

Traditionally, player positions were set and specifically identified: first home, second home, third home, point, cover point, third man, and so on. Now, the positions are referred to as attackers, midfielders, defenders, and, of course, goalie. Teams have four attackers, three midfielders, four defenders, and a goalie. The change is not simply a matter of semantics. Players today are not specialists so much as well-rounded generalists. A low attacker does not simply work around the crease, which is what a traditional first home did. Attackers now cover the entire offensive side of the field. In fact, attackers are looking not only to score but also to redefend—this is known as *riding*—to get the ball back. As a result, they may find themselves anywhere on the field.

How does a player develop her skills on both ends of the field? Based on a five-day practice week, players who are offensively oriented, or most comfortable on the offensive end of the field, should for instance focus three days a week on shooting and dodging, and two days a week developing defensive skills such as the ability to close a double team. Defensive players might work three days a week on footwork, balance, checking, and individual defensive skills and two days a week on shooting and dodging.

Learning offensive skills not only helps a defender to be "complete," but also helps her to be a better defender. If she is privy to the skills that attackers are taught to beat her, then she'll be more effective defending them and "reading" their moves. Traditionally, the skilled stick handlers ended up playing attack. The raw athletic players—those who perhaps lacked in stick skills—were relegated to the defensive side where their tasks were clearly defined: Create a defensive stop, pick up the ball, and deliver it to the player with polished stick skills. Today, there's no place on the lacrosse field for defenders who can't handle the ball. Here are some tried-and-true ways for anyone to develop stick skills: Spend time playing wall ball, get lots of repetitions with a partner, and practice stick tricks. Because today's attackers are more skilled at riding and redefending, defenders must keep improving their ability to handle the ball with both hands, handle it under pressure, and clear it effectively.

A team that's populated with complete players will become a complete team: The *first seven down* are going to be able to hold their own no matter what their "positions" are. No one on a complete team is so pigeonholed that she feels stuck as simply an "attacker" or a "defender." Complete players are convinced that they can help their team on either end of the field; they have the mindset and mental toughness to contribute no matter what the situation.

THE ATTRIBUTES OF EACH POSITION

Attackers

- Are the most skilled stick handlers, feeders, and finishers/scorers
- Create high-percentage scoring opportunities and put the ball in the back of the net, past the goalie
- Feed the ball, setting up teammates to score
- Are the first line of defense, just as the goalie is the first line of offense
- Understand how to "ride" or "redefend" to get the ball back for their team
- Understand how to create space, read a defense, and how to utilize teammates
- Work together as a unit

Midfielders

- Are the fastest players on the field
- Are responsible for contributing on both ends of the field
- Are smart—able to run the offenses that are called, as well as execute various defenses
- Are versatile, fit, and aggressive
- Have polished shooting and dodging skills as well as solid individual defensive skills
- Can close a double team and transition the ball into the offensive end of the field
- Understand how to "ride" or "redefend" to get the ball back for their team
- Know how to communicate, especially on the defensive end of the field

A behind-the-back shot draws cheers from the crowd.

Midfielders are the workhorses of a team—they contribute all over the field.

Defenders

- Are the most relentless players on the field
- Communicate constantly with their teammates
- Defend opponents in the critical scoring area
- Control and contain offensive players
- Have quick feet and the ability to change direction quickly
- Have great balance
- Can maintain correct angles to see both ball and girl
- Can clear the ball successfully under pressure
- Are able to maintain control of body and stick at all times
- Possess the attitude that compels them to wear down and control opponents; are not mere followers, or reactors, but are dictators
- Thwart and take away offensive opportunities
- Anticipate several plays ahead what's going to happen
- Are relentless when a ball hits the ground anywhere near them

Defenders rely on their balance and quick feet.

The Goalie

- Is the *best* communicator on the field; she's the cornerstone of the defensive unit
- Is responsible for stopping opponents' shots
- Starts the offense; when the ball is in her stick, that's the beginning of the offensive push
- Is mobile in and out of the cage
- Is able to pick up ground balls
- Has the ability to clear the ball with both hands
- Is vocal; constructively directs the defense
- Can defend field players when necessary, such as marking an attacker during a ride; is comfortable and confident outside of the goal as well as in
- Regroups the defense after a goal is scored

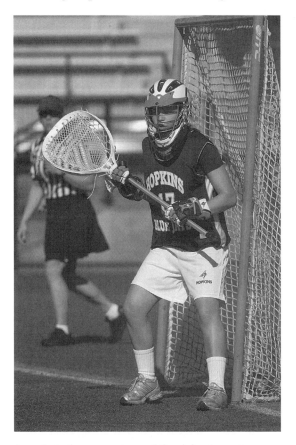

A goalie is the cornerstone of the defensive unit.

THE THINKING PLAYER

Coach Tucker's ultimate goal is to have players who are not known as attackers or defenders, but to have a whole team of complete field players so that she can pick any 11, put them out on the field, and have them hold their own.

Okay, that's pie in the sky. The reality is that players who primarily find themselves on the offensive side will be worked offensively, and vice versa. But each needs to develop respect for what the other does. Coach Tucker says: "I can't tell you how many attack players, when we take the time to teach them defense, share how many revelations they get about how they can turn that knowledge around and use that information to beat the defenders they face. Those lightbulbs are precious. When we teach defenders offensive skills, it gets the wheels turning so they're more prepared for what's coming at them." She tells her defensive players, "Put yourselves in the attacker's shoes. Why? Because once you've learned your opponent's secrets, it's a part of you. It's in your knowledge bank. And that gives you such an edge."

The same is true, of course, for offensive players. When an offensive player sees a defender shift her position in order to force her one way or the other, she's one step ahead of her defender because she's learned how to do that herself. When an offensive player has the knowledge of playing defense and understands defensive skills and tactics, she can predict what the defender is going to do and use that to her advantage rather than being easily contained and controlled.

It is vital to learn, recognize, and respect what an opponent is trying to do. Mastering this can take players to a whole new level of the game. The thinking player holds a distinct advantage over those who are not students of the game. There's no room in today's game for a player who doesn't have the mental capacity to compete.

PLAYER CHARACTERISTICS

The Interactive Player

Coach Tucker enjoys chatty players, especially on the defensive end of the field; she encourages them to give direction, as well as constructive feedback, to their teammates. "In practice, we ask our offensive players, when they beat their defenders, to tell their teammates what they just did to them, so that the defenders have an understanding about why they got beat. We encourage them to immediately discuss and talk through the situation to help each other improve. Very often in practices, players rip each other and that's the end of it. It's more intense and productive when teammates take the time to discuss: 'This is how I blew your doors off; this is what you did that allowed me to take advantage of you.' This interaction reinforces learning, growth, and trust." Players must do this constructively, of course. This type of communication between teammates does not happen overnight, but if it is a part of your philosophy, it can lead to amazing team chemistry and foster consistent communication on the field.

The New Player

Lacrosse is a fairly straightforward game to learn. It's never too late to pick up a stick. The following is a case in point:

Case Study

It's the winter of 2006. Coach Tucker already has settled on her recruiting class for 2007. On a whim, she attends one of the last recruiting tourneys of the year in New England. Her intent is scouting for 2008 prospects (high-school juniors), until she sees a black ponytail flying by and inquires, "Who's that kid?" "That kid" wasn't a junior, but rather a senior who had played lacrosse for only a few months. She had just recently discovered the game; most of her time was spent playing ice hockey with the goal of playing in the Olympics someday. "That kid," with her awkward cradle, sheer strength, lack of experience, incredible speed, fearless attitude, and magnetic energy, ended up with a Hopkins lacrosse scholarship before the day was out.

A team captain knows how to communicate with and motivate her fellow players.

Lacrosse players are not born, they are made! Our sport lends itself to being learned easily and quickly. All it takes is a bit of effort and a lot of heart. A word of advice to those coaches who have raw talent on their teams: patience. Be a cheerleader. In the beginning, when it's not pretty, encourage the new player to keep going. Lacrosse is a sport that attracts athleticism. Any raw talent—whether she's a former rugby, basketball, or ice hockey player—can pick up a stick for the first time in college and within four years, with the help of her teammates and some good coaching, find herself an NCAA Division I champion.

Team Leaders

No matter whether they're appointed by the coaching staff or elected by their teammates, captains are the officially recognized team leaders. That's not to say that other players on the team aren't leaders too. For instance, at Hopkins a cou-ple of years ago, Erinn Dennis, a senior, was not the official captain, but Coach Tucker still remembers her as one of the best leaders ever. The ideal is to have an offensive captain—a quarterback—and a defensive leader who present a united front, a single voice. What's most important is that their teammates respond positively to them. Generally, a leader is sensitive to how she communicates with others and how they respond. Leaders are good at reading body language and mannerisms.

TEAM HIERARCHY

In her 18 years of coaching collegiate lacrosse and recruiting high-school athletes, Coach Tucker has noticed that complete teams adhere to a hierarchy that both respects experienced upperclassmen and nurtures younger players.

Freshmen

You are expected to come in, play your hardest, and emulate the upperclassmen, who, in turn, take you under their wings. You might be responsible for equipment, so don't grouse about picking up balls at the end of practice, bringing out the cones, and gathering the conditioning equipment. These "busy duties" are a rite of passage. Be smart: Keep your self-confidence, recognize your strengths, and bond with the upperclassmen. Think of them as your allies. You, one day, will do the same for younger players. But for now, bide your time and pay your dues. Learn as much as you can. Challenge for playing time. Do whatever you can to help your team succeed.

Sophomores

Remember where you came from; you were a freshman once. Most likely, you have been relieved of such duties as carrying balls. However, lending a hand helps develop camaraderie. Take care of the freshmen. Sophomores have the best understanding of what it's like to be the little ones. If they do something wrong, don't throw them under the bus. Help them to fit in and learn the system. Help provide perspective if they're getting overwhelmed. Assume a nurturing role. Take more personal responsibility for executing consistently what needs to be done within the offensive and defensive units. It's time to demand more of yourself as a player.

Juniors

This is the critical year. You're seasoned and expected to have a solid conceptual understanding of team tactics. Some of you will take on leadership roles, but not everyone can be a team leader. Be the kind of person who others respond to. Try to communicate effectively and constructively. Respect the incoming freshmen and returning sophomores. Continue to play a nurturing role. Your team is only as good as its weakest player. The best way to get respect from younger players is to treat them with respect. This is your time, now, to make a major impact on the field every day at practice and in games. You've earned the right to swagger a bit. Hold yourself to a higher standard.

Seniors

It's your time to lead. You are an extension of the coaching staff. There are natural, in-the-limelight leaders, and behind-the-scene leaders; figure out which one you are. The sheer fact that you made it through three full years at the high-school or college level gives you the opportunity to lead as a senior. Whether you are named a team captain or not, complement your fellow upperclassmen by setting a good example for the younger players. Be a vocal one, or be a quiet one. Be motivating, or be picking up the pieces. But, by all means, be some kind of leader in this, your senior year.

3

The Coach

Watch your thoughts, they become words. Watch your words, they become actions. Watch your actions, they become habits. Watch your habits, they become character. Watch your character, it becomes your destiny.
    —Author unknown

A coach in action.

The Xs and Os are a part of the job. Successful coaches find a way to make an impact on their players in many different ways, on and off the field. Coaches are teachers, motivators, role models, disciplinarians, inspirations, and mentors. Successful coaches break down lessons into easy-to-grasp components, all the while infusing them with positive motivation.

Coaches have different styles, of course, and what works for one might not fly for another. Some are mother figures whereas others are militaristic disciplinarians; both can effectively draw out talent. Coaches need to find a fit, not only for their personas but also for their teams in any given season. A coach's behavior is paramount in setting the tone for a team.

It is important to recognize that teams change each year; players graduate and new players are added to the roster. A team's chemistry changes and the new dynamics must be embraced and factored into a coach's tactics for the season. What are some critical components of coaching?

- Come to practice organized and energized.
- Maintain a positive, constructive approach.
- Stay flexible.
- Show enthusiasm.
- Get to know your players as individuals and as a team.
- Be patient.
- Break the game down into component parts and teach clearly.
- Be a student of the game.
- Create a healthy climate of competitiveness for playing time.
- Demand discipline.
- Provide structure.
- Remember to have fun while developing and teaching your players.

Coaches have to ask themselves, Is the way I handle my team and players effective? Are my coaching and communication styles effective? It's never too late to adjust a coaching style. Some coaches dictate; their communication style is top-down, and that works for them.

Coach Tucker embraces a two-way communication strategy that she calls "coach from the inside out." She considers the athletes that she is working with first as people and then as

Players need discipline from their coach, as well as an arm around the shoulder from time to time.

athletes. She considers their feelings, their personalities, what makes them perform well, and builds around that base. She feels responsible for knowing the individuals who form the cohesive unit that is her team.

THE LEARNING CURVE

As teams change, and as the sport of lacrosse develops, coaches must continue to evolve. It's all about adjusting. Successful coaches have open minds and are true students of the game. They don't ever allow the game to pass them by. They push the evolution of their sport by stealing and applying the best bits and pieces of drills, philosophies, and techniques from a whole range of sports, including basketball, football, soccer, and so on. Successful coaches are innovators who take risks and push the envelope, but all within the spirit of the game. Their creativity can be subtle—tweaking the stance of a center draw specialist, for instance—or dramatic—implementing a high-pressure ride, for example.

Great coaches are students not only of the game but also of the art of coaching; they watch other coaches in all kinds of sports and listen to their interactions and discussions with players, the media, and other coaches. It can be helpful to store away tidbits of important information. Organized coaches might want to write down and file away everything and anything that could inform and influence their own style, whether it's a motivational quote, a faux pas, an exceptional compliment given, or a pithy answer made to the press.

DEALING WITH DETRACTORS

"It's what you learn after you know it all that counts."
   —John Wooden

Coaches have to deal with parents, the media, school administrators, and the public in general. Public relations is part of the job. Everybody's happy after a win, of course. The real test is how a coach behaves after a loss. For instance, are you so angry after a tough loss that you herd your team onto the bus, refuse to allow them to interact with parents and fans, and drive back in silence? Or do you pull them in, offer constructive criticism, and show them by example how to hold their heads up while participating in a postgame tailgate? When detractors feel the need to approach you immediately after a loss, are you confident and firm in your response: "Thanks for your interest. This really is not the appropriate time to discuss today's game." Killing naysayers with kindness can work, if a coach is self-assured. Coaches represent their programs after wins and losses alike. As tempting as it is to retreat to your office after a loss and sit and stew, the right thing to do is to bounce back.

It's a fact of coaching life that you're going to make mistakes and have tough losses. Coach Tucker keeps in mind what her father told her when she first started coaching: "When you're through improving, you're through." "I have found that after a tough loss, it is better to take it on the chin, find the areas to improve, handle the media and critics calmly, and move on," Tucker says. "There is no hiding from adversity—demonstrate this for your players by dealing with it."

COACHING STYLES

Good coaches can be developed. One of the first things to master is communication. As a coach, you're a member of a team-within-the-team: the coaching staff. If you recognize you have a certain style, surround yourself with assistants who balance your strengths and weaknesses. For instance, if you're a taskmaster, a black-and-white disciplinarian, find an assistant coach who respects this style and will complement, not exacerbate or undermine it—a coach with a softer side, perhaps; one who's a listener as well as a communicator. Teams consist of a variety of personalities. Therefore, if you have a mix of personalities on your staff, the odds are greater for real connections to be forged between the coaches and players. Coaches have a choice; they can force players to react to one style of coaching—their style—or they can try to recognize and respect the differences in personalities, motivations, and abilities, and build from there.

READING YOUR PLAYERS

Everyone's fine with compliments. We're talking sticky situations here. How do you get a not-so-welcome message across to a particular player? Keep in mind that your mission is to get the best out of your player, not get the best of your player.

When a major mistake is made on the practice field, or in the middle of a game, address it immediately. Look the athlete in the eyes and gauge reactions. Be aware of the athlete's body language. Readjust. Reposition. Make her move. Walk her three feet farther down the sideline to a different space and start over again. A soft and measured comment can make as much of an impact as any screaming match. Sometimes it's appropriate to get fired up in a player's face and demand better from her; other times, an arm around her shoulder will work. The best coaches visit the entire spectrum of emotion. Ask yourself, "Is the manner in which I'm communicating effective at this moment?" If your gut tells you no, then make a change. The goal is to get through to the athlete. At the very least, you want the athlete to want to listen to you—to be receptive, and not tune you out. You are trying to teach her. Never lose sight of that.

Just as a coach's style and mannerisms are critical to good communication, so are a player's style, body language, and reactions important. Any player who is resistant to feedback, or doesn't want to be called out and encouraged to improve, as well as any who are openly defiant need to be removed from a game, a practice, or a sideline. Address the player privately, later, rather than make a scene or demean her in front of her peers. A removal or sharp reprimand shapes everybody up fast. How? It gets compliance. It sparks understanding. It outlines the boundaries. It reiterates who's in control. It makes a statement. Well-timed statements can be very powerful.

DEVELOPING A PHILOSOPHY

Have a philosophy. Have a method for the madness. Have a mantra. Practice plans do not a coach make. Coaching requires a big-picture perspective. What are your goals? Are you going to be the scrappiest team? Are you going to be up-tempo, pushing the ball? Are you a control team, holding the ball? Are you going to be renowned for your relentless riding ability? Are you after a state championship, or is your focus on developing stick skills in a team full of inexperienced players? Are your sights set on an NCAA championship, or a conference championship? Are you shooting for the Top 5 or hoping to crack the Top 20? It's all about setting realistic, attainable goals.

Important as a philosophy is, don't lose sight of the little, day-to-day things that can make a difference.

- Wear a whistle; use it.
- Keep *your* face to the sun; make sure that when you address your team, they are not distracted by the sunlight and do not have to squint to focus on you.
- Be aware of your environment, notably sun glare and wind, so that your players can comfortably focus on you or on the drill you are doing.
- Keep the drills short and sweet; anything longer than 15 minutes and you'll start losing focus.
- Write down your goals as a coach and your philosophy. Read them before you plan your practices and as you are evaluating your games. Sometimes a loss is worth five wins later in the season if your team learned from the mistakes they made.

Coaches at the highest levels are being paid to win. But even so, they and their teams can enjoy accomplishments, even in the face of a loss. The best coaches spend precious time and energy pursuing *success* in addition to focusing on winning. Success can mean lots of things, not just winning but behaving with class and integrity, displaying good sportsmanship, never giving up, handling adversity with grace, and focusing on making teammates better. A savvy coach can infinitely expand the definition of the word *win*. Your players win every time they push themselves to learn something new about the game of lacrosse, or improve their athleticism or skills, or infect each other with the excitement of being involved with a team. They win every time they follow directions, exhibit confidence under pressure, and handle each other's unique personalities. They win when they come back for more after they thought they were spent and when they deal gracefully with success as well as perceived failure. They win because their characters are, at least in part, being shaped and molded by you, their coach.

Coaching entails organizing and controlling group behavior and creating an atmosphere of good habits through positive energy and reinforcement. Before every practice, when Coach Tucker steps onto the field, she scans all of her players' faces:

> I like to bring the girls in and give them an idea of what we're going to be doing at practice. Are all eyes on me? Do I have their attention? If the group's too quiet, I tell the captains to get some energy into these people. If the group's not focused, I immediately blow the whistle and bring them back in front of me and challenge them. I tell them I'm disappointed in the lack of focus; that always gets them going. Players do not want to disappoint their coach. When we are having a solid practice, I compliment them on their tremendous energy. I've noticed that the players go as the coaches go, and the younger girls

go as the older girls go. If I've had an off day and am not energetic, it can have an impact on the behavior of my team. Even worse is when the upperclassmen aren't engaged and up—that impacts the younger players. The team and coaching staff have to feed off of each other and infuse energy into every minute of practice. Otherwise, it's a waste of time.

If you are in the middle of a practice where everyone is just going through the motions, FIX IT:

> Blast the whistle and bring the team together right in front of you.

> EYES ON ME! Look them all in the face. Get their attention and focus. You need to make a split decision—do you make some demands on what you'd like to see—whether it's more energy, more focus, more consistency—or do you break the monotony of it all and tell them a joke? Diane Geppi-Aikens, the legendary coach of Loyola College and a dear friend of mine, was notorious for the latter. The team would be in the midst of an awful practice and she would be fuming. Her face would get red, her veins would pop out and she would scream, 'Get in here!' The team would gather, heads down, ready to be yelled at and Diane would tell some crazy joke and everyone would crack up. She would then let the girls know what she wanted improved for the rest of practice and inevitably, things would improve.

- Put inflection in your voice.
- Give them the eyeball.
- Make your demands: "I will not accept anything less than . . ."
- Challenge a couple of individual players: "Mary and Alex, you are personally responsible for the energy level of this team

for the next hour of this practice!" When you give a specific player a specific task, the group will likely feed off of them.
- Or, put the team on the end line. Get a couple sprints out of them. When their blood is flowing, they'll be ready to work. Remind them: It's not a punishment; it's a wake-up call.

Here are some words that describe coaching style. Which ones apply to you?

Patient	Psycho
Constructive	Clueless
Enthusiastic	Out of control
Knowledgeable	Disheveled
Trustworthy	Panicked
Inclusive	Condescending
Competitive	Dictator
Dynamic	Boring
Personable	Listless
Flexible	Lifeless
Fair	Maniacal
Direct	Stale
Inspiring	Antagonistic

COACHING RESOURCES

There are personal resources as well as educational and organizational ones. Mentors are the best personal resources. Seek them out and tap their knowledge, experiences, and advice. Another path to take is simply to enhance your life skills in general. Seminars and self-help books abound on such topics as time management, leadership and supervisory skills, effective communication, team building, anger management, dealing with difficult people, and so forth.

US Lacrosse is the governing body of the sport. It has developed a highly recommended coach's certification program and sponsors coaches' clinics nationwide. Visit www.uslacrosse.org for more information. The Positive Coaching Alliance advocates good, positive coaching. It's not as touchy-feely as it may sound; it's all about treating players and opponents with respect and dignity, a time-honored tradition that happens to work effectively. The PCA sponsors seminars and workshops for coaches at all levels. Visit www.positivecoach.org for more information.

Good luck, Coach!

4

The Game

The game of women's lacrosse is fast, fluid, and fun to watch. Courtesy US Lacrosse.

THE FIELD

The rectangular field is marked with a solid-lined boundary (see figure 4.1). The playing area should be 101 meters to 128 meters (110 to 140 yards) from end line to end line and 55 to 64 meters (60 to 70 yards) from sideline to sideline. The goal cages are no more than 92 meters (100 yards) and no less than 82 meters (90 yards) apart. There must also be a minimum of 9 meters (10 yards) of space behind each goal line, extending to the end line and running the width of the field. There must be a minimum of 4 meters (4.4 yards) of space between the sideline boundary and the scorer's table. There should be at least 4 meters of space between the other sideline and any spectator area. There should be 2 meters (6 feet, 6 inches) of space beyond each end line.

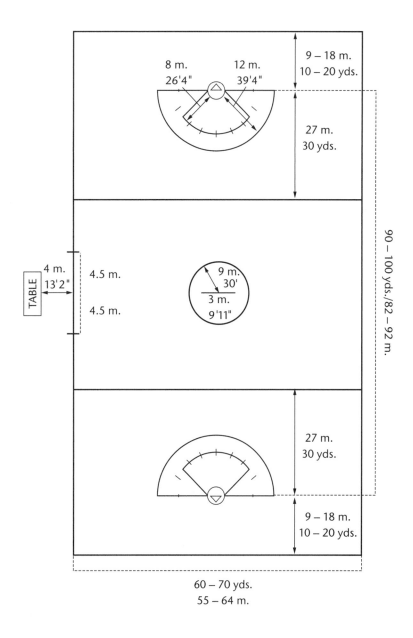

Figure 4.1   Field diagram from the
NCAA rulebook

Where these field dimension requirements are not or cannot be met due to field space limitations, play may take place if both participating teams agree and if the visiting team has been notified in writing prior to the day of the game. However, the minimum distance of 9 meters (10 yards) of space from goal line to end line must be maintained. Soft, flexible cones or pylons must be used to mark the corners of the field.

The playing area must be flat and free of glass, stones, and any protruding objects. It is the host team's responsibility to see that the field is in proper condition for safe play and that the field is consistent with the rules.

When lining a field, all lines must be 5 to 10.1 centimeters (2 to 4 inches) wide, except the goal line, which must be 5 centimeters (2 inches) wide. *The restraining line,* a solid line 27 meters (30 yards) upfield from each goal line, extends across the width of the field. The restraining line, which limits the number of players that can be in the offensive/defensive end at one time, must be clearly distinguishable as the restraining line, for example, the only line on the field, or marked in a different color, or marked with Xs. Cones may not be used for this purpose. There is a center circle, radius 9 meters (30 feet), and through the center of this is a line 3 meters (9 feet, 11 inches) in length, parallel to the goal lines, which, if extended, represents the 50-yard line. This is where the center draw takes place to start each game, to restart the game after goals, and to start the second half.

Two arcs are marked: 8 meters (26 feet, 4 inches) and 12 meters (39 feet, 4 inches) from the goal circles. These are used when fouls occur. They are measured from the center of the goal line: 10.6 meters (34 feet, 10 inches) for the 8-meter mark and 14.6 meters (47 feet, 9 inches) for the 12-meter mark. The *8-meter arc* ends on a line on each side that runs from a point on each side of the goal circle, where, if the goal line were continued, it would cross the goal line. This line is at a 45-degree angle to the goal line extended. The *12-meter fan* ends at the goal line extended.

The 8-meter arc is sectioned off by hash marks 30.5 centimeters (1 foot) in length, perpendicular, and bisecting the arc. These are measured at 4, 8, and 12 meters, respectively, from either side of the center hash mark, which is measured from the center of and perpendicular to the center of the goal line (10.6 meters/ 34 feet, 10 inches). Two additional 30.5-centimeter (1-foot) marks will be made 8 meters from the goal circle, perpendicular to the goal line extended. On each end of the field is a *crease*, or *goal circle*, that measures 8½ feet from the center of the goal line and surrounds the goal cage. Goal cages measure 6 feet by 6 feet.

Each team has a *substitution area* in front of the scorer's table and centered at the midfield line. Two hash marks section off the area; these are placed perpendicular to the sideline 4.5 meters (5 yards) on either side of midfield. The penalty area, where players serve their time after receiving a yellow card, is directly in front of the scorer's/timer's table at the rear of the substitution area. A player serving a penalty must sit or kneel in this area. The *team bench area* extends from the end of a team's substitution area to the team's restraining line, and behind the level of the scorer's table extended. A scorer's/ timer's table is set midfield, at least 4 meters behind the designated playing boundaries on the team's bench side. An accurate visible score is continuously displayed. A visible clock is recommended.

Coaches must remain within their own *coaching areas*, that is, the area on the bench/ table side of the field extending from their team substitution area to their end line, and behind the scorer's table extended. However, college coaches can now come up to the sideline. Non-playing team personnel such as injured players, trainers, and athletic administrators must remain in their team bench area. Violation of this rule is a misconduct foul.

Spectators must stay at least 4 meters from each sideline. No spectators are allowed behind the end lines except in permanent stadium seating positioned behind protective netting or fencing.

An unmarked area of the field about 15 yards around and 10 yards behind the goal circle is "the critical scoring area." This is used to evaluate shooting space.

EQUIPMENT

The Ball

A lacrosse ball is solid rubber, is slightly smaller than a tennis ball, and weighs about 5 ounces. At all levels, women are required to play with a smooth, yellow ball.

There are many different types and styles of lacrosse sticks available today.

The Stick

Women's lacrosse sticks consist of a head, neck, shaft, pocket, sidewall, throwing strings, and sidewall strings. Sticks with plastic heads are the most popular among today's players because they are light, aerodynamic, and flexible. The shapes of the stick heads vary widely, offering advantages such as greater ball control, a quicker release of the ball, a deeper pocket, and the ability to pick up ground balls more easily. The plastic head of the stick is screwed onto the shaft or handle at the neck. Stick shafts are made of aluminum, titanium, wood, or a composite material. Stick heads can have open or closed sidewalls for greater or less flexibility. Most sticks today have at least a partially open sidewall. Wooden sticks are still available and some players still use them. The pocket of a wooden stick is strung with vertical thongs of leather or synthetic material and woven in a criss-cross pattern with gut or nylon strings. The pocket of a plastic stick head is strung with vertical thongs of leather or synthetic material and cross-woven with nylon strings. In the girls' game, only the goalie's stick can be strung with a mesh pocket.

The Pocket

A women's lacrosse stick is considered legal only if the top of the ball is ABOVE the sidewall. Sticks are designed today with smaller sidewalls that allow for deeper pockets and, thus, greater throwing velocity and accuracy. Before a game begins, the umpire checks each player to make sure the pocket of her stick is legal and to assure that she is wearing a mouthguard and goggles. A player with an illegal stick will be asked to tighten her pocket and have it checked again before she is able to take the field.

Stick Length

Women's lacrosse sticks must be between 35½ and 43¼ inches long. A goalie stick should measure between 35½ and 48 inches long and can be strung traditionally, with leather and nylon, or with mesh. The head of a goalie stick is much larger than that of a field player's stick, measuring 13 by 16½ inches.

Mouthguards

All players must wear mouthguards not only during games but also at practices. The rule states that all players must properly wear a professionally manufactured intraoral mouthpiece that FULLY COVERS the upper jaw teeth. There are a number of different kinds of over-the-counter mouthguards that can be molded to fit comfortably. Many players choose custom-fitted mouthguards.

Eyewear

All players must wear eye protection that meets the most current American Society for Testing and Materials (ASTM) standards. There are many types of eyewear/goggles to choose from. It is important that the eyewear you choose fits comfortably.

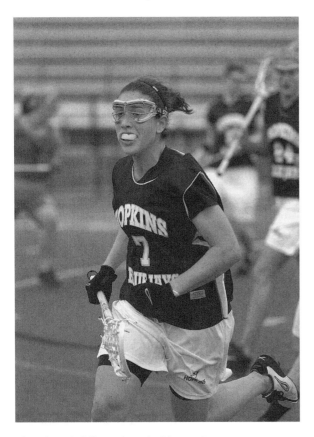

This player is fully equipped with goggles, mouthguard, gloves, and stick.

Other Personal Equipment

Field players may choose to wear close-fitting gloves, nose guards, soft headgear, and close-fitting cloth sweatbands.

Goalie Equipment

Goalies must wear the following protective equipment: a helmet with a face mask, a separate throat protector, padded gloves, a mouthpiece, and a chest protector. Protection for the legs and abdominal area is strongly recommended for collegiate play and is mandatory for high-school and youth play; abdominal protection is also required at the youth level. High-school and youth players must wear padding on the shins and thighs.

PLAYERS AND POSITIONS

A women's lacrosse team generally consists of 25 to 30 players. Twelve players take the field at one time, including a goalie. The remaining team members, on the sidelines, are "support players" ready for substitution. The team on the field consists of one goalie, four defenders, three midfielders, and four attackers. Traditionally, the defenders were called point, cover point, and third man. The traditional names for attack players were first home, second home, and third home. Midfielders were known as defense wings, attack wings, and center. The names of the field positions changed when the restraining line appeared in the year 2000; the change reflects the fact that players now have more flexibility and freedom on the field. Traditionally, for example, first homes rarely left the area around the goal. But attack players of today are encouraged to interchange their positions on the field, playing to the opposite 30-yard line when the opponent has the ball and going over on defense if the situation presents. Lacrosse players today are striving to become COMPLETE—able to hold their own on either side of the field no matter what their "regular" position is.

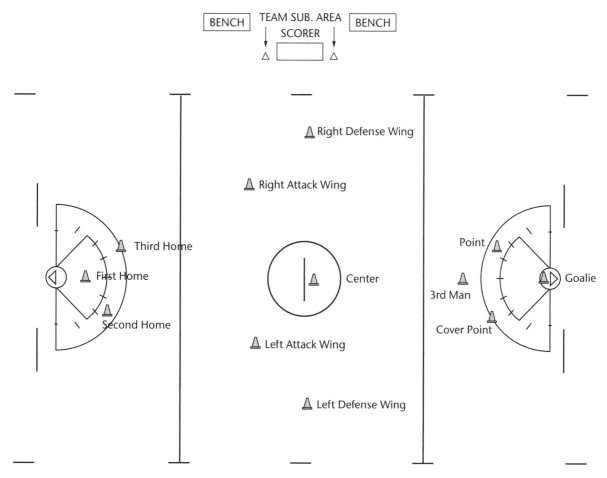

Figure 4.2   Traditional player positions were more specific.

- The *goalie* is responsible for stopping opponents' shots. She is also the player who begins the transition from defense to offense after a save.
- The *defenders* help the goalie by defending opponents in the *critical scoring area,* the area slightly larger than the 12-meter fan in front of the goal that includes a 10-yard area behind the goal. In a player-to-player defense, each defender marks an opposing attacker.
- The *midfielders* are responsible not only for defending their goal area but also for producing on the offensive end of the field. These versatile players do the most running during games; they are responsi-

ble for playing the entire field. The attackers and defenders generally stay on their defensive and offensive ends of the field; however, they are *allowed and encouraged* to move over the restraining line into the opposite end of the field. Any four players can stay back behind the restraining line to avoid the off-sides foul.

- The *attackers* set up the scoring opportunities and assist the midfielders in transitioning the ball into the offensive end of the field. However, attackers have defensive responsibilities. When the other team's goalie makes a save, the attackers are expected to *ride* or pressure their opponents so they can't easily clear the ball

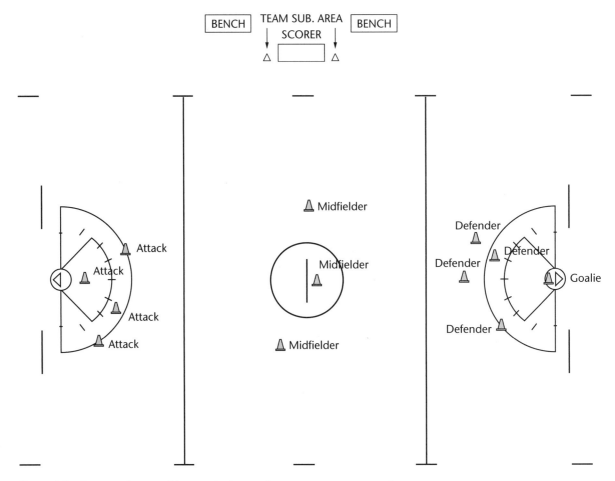

Figure 4.3   Current player positions, as in the men's game, are more general.

out of the defensive end. A *ride* in lacrosse is like a full-court press in basketball. Just as defenders start the offense, attackers start the defense.

• Support players are called on regularly, especially for the midfield positions where players do the most running. The more experience that support players get in practices and games, the faster they will develop game sense and skills.

THE GAME

Length of Game

High-school lacrosse games consist of two 25-minute halves. The game clock runs continuously, stopping after whistles in the last 2 minutes of each half. Some high schools exercise the option of stopping the clock after goals; others keep the clock running. The umpire can also stop the clock for injury or emergency. Halftime is usually 10 minutes. In collegiate women's lacrosse, regulation playing time is 60 minutes, in two 30-minute halves. Halftime is 10 minutes long. The clock stops after every goal, on every 8-meter, and on every whistle in the last 2 minutes of each half.

Scoring

Each goal equals one point. The team scoring the most goals wins. A goal is scored when the entire ball passes completely over the goal line, in between the goal posts, and under the crossbar of the goal cage. The ball can be propelled from an attack player's stick or deflected from a defender's stick or body.

Start of the Game: The Center Draw

A center draw takes place at the midfield on the centerline and is used to start each half of a game and any overtime periods. After a goal is scored, the game is restarted with a center draw at the centerline. At the collegiate level, during the draw, only three players from each team, including the player taking the draw, may be in the midfield area between the restraining lines. However, at the high school level, five players from each team, including the player taking the draw, can be in the midfield area between the restraining lines. Those players positioned around the center circle must have their feet *outside* of the center circle until the whistle blows. All remaining players must be positioned below the restraining lines. All players, with the exception of the two centers, are allowed to move while the draw is being taken, so long as they don't cross into the center circle or step over the restraining line, until the whistle blows. The umpire will raise an arm and say "ready" while starting to back away, to signal the players taking the draw to get ready. The players at the center draw must remain motionless until they hear the whistle. On the whistle, the two players pull their sticks up and away from each other's stick. This motion should send the ball higher than the heads of the players taking the draw, in order for a draw to be legal. A free position will be given to the opponent in the event of an illegal draw. The player who drew illegally is placed 4 meters (4.4 yards) away from the ball carrier to either side at a 45-degree angle from the centerline and toward the goal she is defending. If both players draw illegally, there will be a redraw. Time out must be taken any time the draw is retaken, unless the ten-goal rule is in effect; then there is no timeout for redraw.

The Throw

A throw is used when two players commit offsetting fouls or when an umpire can't determine which team caused the ball to go out of bounds. The umpire positions two players at least 1 meter (1.1 yards) apart with the defensive player closest to the goal she is defending. The umpire tosses the ball in between the two players, who move onto the ball and try to catch it in the air. Players try to get a step ahead of their opponents during the throw (to cut off an opponent's angle to the ball) and try to extend their sticks as far as possible to get to the ball first.

Out of Bounds

When a player in possession of the ball carries or throws the ball out of bounds or when a player is the last to touch a loose ball before it goes out of bounds, the opponents will be awarded the ball when play resumes. When the ball goes out of bounds, the umpire blows the whistle to stop play and the players must "stand." Carrying or throwing the ball out of bounds is a simple change of possession, not a foul. Exception: When the ball is shot and misses the cage, the player nearest the ball will gain possession. If two players are equally close to the ball as it goes out of bounds after a shot, a throw will take place.

Stand on the Whistle

All play is started and stopped with the umpire's whistle. The ball is "dead" when the umpire blows the whistle and all players must stop and stand still except for the goalie; she is allowed to move inside the goal circle. All players may move when the whistle restarts play. The umpire will direct any player who moves illegally to return to her original position.

Substitution

In women's lacrosse, substitution is unlimited. A team may substitute at any time during play, after goals are scored, and at halftime. Teams may not substitute when play has been stopped for a foul or during a free position shot. A player who was substituted for may reenter the game as soon and as often as needed. Players must substitute through the substitution area in front of the scorer's table. Substitutes must not block the view of scorer's table personnel. The player coming off of the field must completely exit the field before her substitute may run onto the field. This applies to every position on the field.

FOULS

For high-school play, consult the *Official Rules for Girls & Women's Lacrosse* published each year by US Lacrosse, a 200,000-member, non-profit organization that serves as the sport's national governing body, and endorsed by the NFHS. Collegiate play is governed by the National Collegiate Athletic Association (NCAA), which writes and publishes the *NCAA Women's Lacrosse Rules and Interpretations*. It is important to understand that these are two separate rulebooks and coaches should make certain they are using the correct rulebook for their level of play.

The following sections describe some common rule infractions in the women's game.

Major Fouls

Major fouls are called when the stick or body is used in a potentially dangerous way. Stick-to-body or body-to-stick contact has always been illegal.

Players may not use their sticks in an intimidating or reckless manner. They may not recklessly check or swing their sticks toward the bodies or heads of opponents. A player may not position her stick to *hold* an opponent's stick or body, impeding progress. Players may not hold or cradle the ball in their sticks directly in front of their faces.

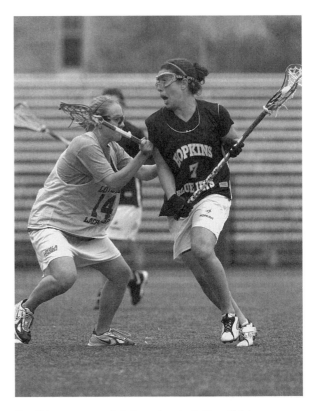

The "shopping cart" defense is a foul: The stick is parallel to the ground and on the body of the opponent.

Some major fouls involve misuse of the body. A player may not block an opponent by moving into her path without giving her a chance to stop or change direction. Players may not push or detain opponents. Ball carriers may not charge opponents, lean into them using their shoulders, or back into them. Players may not set illegal picks in which body contact occurs, that is, picks that don't allow time or space for opponents to stop or change direction. Tripping is illegal. Players may not *false start*, or move, before the whistle starts play.

Several major fouls occur only in the critical scoring area. Defenders may not be in the 8-meter arc for more than 3 seconds without actively marking opponents; they must be within a stick's length of opponents or will be in violation of this 3-second rule. Defenders may not obstruct *shooting space.* Shooting space is the cone-shaped area extending from the ball carrier to the outsides of the goal circle. Defenders may not block the free space to goal when an attacker is intending to shoot or in the act of shooting; however, defenders can be in the cone-shaped area if they are within a stick's length of the opponents whom they are marking. Offensive players may not take dangerous or uncontrolled shots and may not follow through with their sticks in a dangerous manner. Offensive players may not shoot directly at a field player or intentionally at the goalie.

Free Positions

When a major foul is committed in the midfield, the opposing team is awarded a free position where the foul occurred. Time out must be taken when a free position is awarded to the attack player on the 8-meter arc. The player who committed the foul is positioned 4 meters behind the fouled player. The players and umpires are responsible for quickly setting up a free position and restarting play. Players who do not move 4 meters away and have to be consistently reminded to do so are penalized and carded for delay of game.

If the foul occurs within the 8-meter arc, the attack player is positioned on the closest hash mark on the arc and a defender is placed 4 meters behind, on the 12-meter fan. The umpire will clear the arc as well as the penalty lane; all players must clear the 8-meter arc. This allows for a safe execution of the penalty near the goal. On the umpire's whistle, the player with the ball may shoot, pass, or maintain possession of the ball.

If a foul is committed inside the 8-meter arc by the attacking team, the defense will be awarded the ball on the arc and the attack player who fouled is positioned 4 meters behind. All players must be 4 meters away from the ball carrier. Play starts on the umpire's whistle.

Minor Fouls

Minor fouls do not involve dangerous play. A player commits a minor foul when, for instance, she covers a ground ball with her stick, guards it with her feet, or checks an empty stick. Players may not *ward off* opponents with a free hand or arm. Field players may not touch the ball with their hands, use their bodies to keep the ball in the stick, or use their bodies to play the ball. Players may not wear jewelry in a game or intentionally delay the game. For minor fouls, free positions are awarded by moving the fouling player 4 meters away in the direction she approached the player who was fouled. Play restarts on the umpire's whistle.

Indirect Free Position

An *indirect free position* is awarded for a minor foul by the defense that occurs inside the 12-meter fan. The player who committed the foul is moved 4 meters away. The player who was fouled is placed on the 12-meter fan and may not take an immediate shot on goal. She may shoot once an opponent checks her stick or she may pass the ball to a teammate who then can shoot on goal.

Fouls around the Crease

A number of rules govern play around the crease, or goal circle. For example, a field player may not enter the crease or have any part of her body or stick in the crease at any time unless she is "deputizing"—standing in for the goalie. Neither the goalie nor her deputy may hold the ball for more than 10 seconds inside the crease. A player may not, while inside the crease, play the ball in the air or on the ground with her hand if the ball is outside of the crease. A goalie can't cover the ball if it denies the other team the chance to play the ball. Once outside of the crease, she may not step back in while in possession of the ball. If a defender runs into the crease when the goalie is also inside, a minor foul is committed and the attacking team will be awarded an indirect free position on the 12-meter fan out to either side of the goal and level with the goal line. At the high-school level and above, a shooter may follow through with her crosse over the goal circle. Her feet must not touch the goal circle. The shooting motion must be initiated from outside the goal circle, and players directly defending the shooter may reach into the goal circle with their crosses to block the shot or check the shooter's crosse. A defender's feet must not touch the goal circle.

Team Fouls

A team may not have more than seven players over the restraining line in its offensive end of the field, and a team may not have more than eight players (which includes the goalie) over the restraining line in its defensive end of the field. Players may exchange places during play, but it is important to have both feet over the line before a teammate can cross the restraining line. If any part of the foot is over the restraining line, the player will be in violation. When a ball is rolling toward the restraining line, a player may reach over the line with her stick to play the ball, so long as no part of her foot is on or over the line; her foot cannot touch the line.

Yellow Cards

Certain major fouls result in a yellow card being given. Checks to the head or slashing fouls are immediate yellow cards. When a yellow card is given at the collegiate level, the player receiving the yellow card will serve a 2-minute releasable penalty and her team must play short below each restraining line. If the opponent scores, the penalty is released and she can return to the game even if the full 2 minutes have not elapsed. At the high school level, however, when a yellow card is given it is nonreleasable and the offending player must serve the full 2 minutes no matter what. The player receiving the yellow card must sit or kneel in the penalty area, which is in front of the scorer's/timer's table.

Please refer to the NCAA rulebook for complete collegiate lacrosse rules and to the US Lacrosse rulebook for complete high school and youth rules.

UMPIRES

It is the umpires' job to enforce safety and fairness in the game. They use whistles, yellow flags, and sets of green, yellow, and red cards to control the play and safety of the game. According to Pat Dillon, Rules Chair of the Women's Division of US Lacrosse, civilized and professional interaction between coaches and umpires is always encouraged by US Lacrosse, the National Umpiring Committee, the NCAA Rules Committee, and the Women's Division Rules Committee. Umpires should greet both coaches, setting a cordial and friendly tone. Umpires as well as coaches should carry copies of the rulebook in their game bags. Umpires should be willing to take the time to explain themselves to coaches and players when approached in a calm and rational way.

5

Lacrosse Survival Skills

Catching and throwing are two skills critical to the game of lacrosse.

Cradling, throwing, catching, and picking up ground balls—these are some of the fundamental skills of women's lacrosse. At every skill level, there's a profound satisfaction in mastering the basics. Repetition is required. Granted, for some, spending countless hours on the wall can be tedious. However, those athletes who approach the most basic skills with energy, enthusiasm, and a competitive mindset reap the rewards. Think Michael Jordan shooting a thousand foul shots a day. Whether you're involved with the US Elite team or trying out for high-school JV, it's vital to respect and embrace fundamentals. Let us repeat: Repetition required! The most advanced plays in the world aren't going to fly if you can't cradle, throw, and catch.

CRADLING

Cradling, subtle though it may look in today's game, is still the most important of the basic skills in women's lacrosse. The purpose of a cradle is to keep the ball in the stick while the ball carrier is moving quickly up the field or maneuvering through the defense. Maintaining possession of the ball is critical in the game of lacrosse, and possession usually depends upon an effective cradle. Mastering the cradling technique is much easier now that the cradle is a simpler, modified version of its former awkward self. Still, it takes some time to master.

Cradling is a subtle rocking motion with the stick head positioned up, on a slight angle, at one side of the body. Having patience is extremely important and will go a long way. Handling the ball with confidence starts with having an effective cradle with both right and left hands; mastering that takes lots of practice both on the field and off. Challenge yourself to perform daily tasks—everything from brushing teeth to cutting up food—with opposite hands. The rationale is that the more you use your "weak" hand in everyday life, the easier it will be to develop lacrosse skills with both hands. To ensure dexterity with both hands, Coach Tucker introduces several stickwork tricks at the end of this chapter, which are proven to produce confident and creative stick handlers.

The Grip

The grip is all about soft hands. Beware the death grip—squeezing so hard that the knuckles turn white. The fingertips of the top hand are most important in handling the stick. The stick rests comfortably at the point where your fingers meet your palm and is guided by the fingertips. The bottom hand is the anchor; it controls the stability of the stick and is positioned in front of your belly button. Coach Tucker likes to see the thumb positioned up the shaft of the stick while the bottom of the stick rests on the inside of the little finger. The key is a relaxed upper body, including shoulders, wrists, and fingertips. The top hand is the workhorse of the cradle. It should grip the stick *about a third of the way down the handle*. With the stick at an angle, the top hand is off to the side of your shoulder when the bottom hand is at your belly button.

Rocking Motion

The curling motion of the fingers and wrist of the top hand should be smooth and controlled. The top hand will cradle the stick from the player's ear to nose, back and forth, using more wrist than elbow motion. Emphasize a smooth "rocking motion" so that the ball does not bounce around in the stick. Ideally, centrifugal force keeps the ball in the top half of the stick, up by the shooting strings. Keep the upper body relaxed, with the arms loose. A stiff, rigid cradle will lead to the ball popping out—and lots of frustration—as opposed to a smooth, fluid cradle, which will keep the ball in the stick. Coach Tucker recommends the ear-to-nose cradle whenever handling the ball. The "full" cradle, or ear-to-ear cradle, should be reserved for dodging through defenders. The ear-to-nose cradle allows players to pass and shoot efficiently. Remember to give both hands equal time at the top of the stick.

Arm Motion

Keep both arms loose. The top arm moves slightly back and forth with the rocking motion of the wrist and fingers. The bottom arm holds the stick in front of the body—in front of the belly button—and controls the base of the stick. The arms are relaxed and away from the body, not pulled in tight.

Stick Position

Most players hold the stick at a slight angle at the sides of their bodies; the stick head is near

 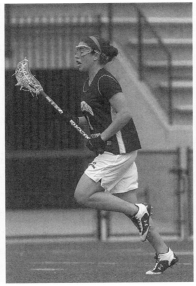 

An effective cradle maintains possession of the ball.

the ear. If a player has no defensive pressure on her, she can carry her stick however she pleases: by her waist, for example, or holding it with one hand out in front. However, when a defender approaches, the player protects her stick by moving it to a more vertical position; the stick head will be by the side of the player's head. Each player, as she matures, will develop her own personal stickhandling style; it'll become her signature. The best players take no small pride in how they wield their sticks.

Two Hands on the Stick

It is important to keep both hands on the stick while cradling. This allows better control and gives the player the ability to pass or shoot quickly. Players may be called for a "warding off" foul if they take one hand off the stick while cradling through defenders and will lose possession of the ball. In an open field, more advanced players like to cradle one-handed with the stick extended out in front of them while pumping the other arm to increase their speed.

Player carrying her stick out in front, one-handed, as she avoids defensive pressure.

Double- and sometimes triple-teaming in the midfield, often called a swarming defense, has become very popular. Players need to develop a cradle that will allow them to maintain control of the ball and run full speed while under heavy defensive pressure. Developing a "tight" cradle for these situations is key. The stick moves in front of the body and the motion is ear to ear or shoulder to shoulder, with the head of the top of the stick around the player's eye level. The top hand is in a choked-up position at the top of the stick. This cradle gives players a few extra seconds to protect the ball, get out of heavy defensive pressure, or find a player to receive a pass without losing control of the ball.

GROUND BALLS

Picking up ground balls and gaining possession makes a tremendous difference in the success of any team. Every ground ball is an opportunity for possession. Three important points to emphasize whenever a player is going after a ground ball:

1. Watch the ball into the stick.
2. Keep moving.
3. After gaining possession, look to pass the ball immediately to a teammate.

Never stand still and wait for a ground ball. Players must attack every ground ball and should be able to pick up ground balls with both their right and left hands.

Stationary Ground Ball

1. Position yourself alongside the ball.
2. Bend at your knees to get low.

As the right-handed player approaches the ball, she puts her right foot slightly ahead of the ball, positions her head over the ball, and bends her knees to get low. She positions the stick head behind the ball and pushes through the pickup with her bottom hand (the top hand is the guide hand, lining up the stick head with the ball, but the bottom hand does most of the work). The stick is almost parallel to the ground as it moves through the pickup. Accelerate through the pickup, and cradle immediately.

Ground Ball Rolling toward Player

When a ground ball is rolling toward a player, she must continue running to the ball as fast as possible. "Running through" a ground ball is an excellent habit. As the player approaches the ball, she extends her stick head to the ground on the side of her body (not out in front of her) so the angle of the stick is almost perpendicular to the ground. Her top hand should be slid about a third of the way down the stick. Having the stick positioned almost perpendicular to the ground provides the maximum amount of surface space the stick has to offer for the ball to roll into. Picking the ball up on the side of her body allows the player to protect the ball from approaching defenders. As the ball enters the stick, the player must give back with the stick toward her body so the ball does not pop out. In a quick fluid motion, she brings the stick up and begins to cradle. The player has a "soft" top hand when picking up a ground ball and a firmer bottom hand for control. Giving back with the momentum of the ball as it rolls into the stick and continuing to "run through" will ensure a smooth pickup.

Ground Ball Rolling Away

There are three important points when picking up a ground ball that is rolling away.

1. Catch up to the ball.
2. Cut off any defenders.
3. Bend at your knees to get low.

Lazy players often reach out in front and bend at the waist, instead of at the knees, to try

Player positions her head over the ball and her foot slightly ahead of the ball in preparation for the ground ball pickup. As the ball meets her stick, she pulls back slightly, immediately brings the ball up toward her head, keeps her stick out in front to protect it from defenders, and immediately starts her cradle.

to pick up a ground ball rolling away. As a result, they end up pushing the ball, thus wasting time, energy, and a potential possession. An efficient player catches up with the ball first, as quickly as possible. When she is alongside the ball, she bends at the knees and lowers her backside to the ground. Her dominant foot is in front of the ball; this guarantees that she is in proper position to pick it up. The player extends the stick head toward the ball, aiming just behind it. At the same time, the player's bottom hand also lowers so that the stick is almost parallel to the ground. Emphasize the bottom hand dropping the stick almost parallel to the ground (the player will almost scrape her knuckles) to effectively push through the pickup. The top hand guides the stick behind the ball while the bottom hand pushes the stick through the pickup, just like shoveling snow. The player stays low until the ball is in her stick; standing up too soon causes the ball to pop out, giving opponents an opportunity for possession. Once the ball is in the stick, the player starts cradling as she runs through the pickup and brings the stick up to her head to protect it from defenders.

Picking Up a Ground Ball under Pressure

As with an uncontested ground ball, the player must run fast to the ball. She should be aware of the position of her opponent so she can cut her off and block her path to the ball. Players need to use their lower bodies to protect the ball. Always run through a ground ball under pressure. Stopping and batting at the ball are bad habits. Slide the top hand up closer to the head of the stick when picking up a ground ball under pressure. This will help protect the ball as you bring it up to your head to start cradling. If other players are around the ball, one option to consider is flicking the ball to a teammate who is positioned away from the crowd. This is a more advanced concept, best used with players who have an understanding of where their teammates are on the field.

CHANGING DIRECTION: THE PIVOT

Learning to pivot enhances a player's ability to change direction quickly. Pivoting is an efficient use of energy. Unenlightened ball carriers run in big semicircles to reposition themselves. This allows defenders plenty of time and room to adjust their positions and continue marking the ball carrier. When the ball carrier pivots to change direction, she plants either her left or right foot and turns on that foot as though it was nailed to the ground before exploding in the opposite direction. A quick change of direction and pushing off of the pivot foot make the ball carrier difficult to defend against. The ball carrier needs to pivot away from the defense and keep her stick protected as she pivots.

How to Pivot

Pivoting to the right requires the ball carrier to run forward and plant her left foot in front with her weight evenly balanced. She then turns on the balls of her feet toward her right until she faces the opposite direction. Her right foot is now in front, and she explodes out of the pivot by pushing off with her left foot and sprinting forward. Pivoting to the left requires the ball carrier to run forward and plant her right foot in front. She turns on the balls of her feet toward her left until she faces the opposite direction. With her left foot in front, she explodes out of the pivot by pushing off with her right foot and sprinting forward.

Lead with Your Stick

It's vital to protect the stick from defensive pressure while changing direction. Lead with the stick while accelerating out of the pivot. A common mistake when pivoting is to leave the stick exposed and behind for defenders to check. Leading with the stick by thrusting it in front of you while you pivot will prevent a defender from checking on the change of direction.

PASSING AND CATCHING

Lacrosse is the "fastest game on two feet" because a ball moves more efficiently in the air than on the ground. The beauty of this sport is inherent in proficient passing and catching. Proficiency requires repetition—lots of time on the wall—and dedication to consistency in catching and accuracy in passing. Creative drills are key to career-long development of passing and catching skills.

Passing

Passing a lacrosse ball is like throwing a baseball. Similar techniques are used to release the ball accurately. When throwing a baseball, a right-handed player does the following:

- Rotates her hips and shoulders
- Reaches back with her throwing arm with the ball above her head (not pushed from her chest)
- Steps toward the target with her opposite foot
- Rotates her hips and shoulders toward the target and into the pass
- Snaps through the pass with her wrist
- Follows through, bending at the waist and completing the rotation of hips and shoulders

The same steps apply when throwing a lacrosse ball. It's a good habit to keep moving when passing; this ensures accuracy and momentum behind the ball.

Set the Feet

The player begins by facing her passing partner. The passer's feet should be offset about shoulder-width apart. A right-handed player will have her left foot in front of her right; a left-handed player will have her right foot in front of her left.

Rotate the Hips and Shoulders

The passer rotates her hips and shoulders so that her shoulders are perpendicular to her passing partner while reaching back with her stick (similar to when throwing a ball). The top hand should be back and above the head (not in front of the body by the chest).

Hand and Arm Position

The passer's arms are out and away from the body with the top hand slid about a third of the way down the stick. The thumb of the top hand is extended up the shaft of the stick, which helps the passer to throw accurately. The other hand (positioned in front of the body) is at the bottom of the stick; the four fingers are wrapped around the shaft with the thumb pointing up. This hand powers the pass.

The Push/Pull Motion

The passer reaches back so that the top of her stick is behind her head and about 6 inches above her shoulder. The bottom hand must stay in front of the body and at chest height. If the bottom hand is raised higher than that, the stick will become parallel with the ground and the ball will either roll out of the stick behind the passer or go straight up in the air on the release. She steps forward with her opposite foot (shifting her weight from the back foot to the front), drives the bottom arm forward, and then executes a push/pull motion by using her top hand and arm to push the stick forward while the bottom hand and arm pull the stick toward the body. This motion makes the stick act like a lever and ensures direct, accurate passes. The passer snaps her wrist through the push motion. The follow-through of the stick should be across the body to the opposite hip, not under the armpit. At all costs, avoid just pushing with the top hand and not pulling with the bottom. The top hand pushes but then quickly develops the snap on the release of the ball out of the stick. This snap helps to add pace and speed to the pass and makes it much more accurate and direct.

Completing the Pass

As the passer steps to complete the push/pull motion, her shoulders and hips are rotating through the pass. Her top arm should extend in the direction of the person to whom she is passing. Collectively, the step forward, the rotation of the hips and shoulders, the snap of the wrist

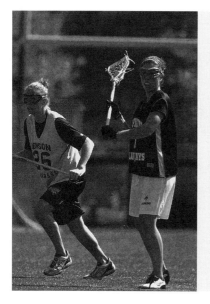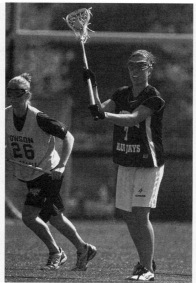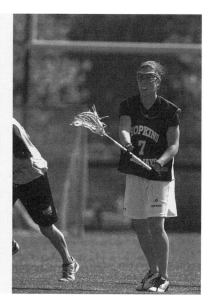

Left: Preparing to pass—arms are away from the body and relaxed, stick is at a slight angle, and player is reaching back to pass. *Center:* The passer is executing a push/pull motion—pushing with her top hand while pulling with her bottom hand. *Right:* The passer releases the ball and continues with her follow-through *across* her body.

through the push/pull motion, and the follow-through of the stick across the body are what give the pass its power. The accuracy of the pass depends upon the follow-through. If the follow-through is toward the ground, the pass will go low. If the follow-through is high, the pass will probably sail over the target. Point the stick exactly where you want a pass to go when releasing the ball. The follow-through is then across the body.

The Flip Pass

The flip pass is a more advanced skill. The player releases from her hip to pass around a defender's stick. Out of the cradle, the passer drops her stick to waist level, parallel to the ground, with the ball resting near the throwing strings. The bottom hand pulls toward the body while the top hand pushes and snaps from the hip. Finish the pass by snapping through with the wrist of the top hand and following

through toward where you want the ball to go, as in the overhand pass. Coach Tucker advises rolling the stick head over as you're pushing with the top hand and pulling with the bottom; this way, the open face of your stick ends up pointing toward the ground, resulting in a much more direct pass than if you didn't roll your stick.

The Riser Pass

This precursor to the riser shot is a more advanced skill. Learning how to catch a ball that's coming from low to high, as well as how to release a riser pass/shot will add to the development of stick skills overall.

Set the feet. The right-handed passer has her feet slightly offset, with her left foot in front.
Hand position. The top hand is halfway down the stick, with the bottom hand controlling the bottom of the stick.

Left: For the riser pass, the stick drops low, parallel to the ground, and the passer bends her knees. *Center:* The pushing/snapping motion of the top hand is complemented by the pulling motion of the bottom hand. *Right:* On the release, the passer rolls over her stick head to ensure accuracy.

Stick position. Out of a cradle, the player drops her arms and bends her knees, dropping her stick parallel to the ground so that the head, facing up, is only inches from the ground.

The push/pull motion. As the player rises from a crouched position, the bottom hand comes up to guide the stick and the top hand starts to push and snap as the player lifts the stick from low to high, ultimately rolling the stick head over to complete the follow-through. The stick head ends up pointing at the target.

The Behind-the-Back Pass

This versatile pass is fun to execute and can be used all over the field. It can also be developed into a shot. Having a relaxed upper body and soft hands serves to improve stick handling skills across the board. The behind-the-back pass forces players to loosen up. Relaxation of the upper body is key, especially rotating the hips and shoulders.

Set the feet. The right-handed passer starts with her feet, hips, and shoulders perpendicular to the player receiving the pass.

Stick and arm position. The passer slides her top hand halfway down her stick, extending the stick back and behind her at waist level, keeping it parallel to the ground. The top arm is outstretched, elbows slightly bent. The bottom hand is at the base of the stick and is positioned above her right hip.

The push/pull motion. The passer steps with her left foot on a diagonal and leans slightly forward. She uses her bottom hand to push while her top hand pulls the stick toward her opposite shoulder, where the pass is released. The midpoint of the shaft makes contact with the opposite shoulder (not the head).

The Lob Pass

The lob pass is executed exactly as it sounds. The passer lobs the ball over the heads of the defenders to her teammate, who generally catches it over her shoulder and while on the run. It is an effective pass in starting an offensive fast-break situation if the player receiving the ball can get a step on her defender. The lob pass can also be used to "switch the field" or send the ball from one side of the field to the other to move the ball into open space, away from defensive pressure.

Set the feet. The lob pass covers a lot of distance, so a passer needs to shuffle into the pass to get momentum behind the rotation of her hips and shoulders. Her feet should be offset about shoulder-width apart. A right-handed player will have her left foot in front; a left-handed player will have her right foot in front. The passer will shuffle forward a couple of steps while rotating her hips and shoulders and reaching back with her stick. The passer may slide her top hand halfway down the stick for leverage.

The release point. To make the lob pass loopy enough, the passer must release the ball while her stick is still slightly parallel to the ground. For enough height, make sure the follow-through ends up pointing toward the sky.

The Reverse Stick Pass

This advanced pass can also be used as a deceptive shot. For a right-handed player, the stick starts on the right side of the body but is then pulled across the body to the left side, where the pass is released.

Set the feet. The right-handed passer starts with her feet, hips, and shoulders square to the receiving player.

Stick and arm position. The top hand is slid about a third of the way down the stick and arms are relaxed and away from the body. The passer cradles on her right and then pulls the stick across her body. Using the fingertips of the top and bottom hand,

the passer rotates the stick head so it is open toward her teammate. Keep the bottom hand further out than the stick head to allow the stick to be at an angle to keep the ball secure.

The push/pull motion. Step with the right foot, and push with the top hand as you pull with the bottom hand. The key is to "snap" the wrist so the pass has some zip. This is a pass that is powered by the arms more than the rotation of the hips and shoulders, so a quick snap of the wrist will make for an accurate, direct pass.

Catching

The catching action actually begins while you're watching the ball in the air and following it into the stick. As players become more proficient with catching, they will see the ball peripherally instead of having to turn their heads. Catching should be active, not passive. Always move toward the ball; don't wait for it. Moving toward the ball prevents an easy interception by a defender and is a great habit to develop.

Set the Feet

The player begins by facing her passing partner. The catcher's feet should be offset about shoulder-width apart. A right-handed player will have her left foot slightly in front of her right foot; a left-handed player will have her right foot slightly in front of her left foot.

Ask for the Ball

As the catcher moves toward the passer, she asks for the ball by giving a target. She holds her stick parallel to her body with her top hand slid slightly down. The stick should be off to the side and slightly in front of her head. The bottom hand is in front of the body with the arm across the body at waist height. The head of the stick is slightly in front of the bottom hand to allow the player to give with the ball on the catch.

Left: The reverse stick pass starts with a strong cradle. *Center:* The stick is pulled across the body and the fingers rotate the stick so the ball is facing the target. *Right:* Notice the passer's bottom hand out in front, ready to pull the bottom of the stick toward the body.

The catcher doesn't point her stick at the passer; rather, she keeps her stick parallel to her body so she can catch and immediately cradle, pass, or shoot.

Watch It In

The catcher follows the ball with her eyes at all times. She watches the ball into her stick and gives back gently with the momentum of the ball as it enters the pocket. As the ball approaches, she does not want to move her stick toward the ball to meet it. She slightly gives with her stick and catches behind her ear in a position to protect her stick and begin cradling right away. Avoid batting at the ball. Run through the catch.

Rotate the Shoulders

As the catcher gives, she rotates her shoulders slightly toward the side on which she is catching. The giving motion with the rotation

of the shoulders helps to ease the ball into the stick, protect the stick from defenders, and allow the catcher to cradle, pass, or shoot right away.

DRILLS, DRILLS, DRILLS!

Cradling and Stickwork Drills

Stickwork tricks are designed to help players become comfortable and creative while handling their sticks. Tricks are fun ways to enhance the ball-handling skills of all levels of players. In fact, a steady diet of tricks will have players handling their sticks in ways they never thought possible. Think outside of the box! Practice really does make perfect, and stickwork tricks really do improve stickwork. These tricks are described for a right-handed player, yet each one should be done with both right and left hands. Make sure to have soft hands and a relaxed upper body when cradling, throwing, and catching.

Toss and Catch

Start with the ball in the stick and the stick out in front of your body parallel to the ground. The top hand should be slid at least one-third of the way down the stick; the bottom hand is at the bottom of the stick for control. Knees bent, body in a balanced position. Toss the ball into the air, rotate the stick with the fingers and wrists and catch the ball on the back of the stick (give with the catch like you were catching an egg). Toss the ball from the back of the stick into the air, rotate the stick with the fingers and wrists (the bottom hand does most of the work, and the top hand is the guide), and catch regularly. Remember to give with each catch and rotate the stick with your fingertips and wrists. This trick improves hand-eye coordination and encourages "soft hands." Remember to use both hands!

Bounce Off of the Shaft

Start with the ball in the stick, and in the right hand. The top hand should be about one inch from the head of the stick for control. Toss the ball into the air, bring the stick parallel to the ground with the stick head by your right ear, and bounce the ball off the stick shaft. Pop the ball straight up off the stick shaft and catch. Repeat 10 times and switch to the left hand. Teaching point: Remember to bounce the ball straight up, not out away from your body, to make it easier to catch.

Bounce Off of the Sidewall

Start with the ball in the stick. Have two hands on the stick. The top hand should be slid about one-third of the way down the stick; the bottom hand should be at the bottom of the stick for control. Knees bent, body in a balanced position. Hold the stick out in front of the body, parallel to the ground. Toss the ball into the air, rotate the stick with the fingertips, and bounce the ball off the sidewall of the stick head. Pop the ball straight up off the sidewall and catch. Repeat 10 times and switch to the left hand. For variation, try bouncing the ball on the sidewall as many times as possible before catching.

Toss and Catch, Front and Back

Start with the ball in the stick and in the right hand. The right hand should be slid about one-third of the way down the stick shaft. Knees bent, body in a balanced position. Position the stick at the right hip, parallel to the ground. Toss the ball across the body to the left side and catch behind the back. After the toss, drop the stick head down, behind your right hip (so the stick is perpendicular to the ground) and then using your wrist, bring it back up behind your back to catch the ball on your left side. Now, from behind the back, use a flip of the wrist to toss the ball in front of the body, bring the stick back to the right side, and catch. Repeat 10 times and switch to the left hand. Teaching point: When moving the stick from in front of the body to behind the back, and vice versa, remember to drop the head of the stick down and perpendicular to the ground and then bring it back up again.

Toss and Catch between the Legs

Start with the ball in the stick and in the right hand. The right hand should be slid about one-third of the way down the stick shaft. Knees bent, body in a balanced position. Position the stick at the right hip parallel to the ground. Toss the ball across the body to the left side and catch behind the back. After the toss, drop the stick head down, behind your right hip (so the stick is perpendicular to the ground), and then using your wrist, bring it back up behind your back to catch the ball on your left side. Now, from behind the back, use a flip of the wrist to toss the ball in front of the body. Instead of catching in front of the body, bring the stick up between the legs and catch between the legs. Use a flip of the wrist to toss the ball into the air and catch behind the back again. Repeat 10 times and switch to the left hand. Teaching point: When moving the stick from behind the back to between the legs and vice versa, remember to drop the head of the stick down and perpendicular to the ground and then bring it back up again.

Cradle and Twirl Drill

Cradle the ball on the right side of the head, from the ear to the nose, with the right hand slid about one-third of the way down the stick. After a couple of cradles, when the stick is back by the ear, TWIRL the stick in a circular motion away from the head using the fingertips. Keep the bottom hand in by the body while the top hand and arm extend slightly out from the body. As the stick is TWIRLED back into the regular cradle position, the ear-to-nose cradle begins again. Remember to make a circle with the stick as it is twirled away from the head and then back to the ear. The ball remains on the *inside* of the circle. Repeat 10 times and switch to the left hand.

Cradle and Extended Twirl Drill

This drill is a variation of the Cradle and Twirl Drill. Cradle the ball on the right side of the head, from the ear to the nose with the right hand slid about one-third of the way down the stick. After a couple of cradles, when the stick is back by the ear, TWIRL the stick in a circular motion away from the head using the fingertips. Keep the bottom hand in by the body, but step with the left foot and extend the top hand and arm out from and *across* the body, really exaggerating the twirl. As the stick is TWIRLED back into the regular cradle position, bring the left foot back so the ear-to-nose cradle can begin again. Make an exaggerated circle with the stick as it is twirled away from the head, really reach with the top hand and arm, and then bring the stick back to the ear. Again, the ball remains on the inside of

the circle. Repeat 10 times and switch to the left hand. Twirling the stick can develop into a way to fake before passing, feeding, and shooting.

Wall Ball Routine

Positioning: About 6 to 8 feet away from a wall.

Grip: Top hand slid at least one-third of the way down the stick; bottom hand out in front of the body. Soft hands; handle the stick with your fingertips. Shoulders relaxed. Turn shoulders slightly with every catch and have more of a rotation on each throw.

Stance: Feet shoulder-width apart and one foot slightly in front of the other (left foot in front when throwing right-handed; right foot in front when throwing left-handed).

Catch: Remember to ask for the ball in front on the side of your head and give back softly (catching behind your ear). Your shoulders should turn when you give back with the ball to protect your stick.

Throw: Bottom hand out in front; use a push (with top hand) and a pull (with bottom hand) motion; remember to snap your wrist. Your shoulders should rotate on your throw to give you power and accuracy. Follow through across your body.

The Routine

1. Right hand up, throw right-handed, catch right-handed. Repeat 10 times. Dip dodge to the left hand and

2. Left hand up, throw left-handed, catch left-handed. Repeat 10 times. Dip dodge to the right hand and

3. Right hand up, throw right-handed, catch right-handed, extended twirl reaching to the left, then reaching to the right. Repeat 10 times. Dip dodge to the left hand and

4. Left hand up, throw left-handed, catch left-handed, extended twirl reaching to the right, then reaching to the left. Repeat 10 times. Dip dodge to the right hand and

5. Right hand up to weak side. Twirl your stick away from your head and throw right-handed; catch on the weak side. Remember to flip your stick over—soft hands so you can give with the catch— push the bottom hand out. Repeat 10 times. Pass your stick through your legs to your left hand and

6. Left hand up to weak side. Twirl your stick away from your head and throw left-handed; catch on the weak side. Remember to flip your stick over—soft hands so you can give with the catch— push the bottom hand out. Repeat 10 times. Pass your stick through your legs to your right hand and

7. Right hand up. Twirl away from your head twice, throw right, catch right, switch quickly to your left, twirl away from your head twice, throw left, catch left, switch quickly to your right, and so on (switch right into your passing position). Repeat 10 times.

8. Right hand up. Drop your stick to your right hip, twirl once and pass sidearm, catch right and dip dodge to your left. Drop your stick to your left hip, twirl once and pass sidearm, catch left and dip dodge to your right. Repeat 10 times.

9. Right hand up. Toss the ball high on the wall so you have to really reach for it on the catch. Catch 5 with two hands on the stick (slid down to the bottom so you get a good extension) and 5 with one hand on the stick (slid almost to the bottom of the stick so you still have some control). Remember to pull the stick in quickly to your head after the catch.

10. Left hand up. Toss the ball high on the wall so you have to really reach for it on the catch. Catch 5 with two hands on the stick (slid down to the bottom so you get a good extension) and 5 with one hand on the stick (slid almost to the bottom of the stick so you still have some control). Remember to pull the stick in quickly to your head after the catch.

Routine Variation

After 30 seconds of wall ball, players should jump rope for 30 seconds. This forces players to throw and catch when they are tired; they will have to really concentrate to keep their throwing and catching accurate.

Passing and Catching Drills

5-Point Passing Drill

- Set up five points around the goal cage as shown in figure 5.1.
- The ball starts in the middle with X_4.
- Five passes—not everyone has to touch the ball.
- After you pass, you must move to productive space: space that is not crowding other teammates or in the middle of the

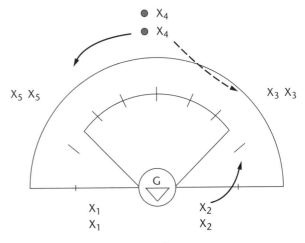

Figure 5.1 5-Point Passing Drill

8-meter arc, space that's in a strong passing lane, or space behind the goal.

- Movement, spacing, and timing are key. Players want to try to establish a rhythm while passing the ball.
- Shoot on the fifth pass.
- Can go from five passes, to four passes, and so on. Can add quick stick passes, and so on.

Pattern Passing Drills

These drills work on throwing, catching, cutting, timing, faking, and shooting. Coaches can set up patterns involving four, five, six, or seven players, depending on how challenging you want to make the drill. As you add more players, this drill will start to mirror your offensive sets. Quick ball movement with accurate passes and consistent catches is the ultimate goal, but many variations can be added (ground balls, cuts to the ball, cuts to the goal, quick stick passes, give and go's, etc.). Players must be able to follow directions and concentrate to execute the patttern effectively and consistently. Encourage your players to communicate with each other throughout the entire drill. Remember, they are trying to make each other look good!

Rotations—Players go to the end of the line they passed to, but not through the middle of the drill. Rotate to the correct line by moving around the outside of the drill so as not to interfere with the pace of the drill or any cutters.

Pattern Passing Drill I

This pattern uses five players. Set up with five lines of players—a line behind X*, X_1, X_2, and X_3. The line for X_4 is off to the side of the field so it doesn't interfere with the drill since X_4 will be cutting to the ball. Players go to the end of the line they passed to, but not through the middle of the drill, rotating to the correct line by moving around the outside of the drill, so as not to interfere with the pace of the drill or the cutters.

The coach tosses a ball to X* who passes to X_1. X_1 catches, gets her feet and hips around, and passes to X_2. X_2 catches and moves the ball quickly to X_3. As the ball is in the air to X_3, X_4 takes a jab step toward X_2 (to fake her imaginary defender) and then cuts hard to X_3 who feeds her the ball. X_4 catches and shoots. The next players in line step up and the drill starts again. Focus on establishing a rhythm with the passes; challenge your players to catch and quickly get

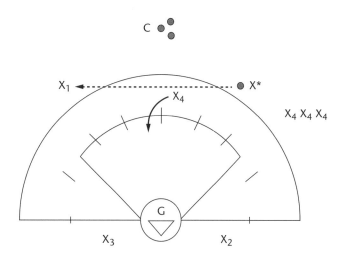

Figure 5.2 Pattern Passing Drill I

their feet and hips around to move the ball to the next player. Communication is a must!

Pattern Passing Drill II

This pattern uses six players. Set up with six lines of players—a line behind X*, X_1, X_2, and X_4. The lines for X_3 and X_5 are off to the side of the field so they don't interfere with the drill since X_3 and X_5 will be cutting to the ball. Players go to the end of the line they passed to, but not through the middle of the drill, rotating to the correct line by moving around the outside of the drill, so as not to interfere with the pace of the drill or the cutters.

The coach rolls a ground ball to X*, who picks it up on the run, gets her eyes up immediately, and moves the ball to X_1. X_1 catches, gets her hips and feet around, and quickly moves the ball to X_2. X_2 catches and redirects the ball (quick stick) to X_3 who is cutting down the middle of the 8 meter. Instead of shooting, X_3 passes to X_4. X_4 fakes opposite and then feeds the ball to X_5 who is cutting around the backside of the crease. X_5 catches, moves the goalie (fakes) and shoots. The next players in line step up and the drill starts again. Focus on quick ball movement, timing of the cuts, and convincing fakes.

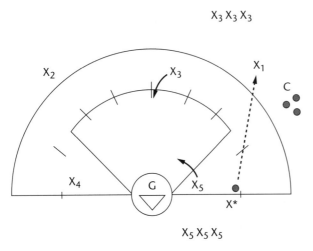

Figure 5.3 Pattern Passing Drill II

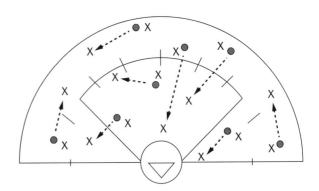

Figure 5.4 Fan Passing Drill

Fan Passing Drill

This drill develops the ability to find an open player and move the ball quickly. It also develops the ability to move without the ball and make decisions when there are a lot of distractions.

This drill can be set up with a smaller number of players (5 v 5) or can use your whole team. For this drill we will set it up as an 8 v 8 inside the 12-meter fan.

Set up all 16 players inside the 12-meter fan. Half have a ball and the other half do not. On the whistle, the players begin moving around the 12-meter fan, keeping their eyes up, maintaining space and looking for open players. The players with a ball must pass to an open player and then cut to receive a pass from someone else. Players must see the field and anticipate passes and cuts. Drill continues for 5–7 minutes.

Variations—quick stick passes, ground balls, reverse stick passes, behind the back passes; be creative and have fun!

Ground Ball Drills

Competitive Ground Ball Drill

Set up with groups of three on either side of the goal cage about 25 yards out (see figure 5.5). A coach has the balls in the middle of the

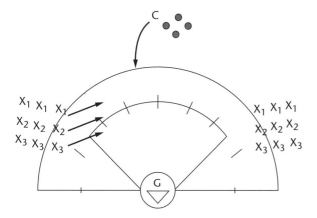

Figure 5.5   Competitive Ground Ball Drill

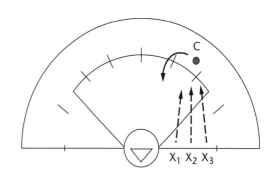

Figure 5.6   Pressure Ground Ball Drill

two groups. The coach rolls a ball out for one of the groups of three to fight for. Whoever gets the ball is on offense; the other two players become defenders. The attack player goes hard to the cage, trying to avoid the double team. The attack player must not force the ball through the double team but must look to *back out* of the pressure first and then look to beat the double team by running off of one of the defenders' shoulders to cut the other defender off.

The two defenders try to close the double team and prevent the ball carrier from getting off a good shot. The defenders must communicate with each other while they close the double team and look for the check. They must be careful not to cut each other off, so they must stay on the sides they originally chose and continue to turn the attacker back toward the helping defender.

Pressure Ground Ball Drill

The objective of this drill is to improve players' ability to cleanly pick up and maintain control of the ball under heavy defensive pressure. As the level of play increases, the speed of picking up ground balls becomes crucial. This drill, like the competitive ground balls drill, emphasizes full-speed ground ball pickups with a bit more detail and from different areas on the field.

The player will need to get low and pick up the ground ball cleanly without slowing down and will need to maintain control of the ball after the pickup as defensive pressure will continue.

Depending on the size of your team you will want to break your team up in two groups. Each group will form three lines, with the lines beginning on the goal line extended (facing the center of the field) and about 6 meters off the goal circle. (See figure 5.6.)

All players, including the goalie, can be involved in this drill. Three players will be working at one time; the drill is fast-paced and has a *high fitness component,* which aids the coach when working on team fitness. The fitness component is hidden in the drill and the fun overrides the effort it takes to complete the drill.

In this drill there will be three players going after a ground ball (toward or away). The object is for the middle player to get the ball and maintain control while the two outside players apply heavy defensive pressure. Any player can gain control of the ground ball, but the initial offensive player should be the middle player in the line of three (in this drill, she is X_2). If X_1 or X_3 gets control, that is okay. Once a player gains control, she tries to make a move and go to goal while the other two players apply defensive pressure.

Goalie involvement: Full—the goalkeeper can go after ground balls and play in the net. The drill begins with players about 10 feet apart on the goal line extended. The coach is 15–20 yards away; she rolls the ball (ground ball toward) or blows her whistle to release the three players to go after the ground ball.

The key to gaining control is that X_2 takes off at full speed and uses proper ground ball technique to get the ball off the ground and go to goal. The player needs to be focused on getting a clean ground ball on the first try at full speed. She should begin to get her stick in position early and ensure that the stick is parallel to the ground. This position puts her at an immediate advantage over the defenders. Boxing out the closest defender increases her chance of getting the ground ball and minimizes the defenders' ability to check.

Teaching cues are "knuckles to the ground" and "accelerate the stick head under the ball." Encourage defenders to use proper defensive techniques and apply heavy pressure to the player attempting to get the ground ball. If one of the defenders can get the ground ball, then she gets to go to goal.

Key drill aspects:

- Players are always going full speed.
- Players attempt to get the ball cleanly.
- Players are making adjustments to not lose body position as they approach the ball.

- Offensive players must make aggressive moves to the goal once they gain control of the ball.
- Defenders are using good defensive positioning and techniques before and after the ground ball pick up.

X_2 is the player designated to get the ground ball if possible. X_1 and X_3 apply defensive pressure. The player who gains control turns and goes to goal while the defenders double-team the offensive player.

Skills practiced:

- Full-speed play
- Boxing out
- Awareness of defenders
- Going to goal

Variations:

As your players improve their skills, incorporate the following variations to increase difficulty:

1. Alternate ground ball to and away.
2. Start with defenders X_1 and X_3 a step behind X_2 to allow X_2 to get a step on them.
3. Add an offensive player once the ground ball is picked up and make the defenders adjust.
4. Begin with no checking, and then move to checking.

6

Individual Offensive Skills

Regina Oliver is an explosive player for Team USA. Courtesy US Lacrosse.

Squaring to a defender, dodging, shooting, feeding, setting picks, and cutting are individual offensive skills that require lots and lots of practice to master. Players can develop their own offensive styles as they work on their skills to add a bit of personality to their play. Some offensive players are naturally flashy, some are workhorses, and some are high-energy, whereas others are more behind-the-scenes. All can be equally effective.

In the past, far too many players have gotten into their heads that they play only offense. The modern coach will challenge players and expose them to playing both offense and defense. In high school, a coach may have a freshman with tremendous offensive talent but limited defensive skills.

The offensive player moves to the ball to catch it but, immediately after the catch, she squares her shoulders toward her defender so she can run directly at her and beat her to either side.

That coach might move this player into a more defensive position for the freshman season to help her acquire the defensive skills necessary to becoming a "complete player." The "I-only-play attack" days are long gone. Coaches today advise solid attack players to add defensive skills to their arsenals, and vice versa. Imagine a player going through tryouts for the one spot on the varsity squad. Those spots are usually reserved for the complete player. It would be a shame if the exclusively offensive-minded player got passed over because she never chose to acquire all the lacrosse skills needed to play the modern game.

SQUARING TO A DEFENDER

This is a skill that separates good attack players from great ones. Squaring to a defender can happen anywhere on the field, but is a skill that is extremely effective in a settled offensive situation. As the ball is being passed around by the offense, the attack player who catches the ball while facing her defender—also known as "square" to her defender—will have a distinct advantage as she dodges.

On offense, get in the habit of thinking three steps ahead. Anticipate the movement of the ball and, if you think you will be receiving the ball, curl *upfield* first so that when you catch the ball you will immediately turn toward the defender and head directly at her in a north-south direction. Most players catch the ball and take several steps "flat" across the field (east-west). This allows defenders to get set. If you catch the ball and attack a defender immediately by putting yourself in a position to square up, this allows you to dodge in either direction and gives you a tremendous advantage. Squaring up to a defender right out of a catch puts the defensive player on her heels and is an aggressive offensive skill.

The most effective attack players are efficient managers of time. Those who shorten the amount of time they give defenders to make adjustments are the greatest threats. Great teams and players always act as if they are on the attack, forcing defenders to constantly adjust.

DODGING

A fancy dodge may be unnecessary if a ball carrier can simply kick it into fifth gear and run by her opponent. That said, every player on the field, no matter what her position, must understand and have the ability to dodge effectively. For an attack player eluding a defender on the way to the cage, or a defender clearing the ball past an attacker who is pressuring her, dodging is a vital skill. Before getting into specific dodging techniques, coaches and players must understand the distinction between *speed* and *quickness*. If a player has sheer speed, she doesn't need a lot of fancy moves in her repertoire to beat her opponents. That player needs to recognize that she's faster than her opponents and therefore simply needs to make a move, such as a stutter step, while exploding upfield. Even if a player is not *faster* than her opponent, she still may, in fact, be *quicker*. This player uses fast feet for a quick first step to get ahead of her opponent and then maintains that position.

The purpose of a dodge is to gain an advantage. Dodging is not about making preconceived moves, but, instead, is about learning to "read"

This player digs her shoulder in and dodges hard.

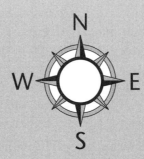

An offensive player's job on the field is to go to goal; this means traveling *north* and *south* on the field. Defensive players want to push the offense off-course, in an *east-west* direction, which forces them away from goal. This is important, especially in the context of dodging. If dodges aren't executed correctly, the offensive players help defenders by moving themselves east-west. A player who properly executes her dodge won't veer off her north-south course.

the defense and adjust to gain that advantage. Dodging effectively "eliminates" a defender, putting her behind the play and allowing the dodger to gain the time and space she needs to pass, shoot, or cut.

Several basic dodges are effective. Beyond the basics, players will add their own variations and embellishments to dodging, so coaches should encourage players to be creative. The main objective of a successful dodge is to get an opponent off-balance and out of her defensive stance. Players can use change of speed, change of direction, and quick movements of their feet, head, shoulders, and sticks to accomplish this. This is critical: Once an opponent is off-balance, the ball carrier needs to get a step on her and then dodge to the *opposite* side. Too often, players fail to read the defense by not recognizing where an opportunity is. Ball handlers want to "set up" their defenders by faking moves and taking jab steps. When a player sets up her defender—she gets a defender to bite on a move to the left—she creates an opportunity to beat the defender on her right side. Setting up a defender helps a ball

carrier to predict where the defense will move, and she can react accordingly.

The Face, or Pull, Dodge

The face dodge, or pull dodge, is the easiest to teach and learn. It is a dodge that can be used in the midfield as well as in settled situations.

Set Up the Defender

As the dodger approaches her defender, she wants to "set up" the defender by making a move and/or faking a pass or shot with a slight movement of her feet, head, and stick. This will often cause defenders to raise their sticks and straighten up, taking them out of their defensive stance.

Stick Position

The dodger wants to keep two hands on the stick with the stick positioned parallel to the body and off the right shoulder (for a right-handed player). Once the dodger sets the defender up, she pulls hard across her face to the opposite side, keeping the stick parallel to her body and protected from the defender. She keeps the stick in her strong hand, protected by her shoulders and then brings it back to her strong side once past the defender.

Footwork

On the approach, the dodger jogs at the defender's left shoulder to "set her up" with a jab step or fake pass. When the dodger is within a stick's length of the defender, she plants her right foot (for a right-handed player), pulls her stick hard across her face protecting the stick with her shoulders, and explodes past the defender's right shoulder. She can take the smallest step to the side with her left foot (east-west) in order to achieve her goal of moving upfield, with a powerful next step in the north-south direction. As soon as the dodger gets a step ahead of the defender, she cuts off the defender by staying on the same north-south course, leaving the defender behind. Imagine that the offensive player is on a set of railroad tracks. She approaches the defender, dodges off the tracks, and then seals the defender off by getting back on the tracks and using a tight cradle while leading with the stick. A dodge is truly effective only when a defender is left with a view of the dodger's back.

Lead with the Stick

It is critical to "lead with the stick" out of every dodge. Once the dodger explodes past the defender, she holds her stick in front of her shoulders for protection, sensing that the defender is recovering and still a threat. She keeps her stick in front of her until open space is gained and she can pass or shoot.

The Dip Dodge

The dip dodge utilizes both hands and is named for the way the ball handler switches her stick from one hand to the other This dodge is most effective if players handle the ball well with both their left and right hands.

Set Up the Defender

As the dodger approaches her defender, she wants to "set up" the defender by faking a move, pass, or shot with a slight movement of her feet, head and stick. This often causes defenders to raise their sticks and straighten up out of good defensive positioning.

Stick Position

The dodger wants to keep two hands on the stick as she approaches the defender. The stick is parallel to the body and off the right shoulder (for a right-handed player). Once the dodger sets up her defender, she takes her left hand off the bottom of the stick and, with her right hand, "dips" the stick in front of her body as if she is scooping the air in front. She turns her shoulders slightly to protect the stick as she brings it to her left side. Once the stick is at her left side, she grasps the top of the stick with her left hand and places her right hand on the bottom of the stick and begins to cradle.

Footwork

On the approach, the dodger jogs at the defender's left shoulder to "set her up" with a quick jab step, fake pass, or shot. When the dodger is within a stick's length of the defender, she plants her right foot (for a right-handed player), dips her stick across the front of her body with her right hand while protecting the stick with her shoulders, switches the stick into her left hand, and explodes in a north-south direction past the defender's right shoulder. As soon as the dodger gets a step ahead of the defender, she continues to cut off the defender, who is left behind the play.

Lead with the Stick

It is critical to "lead with the stick" out of every dodge. Once the dodger explodes past a defender, she should hold her stick in front of her shoulders to protect it. The stick remains in front of the dodger until she gains open space and can pass or shoot.

Switch Hands Dodge

The switch hands dodge is much like the dip dodge, except instead of dipping the stick across the front of the body to change hands, the dodger pulls the stick from one side of her body, across her face, to the other side of her body and then switches hands. For example, a right-handed dodger pulls the stick across her face from her right side to her left side. As the stick is moving from one side of the body to the other, the dodger slides her left hand up to the top of the stick and then grasps the bottom of the stick with her right hand, completing the switch. She cradles right away with the stick in her left hand.

Lead with the Stick

Again, it is critical to "lead with the stick" out of every dodge. Once the dodger explodes past the defender, she holds her stick in front of her. The stick remains in front of the dodger until open space is gained and she can pass or shoot.

Sword Dodge

The sword dodge is like the dip dodge and the switch hands dodge except, instead of dipping the stick across the front of the body or pulling across the face to change hands, the right-handed dodger will slide the stick down to her left hand, which is at her waist (like sliding a sword into its sheath), and then bring the stick up in her left hand to her left side while the right hand grasps the bottom of the stick. Two smooth motions make it happen: the slide down from the right side, and the slide back up to the left side. The footwork and the method of protecting the stick with the shoulders are the same.

Having several different ways to execute a similar dodge gives players options to try as they work on their skills. Some players may be more successful with one technique versus another.

Be creative and try as many different ways as possible to beat defenders.

The Roll Dodge

The roll dodge is used mainly in settled situations. Players can roll dodge to the left or right, depending on field position and where they want to go.

Set Up the Defender

As with all dodges, the dodger wants to "set up" the defender by faking a move, pass, or shot with a slight movement of the feet, head, shoulders, or stick. This will often causes defenders to raise their stick and straighten up, taking them out of their defensive stance.

Stick Position

The dodger keeps two hands on the stick as she approaches the defender with the stick positioned parallel to the body and off the right shoulder (for a right-handed player).

Footwork

On the approach (for a right-handed dodger), the dodger jogs at the defender's left shoulder to "set her up" with a jab step, or fake pass. When the dodger is within a stick's length of the defender, she plants her left foot (for a right-handed player) in front of and in between the defender's feet. The planted left foot is the pivot foot and the right foot moves next. The dodger rolls to her right swinging her back foot around the defender. As the dodger rolls to her right, she keeps her back to the defender and her stick in between her shoulders. The right foot will now be to the side and slightly behind the defender as the roll is completed, and the dodger explodes forward with the left foot while cutting off the defender with her body.

Lead with the Stick

As the dodger explodes past the defender, she keeps her stick in front of her and in between her shoulders to protect it. The stick

Top: The offensive player "sets up" her defender for the roll dodge by driving hard upfield.
Bottom: The dodger switches hands, pushes off of her right foot, and explodes toward the cage.

remains in front until open space is gained and she can pass or shoot.

The Rocker Step

This quickly executed dodge tricks the defender into stepping one way while the dodger explodes in the opposite direction.

Set Up the Defender

The right-handed dodger wants to "set up" her defender by driving hard with the ball and letting the defender make contact with her. In this case, the closer the defender, the better the chance of beating her.

Stick Position

The dodger keeps two hands on the stick as she approaches the defender with the stick positioned parallel to the body and off the right shoulder (for a right-handed player). Be ready for the defender to make contact with her knuckles

Left: The dodger "sets up" her defender for the roll dodge by taking a hard step forward with her left foot. *Right:* She puts on the brakes and "rocks" back onto her right foot, making her defender think she is rolling over the top.

or forearm on your left side, which is what you are looking for.

Footwork

On the approach (for a right-handed dodger), the dodger jogs at the defender's left shoulder to "set her up." When the dodger is within a stick's length of the defender, she drives toward the cage looking for the defender to step up and make controlled contact with her. Once contact is made, the dodger "drives" for a couple more steps and then plants her left foot and drop steps with her right foot—looking over her shoulder and rocking backwards, making it seem like she is going to roll around the defender. As soon as the defender shifts her weight and "bites" on the rocker step, the dodger leads with her stick (brings the stick quickly in front of her face) and explodes off her left foot, digging her left elbow into where the defender was and exploding to the cage.

Lead with the Stick

As the dodger explodes past the defender, she keeps her stick in front of her to protect it.

The stick remains in front until open space is gained and she can pass or shoot.

SHOOTING

Great shooters are made, not born. Shooting takes practice, and lots of it—and then some more. It's so much more involved than simply throwing a ball at a cage. All players need to practice shooting, no matter what their positions. When a team is coming out of transition, the defense isn't set yet so the first seven players, no matter what positions they normally play, who make it down to the offensive end of the field have the best opportunity to put the ball in the cage. That's why defenders need to know how to shoot.

When learning how to shoot, players build on skills they've already learned, namely, how to pass. The overhand shooting motion is similar to the passing motion. This section covers basic as well as advanced shooting techniques. The types of shots the attackers will use depend on where they are on the field and where the defense and goalie are positioned. Shooters need to develop a repertoire of shots because players who have only one type of shot are too easily defended. When Coach Tucker scouts other teams, she singles out those players who execute the same shots over and over, and those are the ones her team plans to shut down, which is easily done by minimizing that one shot. When a one-shot player is out of her comfort zone, she's lost.

Three critical components of shooting are *power*, *placement*, and *creativity*. Shooting drills need to develop all three components equally and should be practiced often.

Power

The power of shots is affected by release points. Shooters can release the ball from a vari-

Arms away from the body will give greater power to your shot.

ety of points: overhand, three-quarter arm, side arm, and risers (shots from low to high). The most accurate and powerful release point is the overhand shot. This should be taught first and practiced consistently.

Players want to go "down the pipes" when shooting, to travel north-south, and not veer off to one side or another. "Down the pipes" refers to the pipes of the goal cage. Shooters need to align themselves between the goal pipes for the best angles and the most opportunities to score.

Placement

You'll often see a shooter execute a terrific dodge, find herself in front of the goal, shoot, and miss the cage completely. Or, the player shoots the ball directly into the goalie's stick and wastes a golden opportunity to score. This happens at every level of the game because the shooter fails to do one thing: look before she shoots. Placement of shots is critical to scoring. Players must be in the habit of "leading with their heads" before they shoot; the head has to turn first to find the cage and see the goalie and net before a shooter shoots.

Lead with Your Head

As the shooter draws her stick back to begin the shooting motion, and before she steps into her shot, she must lead with her head and look at the cage to find the open net. She is looking to see where the defense is, looking to see where the goalie is positioned, and looking to see the open areas of the goal to shoot for. Leading with your head combined with following through where you want the ball to go will greatly increase the accuracy of your shots. Ask yourself, "What do you see when you look at the goal?" If you answer, "The goalie," take a moment to adjust and see the net behind the goalie; that's what you are shooting for. Great shooters perfect their shots and accuracy not only by looking at the open area left uncovered by the goalkeeper, but also by concentrating on one of the small squares made by the netting to ensure pinpoint accuracy. Try it! As shooters become more accurate, they can work on deceptiveness. Deceptive shooters can look one way and accurately shoot in the opposite direction.

Creativity

Successful shooting requires creativity. Offensive players should practice taking shots from many different locations on the field: low-angle shots, outside shots, high shots, bounce shots, shots right on top of the crease, and so on. Behind-the-back shots, around-the-world shots, extended-stick shots, between-the-legs shots—all are creative ways to surprise a goalie and score. They also make for fun shooting practices. Fakes are another way to be creative while shooting. Using a head-and-shoulders fake high and then shooting low is effective. The objective in using a fake is to get the goalie moving so you can shoot around her. Dipping the shoulder and stick low and shooting high will catch a goalie by surprise. These are all methods offensive players can use to be creative when shooting.

Visualization is key when you're working on shooting alone, or without a goalie. As good as a shooting net is, it's even better if you can visualize a goalie in the cage who you must move in order to shoot around.

The Overhand Shot—Power

Coach Tucker insists that the overhand shot is your bread-and-butter shot. Even though it's not the flashiest, it's the most efficient. Players must focus long and hard on learning the correct technique for the overhand shot because it offers the best opportunity to score. Every player needs a solid, powerful, and accurate overhand shot. This shot affords a quick release, allowing shooters to protect their sticks from defenders. It also offers multiple release points—high, off-hip, and low.

The Stance

The shooter begins by facing the goal with her feet offset and shoulder-width apart. A right-handed shooter will have her left foot in front, and a left-handed shooter will have her right foot in front.

Hips, Arms, Hands, and Feet

The shooter rotates her hips so her shoulders are perpendicular to the goal as she reaches back with her stick. Her arms should be away from her body, not in tight by her side. Her top hand should be slid about one-third of the way down the stick while the bottom hand is at the bottom of the stick. The thumb of the top hand is extended up the shaft of the stick, which will help assure accuracy. As the shooter pulls the stick back, her top hand should be about 6 inches higher than the shoulder and her bottom hand should be slightly below the shoulder. This will keep the stick at an angle to control the ball. As she rotates her hips and reaches back with her stick, she transfers her weight to her back foot. When she begins the shooting motion, she shifts her weight from her back foot to her front foot and steps toward the goal with her front foot. Her stick is positioned behind her head, which will make the goalie lose sight of the ball for a second and have a harder time finding it when the shot is taken.

The Shooting Motion

The shooter first drives the bottom hand forward while stepping toward the goal and rotating her hips toward the goal. She then snaps the top hand forward toward the cage while pulling the bottom hand back toward her body. The *push and snap* of the top hand and the *pull* of the bottom hand act as a lever and provide the power and accuracy for the shot.

The Follow-Through

The shooter completes the shooting motion by following through across her body as her hips, shoulders, and back foot complete their rotation. Initially, the top arm should extend toward the spot the shooter is aiming for, assuring the accuracy of the shot. As the shooter completes her follow-through, her bottom hand (left hand) should finish behind her left hip, with the left elbow up and away from the body. The stick head will end up facing the ground, at the lead foot (left). Note: PUTTING YOUR LEFT HAND "IN YOUR BACK POCKET" AND FOLLOWING THROUGH ACROSS YOUR BODY IS VITAL FOR AN ACCURATE, CONSISTENT OVERHAND SHOT. The momentum of putting the body behind the shot—rotating hips and shoulders as the shooter steps into the shot—will cause the shooter to step forward with the back foot to keep her balance.

The overhand shooting motion is very similar to the passing motion and can result in a high shot or a low shot, depending on the release point during the follow-through.

As mentioned earlier, the three components of shooting are power, placement, and creativity.

Additional release points can increase power and enhance unpredictability, but they also can be construed as lazy shots if they're not done for a specific reason. For instance: Dropping a stick to the hip to avoid a defender and shoot around the goalie is desirable; there is a valid reason for this release point used at the appropriate time. But if a shooter finds herself being driven off-angle by a defender and she drops her stick to her hip and tosses the ball at the cage, that's lazy. The additional release points include a three-quarter arm shot, a side-arm shot, and riser shots (shots from low to high). All of these release points use the same push/pull concept: The stick works as a lever. Having the ability as a shooter to read the defense and goalie, and change the release point of the shot while on the fly, are hallmarks of a solid shooter.

The Bounce Shot

A follow-through toward the ground will result in a hard bounce shot. Any goalie will admit

Preparing to release the shot: arms away from body, lead with the head, and step into the shot.
Releasing a strong overhand shot—notice the ball up in the shooting strings. The follow-through—the shooter is following through across her body and leaning into the shot.

that low, hard bounce shots are tough to save. The shooter can bounce the ball at the top of the crease, looking for the ball to bounce over the goalie's shoulder as she drops down to save it. The shooter can also bounce the ball right behind the goalie's feet toward either corner of the cage for another high-percentage low shot. A more advanced technique is putting a "spin" on bounce shots. The shooter can spin the ball as it comes out of her stick, like a top spin in tennis. To put a top spin on a bounce shot, the shooter will twist the stick over the top of the ball during the release and follow-through, causing the ball to skip when it hits the ground. As in tennis, "slicing" the ball will put a *backspin* on it when it hits the ground. To execute this with a lacrosse stick: At the last second, during the release, roll the stick underneath the ball so it has a back spin as it hits the ground.

The Riser Shot

A great shooter is able to move the goalie and shoot around her. An extremely effective shot that forces a goalie to move is the riser shot. This shot requires space on the stick side; it is not a shot to be attempted in the middle of the 8-meter arc surrounded by defenders. As with the riser pass, the concept is to drop the stick low and, ultimately, to release the ball high. Most goalies will drop into a crouch when expecting low shots. That's why, if you polish the techniques needed to drop your stick low and then place the ball in a top left or right corner, you're golden.

Set the Feet

The right-handed shooter has her feet slightly offset, with her left foot in front.

Hand Position

The top hand is halfway down the stick, with the bottom hand controlling the bottom of the stick.

Stick Position

Out of a cradle, the shooter drops her arms and bends her knees, dropping her stick parallel to the ground so that the head, facing up, is only inches from the ground.

The Push and Pull Motion

The shooter springs up from the low crouch. Her bottom hand comes up to guide the stick, and the top hand starts to snap as the shooter lifts the stick from low to high, ultimately rolling the stick head over to complete the follow-through. The stick head ends up pointing at the target, a top left- or right-hand corner of the cage. Riser shots gain power from shooters bending their knees to get low and then springing up during the release.

The Quick-Stick Shot

A quick-stick shot is exactly what it sounds like: The shooter receives the feed—good, bad, or indifferent—and in one motion redirects the ball toward the cage. To do so, the shooter gives back with the ball on the catch and immediately snaps through the shot to redirect it to the cage (without cradling) using the push/pull motion. This is an advanced shot that takes lots of practice to master. The feeder generally sends a high pass to the shooter, who is able to watch the ball into her stick, give back slightly to gain control of the ball, and then immediately redirect the ball on cage with a snap of her wrists. Not all feeds are on the money, however. That's why quick-sticks should be practiced with feeds above the shoulder, at the waist, and at the feet. This will help you prepare for any ball thrown to you. Quite often, you'll see two offensive players setting up this shot: The feeder will roll the crease while the shooter positions herself on the back post; the feeder lobs a cross-post feed, which the shooter controls and redirects on cage.

FEEDING

Feeding is the ability to pass the ball accurately to a teammate, giving her a quality opportunity to score. The four elements of a successful feed include creating space from the defender, seeing the field, timing the feed, and protecting the stick.

Creating Space from the Defender

Players must be able to feed with and without defensive pressure. In order to do so, feeders must be constantly moving to make it difficult for defenders to play them. This will reduce the possibility of their feeds being blocked or intercepted by the defenders. Players must be able to drive toward their defenders and then drop-step away from them to create the space needed to feed and to get the defender out of her defensive stance. This is like a football quarterback, who must execute a three- to five-step drop away from the line in order to see the field and choose his target. Experiment by driving toward your defender and then taking a three- to five-step drop back to free up your hands and stick to feed. It is critical that you push off of your back foot after the initial drop step in order to pass the ball accurately to your teammate. Do not pass off of your back foot while retreating. Be sure to plant the back foot and step into your feed to ensure a crisp, accurate pass. After executing the drop step, players might want to consider curling upfield before passing to open up their passing lanes. When executing the drop step to gain space for a feed, always remember to protect your stick by keeping it behind your shoulders. Think shoulder-shoulder-stick as you drop back.

Seeing the Field

Feeders must be aware of where their teammates are on the field and anticipate cutters. To do so, feeders keep their heads and eyes up, constantly scanning the field to read where the next cutter is coming from. All the while, feeders must be prepared to dodge if their defenders get lazy.

Timing of the Feed

Good timing is the key to feeding. The feeder is responsible for giving the shooter an opportunity to score. If the feed comes too early, the cutter will not be ready; if the feed comes too late, the cutter may no longer be at an angle to score, or the defense may have already recovered.

Stick Protection

Using fakes, changing the level of your stick on the feed, and protecting your stick while assessing cutters are important factors for the feeder to consider. Feeders must remember to turn their shoulders for protection and hold their sticks back behind their heads. Remember: shoulder-shoulder-stick!

The offensive player is protecting her stick by keeping it behind her shoulders. When she beats her defender, she can either shoot or feed.

PICKS

Picks are used in many sports to create offensive opportunities. Setting a pick requires communication between two off-ball players, such as a hand signal or eye contact. A player opposite the ball recognizes that her teammate could set a pick for her. She motions to her teammate on the ball side with a slight hand signal (for example, a come-here motion). Her teammate recognizes the cue for setting a pick.

The picker runs to a spot on the field and stops, with her stick straight up and down. Her teammate (the cutter) runs the defender into the pick, allowing the picker to block the path of the defender and the cutter to gain an advantage into open space. In the game of lacrosse, picks can be set *off the ball* and *on the ball* to free up teammates for shots on goal or to produce favorable situations for the offense. It is important to set a proper pick: one that consists of stationary position and the element of surprise. A defender has a much greater chance of adjusting if she is easily able to see a pick coming. (If a defender can't see the pick at all, it's considered a blind pick, which is illegal.) When setting a pick for a teammate who has the ball, the picker must be prepared to accept contact and, after the pick is set, to move as quickly as possible to open space. This will negate the defensive strategy of switching. The player for whom the pick is being set must be ready to draw a double-team and move away from the defensive pressure in order to pass the ball to her open teammate.

It's best to focus on setting picks off-ball. Picks can be set all over the field but are used most often in settled offensive situations. Players need to recognize where the ball is and be able to set picks opposite the ball. A pick is meant to free up a teammate enough for her to get a step on her defender and receive a pass into open space moving toward the goal. When setting a pick it is important to keep the stick straight up and down, not parallel with the ground. Having the stick parallel to the ground when setting the pick is a foul and will result in a change of possession. To avoid setting a blind pick (a pick that is set directly behind the defender), the pick must be set off to one side or the other of a defender. Remaining stationary until a teammate runs off of the pick is also critical to setting a successful pick. You may not move to block the path of the defender once the pick is set; this is called a moving pick and is also a foul. Once you've set a pick, you're job isn't finished: Now it's time for you to flash off the pick opposite to where the cutter ran so you can be another option for the feeder.

DRILLS, DRILLS, DRILLS

Dodging Drill

The Mirror Drill

This drill works on the dodger's ability to "read" her defender and dodge to the opposite side. It helps the dodger to "set her defender up" and works on many different dodges.

A dodger with a ball and a defender are set up in pairs.

The dodger and defender are positioned back-to-back with about a foot of space between them. The dodger has a ball in her stick and the defender is in her defensive stance with her stick up.

On the whistle, they both turn and the dodger "reads" the defender's stance and explodes to one side or the other, executing a face dodge, a roll dodge, a sword dodge, and so on. The defender is trying to step up and stop the dodger.

Keys to the Drill

- Quick feet on the turn by both the offense and defense
- Ability to read which way the defender is leaning and dodge (beat her) to the opposite side
- Use of head and shoulder fakes to get defender off-balance
- Exploding out of the turn to get a step on the defender and cut her off

Variation

The dodger and defender are positioned 10 feet apart, back-to-back. Now they have more room to work with. The dodger can build up speed and then make her move to beat the defender. She can work on her fakes and "setting up" the defender. The defender has more time to establish her defensive position. She can work on staying balanced and not falling for fakes.

Individual Shooting Drill

Drop-Step Drill

This is a drill that works on an individual player's shooting technique. The shooter gets lots of shots in this drill. Focusing on the correct shooting technique is critical and repetition leads to proficiency.

The drill is set up for right-handed shots first. The shooter's back is facing the cage and she is positioned about 5–7 yards in front of the goal. Her stick is up, ready to catch, turn, and shoot.

Her coach, or another player, stands in front of her with a bucket of balls. (See figure 6.1.)

One after another, the coach tosses a ball to the shooter, who

- Gives back slightly on the catch.
- Drop steps with her left foot as she pivots with her right foot.

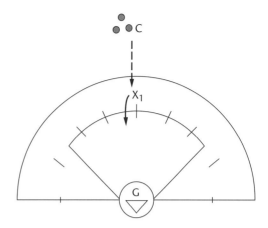

Figure 6.1   Drop-Step Drill

- Is reaching back with her stick with her arms away from her body.
- Steps into the shot with her left foot, rotates her hips, drives her bottom hand forward, and pulls with her bottom hand as she pushes and snaps with her top hand to release the shot.
- Snaps her wrist and follows through across her body, with the stick head ending up at her left foot.
- Remembers to bend at the waist to put her body behind the shot.
- Resets, facing the feeder, and shoots again. And again. And again!

Coaches can give the shooter specific places to shoot to work on accuracy. Fakes can be added before the shot is released.

Team Shooting Drills

2-Pass Weave with a Shot

Players are set up in three lines at the 50-yard line. Balls are in the middle line.

X_2 passes to X_3 and then cuts behind her.

X_3 passes to X_1 and then cuts behind her.

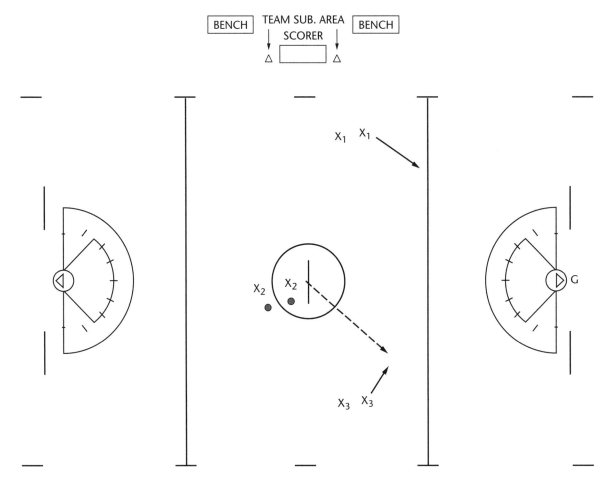

Figure 6.2   2-Pass Weave with a Shot

X_1 sets her feet to shoot, or shoots on the run. (See figure 6.2.)

Key points:

- As X_2 passes to X_3, she wants to angle her pass toward the cutter.
- X_3 and X_1 players must do the same—angle their cuts toward the ball carrier/center of the field; this will help keep the passes accurate.
- The player in the center line can choose which side to pass to initially, so players can work on shooting from both sides of the field and with both their left and right hands.

- Encourage players to shoot with power, either on the run or after setting their feet.

Give-and-Go Shooting Drill

For this drill you'll need 6 cones and a bucket of balls. Set up cones as shown in figure 6.3, about 20 yards apart, four in a square around the goal cage and two about 2 yards apart at the top of the 12-meter fan. There is a line of players at each of the outside cones.

Balls start with X_3 and X_4. X_3 is passing, catching, and shooting left-handed, and X_4 is passing, catching, and shooting right-handed.

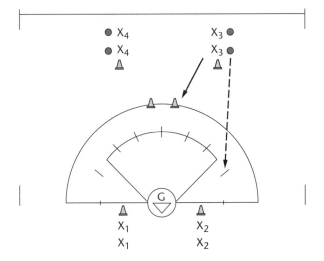

Figure 6.3   Give-and-Go Shooting Drill

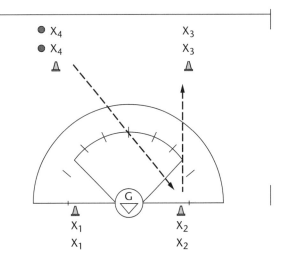

Figure 6.4   Box Passing and Shooting Drill

X_3 passes the ball to X_2 and then cuts to the middle cone and pops back to the ball looking for a feed.

X_2 catches, moves her feet to curl upfield, and feeds the ball back to the cutter (X_3) who catches and shoots right away. The same thing is happening with X_4 and X_1, except X_4 passes, catches, and shoots with her right hand.

Players rotate clockwise so everyone feeds, shoots, and uses both hands.

Box Passing and Shooting Drill

Set up four cones around the goal cage in the shape of a square about 20 yards apart, as shown in figure 6.4. There is a line of players at each cone. The balls start with X_4.

The first four players step up and, on the whistle, begin passing the ball quickly amongst themselves—quick passes, direct passes, accurate passes. Players must keep their feet moving and angle themselves in such a way as to catch and move the ball quickly and accurately. They are trying to establish a rhythm as they pass.

On the next whistle, whoever has the ball must shoot.

If the ball is dropped before the second whistle, that group of players is out and goes to the end of the line and a new group steps up to start the drill.

Four Corners with a Shot Drill

This drill works on shooting, feeding, picking, and cutting.

Set up four lines in a square around the goal cage. (See figure 6.5.) The ball starts with X_4.

X_4 passes to X_3 and then drifts into the middle of the 8-meter preparing to set a pick.

X_3 passes to X_2 and stays high outside of the 12-meter waiting for the pick.

X_2 passes to X_1 while X_4 sets a pick at the top of the 8-meter for her waiting teammate, X_3.

X_1 catches, curls upfield, and feeds the ball to X_3, who is cutting off of the pick set by X_4.

X_4 then flashes to the opposite side of the cutter looking for a feed or a rebound after the shot.

Feeding Drills

Partner Passing Drop Step Drill

In pairs, add drop steps of three to five steps after each catch to work on a feeder's ability to

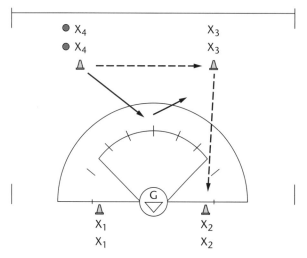

Figure 6.5   Four Corners with a Shot Drill

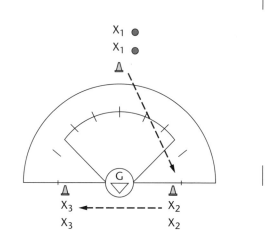

Figure 6.6   Triangle Feeding Drill

create space from her defender before she feeds. Stepping into the feed is important to work on as well.

Catch, drop-step, and then step into the pass back to your partner.
On the drop steps, position your stick shoulder, shoulder, stick to get in the habit of protecting the stick.

Variation:

Add a curl upfield after the drop steps to work on improving angles to feed. Progress to setting the pairs up in front on the goal for lots of feeds and shots.

Triangle Feeding Drill
Set up with three players in a triangle around the goal cage. (See figure 6.6.)
The ball starts with X_1.
X_1 passes to X_2, who swings the ball to X_3.
X_3 catches and curls upfield to feed the ball to X_1, who is cutting to the ball.

Variations:

Add drop steps before the feed.
Change the point of the feed: Have the ball start with X_2, who passes to X_3, who passes to X_1, who feeds from the top of the 8-meter to X_2, cutting around the crease.

Ladder Feeding Drill
    This is a great drill that incorporates a lot of individual offensive skills. (See figure 6.7.) Directly behind the goal cage there is a conditioning ladder. There are four cones set up: two at the top of the 12-meter arc and two just outside the goal crease on the goal line extended. The drill starts with X_1 picking up a dead ball and running through the power ladder. S_1 is anticipating a feed from X_1, so they need to time their cut. Once X_1 is out of the ladder she challenges toward the cone on the goal line extended, then quickly drop steps and feeds the ball to S_1 who shoots on the cage. Then X_2 starts the drill from the other side. The players rotate clockwise from cone to cone. This drill has many game-like vari-

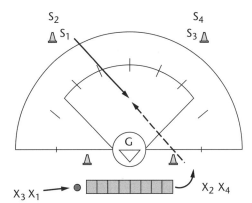

Figure 6.7   Ladder Feeding Drill

ations. You can replace the goal line cones with active defenders to make it more game-like. You can have defenders chase the shooters putting pursuit pressure on them. You can eliminate the ground ball pickup and have the opposite low line feed the ball or have a feed come from the shooting line high to the low feeding line. There are endless possibilities.

7

Individual Defensive Skills

Defenders must be aggressive, strong, and ready to help each other.

You've probably heard the saying "Offense wins games, defense wins championships." We believe this to be true and encourage you to hone defensive skills no matter what position you play on the field. At the higher levels of play, every player must be able to be an offensive threat, as well as create a stop on defense. Challenge yourself to develop as a complete player, with an ability to hold your own on both ends of the field.

It is the mission of the defense to prevent the offense from scoring. The defense does this by creating defensive "stops" or situations where the defense has slowed the offense down and prevented a shot on goal. Successful team defense comes from fundamentally sound individual defense and solid communication skills. Defenders need to be the ultimate communicators; this communication starts in practices. Silence in practice almost always results in defensive breakdowns and silence in games. Defenders who chat it up with a purpose ultimately bond as a unit and are tough to beat.

HOT SPOTS

It's vital at all times that everyone on the defensive unit knows the exact location of the ball. The reason: Defenders cannot focus solely on the ball or solely on "their" particular opponents; they have to focus on both. Communication is key to being able to do these two things at once. Hot spots are numbered locations surrounding the 8-meter, used to designate specific areas on the offensive and defensive ends of the field. Hot spots help seven players to coordinate what they want to do as a unit at any given moment. The goalie, as well as the player on the ball, voice the hot spots to describe to her teammates the exact location of the ball on the field. The goalie might yell: "Ball's in the three, ball's in the three! Where's the slide? Who's the help?" Additionally, a hot spot could signify where a defender wants the ball to come: "Bring her to the six spot; the double's here. I'm your double. Bring her to the six spot." The hot spots serve to clarify positioning on the field and facilitate communication.

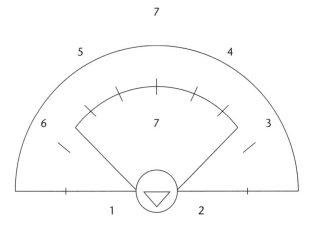

Figure 7.1   The Hot Spots

DEFENSIVE TERMINOLOGY

The single most important thing defenders can do for each other is communicate. Everything else will fall into place if defenders are able to direct each other and have an understanding of what others are doing or are about to do.

We encourage coaches and players to create their own list of defensive terms that their team will use consistently on the field to keep everyone on the same page. Keep it simple—defenders don't have a lot of time to speak in sentences when attackers are driving to the cage. Here is a sample of the defensive terminology used at Hopkins:

Ball is in the ___
I have ball in the (insert hot spot # here).

Hot
I'm the First Slide.

2nd
I'm the Second Slide.

3rd
I'm the Third Slide.

Bring her
I'm waiting to double, bring the ball carrier to me.

Double
I'm doubling the ball.

Step right
Step upfield with your RIGHT foot on a 45-degree angle.

Step left
Step upfield with your LEFT foot on a 45-degree angle.

Hold
Hold your player where she is, *or* I don't need help.

No slide
I'm in good positioning on ball and don't need a slide.

Blue jay
Look for a check from behind on dodges/challenges.

Feed
Ball has just been fed into the 8-meter.

SOAP
Shut Off Adjacent Player.

Turn her
Turn your player back toward your teammate waiting to close the double.

Ball side
Position yourself between the player you are marking and the ball.

Goal side
Position yourself between the player you are marking and the goal.

Jump
Look to double the ball off of a screen or a criss-cross move by the offense.

Get in
Get to the top/middle of the 8-meter as fast as possible.

DEFENSIVE POSITIONING

Defenders want to take something away from the ball carrier, such as a strong pass, a lane to the middle of the field, or a good angle from which to shoot. Defenders, ideally, should dictate to the offense. The main job of a defender is to "contain" an offensive player by keeping her in between her shoulders. Having a strong defensive stance and solid defensive positioning allows a defender to contain her opponent and force her to an area she chooses. *Containing is far more important than checking.*

Defensive Stance

A defender's main objective is to control her offensive opponent. She wants to dictate to the attack player, not react to her. A defender does not want to allow an attacker to throw her off-balance and beat her. A strong defensive stance is the key to effective defensive positioning and

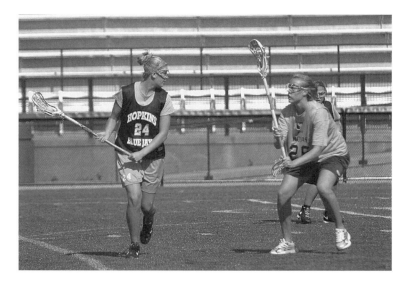

The defensive stance: feet are shoulder-width apart, arms away from the body, stick up, and knees bent in a balanced, sitting position.

the key to "containing" or controlling an attack player. A defender needs to maintain her "center" with balanced body weight; her knees are slightly bent and her butt is tucked in, similar to being in a sitting position. She maintains her balance by keeping her feet and hips under her shoulders. The defender's arm position is summed up by "arms away, elbows locked." Short steps, not long strides, ensure balance. If a defensive player keeps her core centered—shoulders, chest, and hips—and keeps her attack player in between her shoulders, she will rarely get beat.

A defender can't afford to be distracted by, or react to, her opponent's head and shoulders, or stick. To maintain a strong defensive stance and prevent getting faked out, a defender needs to focus on her opponent's midsection: her belly button. The rest of the picture she'll see in her peripheral vision.

Stick Position

The stick is an extension of the defender. She needs to keep it under control and use it wisely. Stick position is important in maintaining a strong defensive stance: It should be straight up

Stick-to-body contact is a foul. Avoid "shopping cart" defense.

and down, or slightly off to the left or right, at 10 o'clock or 2 o'clock. At all costs, avoid the "shopping cart" defense, where your stick is at hip level and parallel to the ground, like you are pushing a cart. Defenders who carry their sticks at their waists have no chance of blocking a pass or shot, or making a check. The ball-carrier can easily pass, feed, or shoot around a defender who has her stick at her waist.

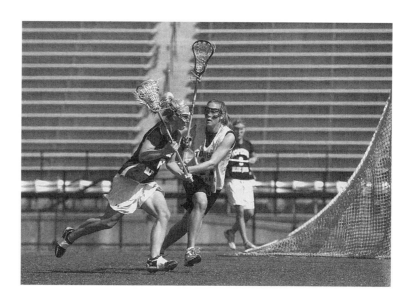

This defender has established good body position and excellent stick position. Notice her arms away from her body.

For the sake of safety and efficiency, defenders need to pay attention to the angles of their sticks: They can't be thrust too far forward in an opponent's face, or pulled too far back.

Defenders grip their sticks with their top hand about two-thirds of the way down the stick and with a firm bottom hand at the bottom. A defender's balance and ability to change direction can be adversely affected by a grip that's spread out rather than compact. The top hand is the guide and the bottom, the control.

Maintaining Balance

Keeping an opponent in between your shoulders depends on two things: being able to move your feet with quick, short steps and keeping your feet and hips underneath your shoulders as you move. A defender will establish a strong defensive stance if she can also keep her top hand slid two-thirds of the way down the stick and arms away with elbows locked. As a defender, you're entitled to that space between your chest and stick; guard that space because that's how you are able to control the attack player. If a defender bends her elbows and hugs her stick—"breaks her arms"—and loses that space in between her chest and stick, she's less able to control the attacker and more vulnerable to getting beat. What happens if you break your arms? Concentrate on backing yourself up with your feet as opposed to pushing out with your arms. This strategy reestablishes a strong defensive stance that won't result in a foul. Remember to concentrate on your opponent's midsection—don't be distracted by head, shoulder, and stick fakes!

Taking Something Away

With their defensive stance, defenders want to "take something away" from the attackers and not concede a path to the goal. Defenders must "step up" with either their left or right foot as the attacker challenges to dictate to the attacker where the defender wants her to go. Whether the defender steps up left or right, her next step must be at a 45-degree angle. Defenders must avoid opening up their hips and allowing the attacker to drive to the cage, and avoid at all costs backing directly up toward the goalkeeper. The on-ball defender must be listening for her teammates to tell her where the help is and must also listen for her goalie's directions. The goalkeeper can see the offensive play developing; she is the main source of communication on defense.

ON-BALL DEFENSE

Defenders are responsible for *"marking"* or *"guarding"* offensive players. Defenders' primary objective is to control offensive players and keep them from scoring, without compromising safety, of course. Contact is part of the game; however, the focus needs to be on body-to-body contact (for example, using a forearm or knuckles to control an offensive player) and not stick-to-body contact. It is a major foul if a player initiates stick-to-body or body-to-stick contact.

A defender is entitled to her space. If she's able to lock on to her attacker and, using controlled body-to-body contact, dictate where that attacker can go, then she's playing solid, under-control defense. She is guiding the attack player with her body—with her feet, her defensive

Stick-to-body contact is a foul.

An example of good forearm defense. The defender is making contact with her forearm, and her stick is up.

positioning, and her forearm or knuckles. She's not bruising her attack player with stick-to-body contact. If defenders weren't able or allowed to touch opponents, then attackers would drive down the field unimpeded and go to goal at will. However, coaches, players, and officials all need to take responsibility to make sure players are focusing on body-to-body defense instead of stick-to-body. Wanton stick-to-body contact results in injuries and fouls—and that's not good lacrosse nor does it bode well for the future if women want to continue playing unencumbered by helmets and protective pads.

Defenders are also responsible for creating defensive "stops," or opportunities to slow down the ball or gain possession of the ball through interceptions, blocks, checks, or ground-ball pickups. Initially, on-ball defenders want to "contain" their opponent, or position themselves in a way that controls their opponent's moves. Next, defenders want to "take something away" from the ball carrier: a strong pass, a lane to the middle of the field, or a good angle

to shoot. Defenders can position themselves on ball carriers' strong sides and force them to pass or shoot with their weaker hands. Through well-executed individual defensive positioning, defenders can influence the movements of an offensive player with the ball by forcing her into a double-team, away from the line of center, toward the sideline or end line, or to a non-dominant side.

MIDFIELD DEFENSE

On-Ball

Hip-to-Hip Positioning

When running with the ball carrier in the midfield or in transition, the defender positions herself to the side of the ball carrier, on the ball carrier's hip, shoulders almost square to the ball carrier. The defender's arms are away from her body with elbows locked (keeping space between the chest and stick); the top hand is slid two-thirds of the way down the stick, and the stick is straight up and down, ready to block a shot or pass or to make contact using knuckles or forearm. The defender's feet are traveling in the same direction as the attacker's.

The defender does not position herself in front of the ball carrier, as she wants to avoid running backwards and allowing the ball carrier to beat her to open space. The defender does not position herself behind the ball carrier because there she forfeits her chance to dictate; the ball carrier will cut off the defender, leaving her to chase.

Players need to assess their opponents. Which is her strong hand, and how speedy is she? By positioning themselves properly, defenders can force opponents to play with their weaker hands. Here's how. The defender positions her feet in the same direction as the ball carrier's. She slides her hand two-thirds of the way down her stick and aligns herself alongside the ball carrier's hip as the ball carrier runs down the field. While maintaining her balance, the defender extends her arms and hands out in front of the ball carrier when playing hip-to-hip defense. This is much more effective than reaching her stick across the opponent's path, which usually results in a foul. If a defender is on an opponent's weak side and the opponent is using her strong hand, then the defender's mission is to step across the opponent's path to "turn" her, slow her down, and force her to switch to her weak hand. The satisfaction a defender gets from dictating an attacker's movements and slowing her down rivals the elation an attacker feels when she rips a defender on her dodge, shoots, and scores.

Off-Ball

As the ball carrier and her defender are moving down the field, the remaining defenders must position themselves accordingly, based on where the ball is and where opponents without the ball are. Generally, off-ball defenders position themselves goalside, which means that they are closer to the goal than their opponents. A rule of thumb: The closer you and your opponent are to the ball carrier, the tighter you should mark your opponent. If the ball carrier is relatively far away from you and the player you are marking, then you can sag in toward the goal you're defending. Defenders' sticks belong up and in the passing lane, and their top hand should be positioned about two-thirds of the way down their sticks to increase their reach. A more advanced technique, which ensures that a defender's stick is up and in the passing lane, involves removing the top hand from the stick and holding and controlling the stick solely with the bottom hand. Many defenders like to take one hand off of their sticks when they are off-ball to give themselves more reach, cover more of the passing lane, and make themselves seem bigger.

Off-ball defenders in the midfield need to keep an eye on the ball as well as the girls they are marking. In order to do this, they position themselves at angles that allow them to see both without having to turn their heads. Coach Tucker consistently reminds defenders to *take a step back* so they can increase their angle to see both ball and girl.

SETTLED DEFENSE

On-Ball

Defensive Positioning from the Wings (3 and 6 Spots)
Forcing Away from the Line of Center: When defending the ball carrier from the right wing, or the 3 spot, the defender positions herself right shoulder to right shoulder as she faces her opponent. Her stick is up and slightly to her left (10 o'clock) and her left foot is slightly in front of her right foot. This will automatically

place the defender slightly higher upfield than her opponent. When forcing away from the line of center, the defender wants to dictate where her opponent can go—she wants to take away the center of the field and force her opponent down and toward the sideline. From the start, this defensive position takes away the center of the field.

As the attacker approaches, stay on the balls of your feet, balanced with an active, controlled stick. Ideally, the defender wants to make the first move, NOT react to her opponent's move. Timing is critical. If the defender steps too soon, the attacker will have enough space to dodge and the defender may not be able to recover. If the defender steps too late, she'll be reacting to the dodge, not dictating, and find herself a step behind. Make it a habit to take a small step with the left foot first as the attacker approaches to naturally take away the center of the field and to discourage the attack player from dodging topside. Concentrate on the attacker's midsection—don't be fooled by a head, shoulder, or stick fake.

The defender makes contact with her knuckles or forearm as she moves her feet to lock on while keeping her stick up. She steps to drive the attacker away from the line of center, down and toward the sideline. Focus on containing, not checking. The priority is to maintain strong body position, with the attacker in between the defender's shoulders, forcing an off-angle shot.

If the opponent continues to try to dodge topside, the defender locks her elbows, holds her position, and keeps stepping left to take away the middle of the field. Force the attacker to turn and put her stick in her left hand. Do not back up as she approaches; avoid being back on your heels. Once she turns, drive her down and out toward the sideline. A defender must make contact with her opponent to hold ground. Keep elbows locked, arms away from

the body, and knuckles or forearm on the back or side of an opponent. Drive with the legs and take very small, quick steps. Try not to bend at the waist as that can affect balance. Balance is critical. As a defender is driving her opponent down and out, she listens for the double team coming to help. She stays on her opponent's back hip as the double team comes from her right. If an opponent tries to roll back to the middle of the field, step up with the left foot and force her back down. Remember to maintain balance by sitting, not bending at the waist, and keeping elbows locked. Drive with the legs with quick, short steps. Keep your feet moving under you. Do not cross your feet over each other, or you will lose your balance. Reverse this technique when defending from the left side, or the 6 spot.

Forcing Over the Top to the Double Team: When defending the ball carrier from the right wing, or the 3 spot, with the intent of forcing her opponent over the top of the 8-meter to a double team, the defender lines up her left shoulder to her opponent's left shoulder when facing her. Her right foot should be slightly in front of her left foot. Her stick is up and slightly to the right (2 o'clock). This will automatically place the defender slightly lower than her opponent, who thinks she is being given the middle of the field. The defender is dictating where her opponent can go—she is giving her the center of the field and forcing her toward the double team. As the attacker approaches, stay on the balls of the feet, balanced, with an active, controlled stick. Ideally, the defender wants to make the first move, NOT react to her opponent's move. Again, timing is critical. If a defender steps too soon, the attacker will have enough space to react and dodge. Defenders often step too late and miss the chance to dictate, falling a step behind. Make it a habit to take a small step with the right foot first as the attacker approaches to naturally take away the sideline and to encourage the attack player to dodge topside. Focus on the attacker's midsection—her body will follow her hips—don't get beat by a head and shoulder fake.

Once the defender locks on to the attacker with solid knuckle or forearm positioning and her stick up, she takes small, quick steps over the top of the 8-meter arc, driving the attacker east-west toward the double team, keeping her in between the shoulders. Defenders MUST avoid opening up their hips, drop stepping, and allowing their opponents to "turn the corner" and drive north-south toward the cage. Focus on keeping the hips facing the 50-yard line to keep your body in the right position to "bring" the ball carrier to the double team waiting at the top of the 8-meter.

After stepping with the right foot, then left, a defender makes contact with her opponent by keeping her arms away from her body, her stick up, and her elbows locked. If defenders break their elbows and extend their arms again, they'll likely be called for a foul. No shopping cart defense; no sticks at the waist! A defender uses her legs to hold her position and step across the path of her attacker, leading with her left foot and along the top of the 8-meter. Try not to back up as the opponent approaches. Stay balanced and on the balls of the feet. Make physical contact (knuckles or forearm) and maintain this contact with elbows locked and quick feet. Drive the attacker east-west over the top of the 8-meter to the double team. Stick up! Listen for the double team. Stay on the attacker's back hip and drive her to help. If she tries to roll back toward the sideline, step up with right foot forward and force her back to the middle of the field.

To maintain balance, and your ability to step left or right quickly, avoid bending at the waist and pushing with the arms. Drive with the legs, elbows locked, taking quick, short steps. Reverse this technique when defending from the left side, or the 6 spot.

Crease Defense (1 and 2 Spots)

When defending the ball carrier from behind the cage in the 1 spot, a defender waits at the goal line extended, on the balls of the feet, feet about shoulder-length apart, with an upright, active stick. She gives the attacker about 2 feet between her and the crease to entice her to dodge to the inside. If the attacker tries to dodge to the inside, step left and force her into the crease, or draw the charge. Another way to set up as a crease defender is to keep the left foot slightly behind the right and turn hips toward the crease while meeting the dodger at the goal line extended. If she challenges to the inside, step with the left foot and drive her into the crease. However, if she drives to the outside, step with the right foot toward the sideline; this keeps the hips square.

Remember to stay balanced and take small steps. Attackers are always trying to throw their defenders off-balance, especially with head, shoulder, and stick fakes. Don't fall for them—concentrate on the hips. When an opponent approaches, make her react by taking a small, quick step with the right foot or throwing a short, quick, fake check. The objective is to not let her get to the middle of the field. Keep her outside the 8-meter by making contact with her at the goal line extended, stepping on a 45-degree angle with the right foot, and driving her away from the 8-meter using legs and core strength. Use the 8-meter line as a guide—step up along the 8-meter line without opening the hips or allowing the attacker to step inside the line. Keep both the hips and shoulders facing the sideline; do not open them up and let them face the 50-yard line as this will give the ball carrier a lane to the cage.

A defender's stick is up at all times, ready to block a feed or a shot. A shopping cart defense (with a stick at the waist) is not effective. The attacker will feed or shoot over a defender who doesn't keep her stick up. Take quick, small steps to keep an opponent in between the shoulders and contain her. Stay balanced. Balance separates good defenders from great defenders.

Making contact with the knuckles or forearm is critical. Lock the elbows and keep arms away from the body (so there is space to recover if need be), while keeping the stick up. Opponents will apply pressure physically as they try to get to the middle of the cage. It's the defender's job to hold her ground and, with her elbows locked, drive the attacker out, using her legs and core strength. Avoid leaning on the attacker as she makes contact and drives to the cage. Smart attack players will feel their defender leaning and step away (to make the defender fall forward) before exploding to the cage. Focus on the ball carrier's hips, not her head, shoulder, or stick. Keep the feet moving and stay balanced, keeping the attacker in between the shoulders, listening for the double team.

Blocking and Intercepting

Blocking and intercepting are rarely given their due in organized practices; however, they are invaluable defensive skills. They both require anticipation, good timing, and hand-eye coordination on the defender's part. Dominant defenders make it a point to consistently attempt to block and intercept at every practice and every game; gaining and maintaining possession of the ball is always on their minds. Defensive players who are proactive instead of reactive, those who embrace learning and practicing these particular skills, tend to stand out because they influence the outcomes of games.

Blocking: The defender is positioned a stick's length away from and slightly to the side of the ball carrier when blocking a pass or shot to avoid getting hit with the ball or the follow-through. She mirrors the ball carrier's stick with her own, with either one or two hands on her stick, depending on the height required. As the ball carrier releases the pass or shot, the defender keeps her eye on the ball, extends her stick vertically by sliding the stick through the top hand to meet the ball as it leaves the stick, and blocks or deflects the pass or shot. The timing of the stick extension is critical and coincides with anticipating when the ball carrier will pass. Don't be tempted to angle the stick too far forward toward the ball carrier. Keep it straight up and down,

By sliding her top hand down the stick and maintaining good body position, the defender is able to block the pass of her opponent.

mirroring the attacker's stick. Too much of an angle cuts down on the timing of the block and can leave the defender off-balance, allowing the attacker to gain an advantage. Once the ball is blocked, the defender must step in front of her opponent, cutting off her path to the ball, and pick up the ground ball.

Intercepting: The offense is flying down the field on a fast-break. From across the field, you detect the ball carrier's intent to send the ball to a player near you. You watch as she brings her stick back and launches the ball; everyone's eyes are on it. Nobody notices as you begin to react. Just as your opponent attempts to catch

the ball, you explode in front of her and snag the pass, thwarting what was sure to be a clean catch and goal. Your decision to act aggressively results in a change of possession and, more importantly, game momentum.

Intercepting a pass is one of the most exciting skills a player can execute because it requires the element of surprise. Interceptions happen when a player "reads" or anticipates where the other team is going to pass the ball and then steps in front of the intended receiver and catches the pass, gaining possession from the opponent. When intercepting a pass, the top hand is slid as far down the stick as possible (for greatest reach) while still maintaining control. The trick is to react precisely when the passer brings her stick back to pass—not *after* the ball has been released! The intercepting player bursts into the passing lane while stepping in front of the intended receiver. Once the interception is made, the player brings her stick in front of her and cuts off her opponent to protect the ball. As always, she accelerates through the catch.

Off-Ball Defense

Maintaining Angles

While one defender marks the player with the ball, six other defenders need to be aware of what the ball carrier is doing and whether or not their teammate playing the ball needs help. If the on-ball defender has control of her opponent—if she's able to keep the ball carrier between her shoulders and dictate her movements on the field—then she does not need help and the other defenders can "hold." An off-ball defender must watch the ball *and* her opponent at the same time; she positions herself at an angle that allows her to see both without having to turn her head to see either the ball or her girl.

One of the most common tactical errors defenders make is to turn their heads to find the ball, losing sight of the players they are marking;

Extra effort pays off! Extending her stick, this player is able to intercept the ball and gain possession for her team.

once they do, the attackers have an advantage. Attack players are taught to cut hard behind the defender and to the cage if they see the back of a defender's head. By maintaining a triangle between themselves, the ball, and their opponents, off-ball defenders can see both the ball and their opponents at the same time and react accordingly. In a settled defensive situation, defenders on the ball side should have their backs facing the *line of center* (an imaginary line that splits the field in half from one center of the goal to the other) while defenders on the off-ball side should have their chests facing the line of center. (See figure 7.2.) This positioning discourages "ball-watching" and "girl-watching."

Coaches' Tip: Ask your defenders to take one step back to increase their angle and see both ball and girl. Most defenders don't give themselves enough of an angle and end up having to turn their heads. That one extra step can make a big difference!

Off-Ball Stick Position

A critical component of off-ball defense is the ability of the defensive players to keep their sticks up and in the passing lane. They do this with either one or both hands on their sticks; the objective is to keep sticks straight up and down, in the passing lanes, protecting the middle of the 8-meter. They want to make themselves as big and tall as possible and create as many distractions as possible to thwart the feeders and cutters. This isn't the place for shopping cart defense: No sticks at the hips! At Hopkins, we have our players hold their sticks straight up and down at all times during practice—even when we pull the team in to speak with them. Our players remind each other in the team huddle—sticks up! It is habit-forming. Although this may sound a bit odd, it creates a focus on defense. That focus begins in practice and may lead to having the stick in an attacker's passing lane and ultimately gaining a defensive advantage.

Encouraging your players to keep their sticks up in every huddle develops a good habit. Keep sticks up!

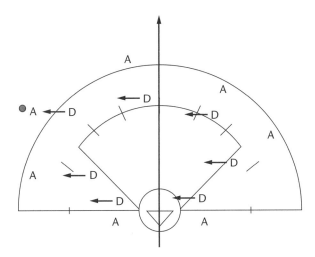

Figure 7.2   The line of center is an imaginary line from the center of one goal to the other, and it splits the field in half.

Defending a Cut through the 8-Meter

Off-ball defenders want to prevent cutters from moving easily through the 8-meter arc. Keep in mind that great defenders don't react to attackers' movements, they dictate them. Too often, defenders are content to "follow" attack players as they cut for the ball; as a result, they find themselves trailing the cutters, having done nothing to control their players. If the off-ball defender's girl cuts, she needs to anticipate the cut and *step up* into the path of that cutter, forcing her to change the path of her cut. By stepping up and *squaring her hips* to the cutter, a defender will effectively disrupt a cut, slow down the attacker, and gain good body position.

Defenders should avoid *opening up their hips* and giving an attacker the open lane for cutting. Defenders want to step at 45-degree angles, not open their hips and give the attacker a lane to the cage. Players can develop a good conceptual understanding of controlling cutters by practicing this skill without sticks, at least to start; this forces them to get their bodies and feet in the right positions without relying on their sticks. The key to controlling a cutter is to anticipate her move, step across her path, and redirect where she goes.

Defensive Slides

In settled defense, when the ball carrier challenges her defender one-on-one to the cage, an adjacent off-ball defender slides, meaning she moves toward the player with the ball to help her teammate, which results in a double team. This leaves the sliding player's opponent open, so the next adjacent defender must slide (move) to cover the open defender. This, in turn, leaves her player open. The defenders continue sliding until one defender on the *backside* (the side opposite the ball) is left covering two offensive players. (See figure 7.3.)

When sliding to double-team, players must commit to remain in the double team until they come up with the ball or the ball gets passed.

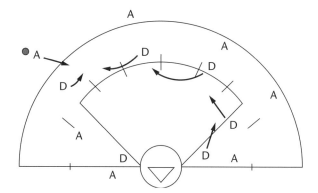

Figure 7.3   Defensive movement when the ball carrier challenges to the cage. Notice the player open on the backside (farthest away from the ball).

Once the ball is passed, the defensive unit must "reset" back into player-to-player defense. One way to reset is to have a defender who was in the double team sprint to the middle of the 8-meter, toward the backside, where she expects the open player to be. All the while, her teammates are communicating to her about the location of the open player.

A more advanced way to "reset" depends on the double-team defender who is opposite and away from where the ball moves. She slides to the next adjacent player and "bumps" the remaining defenders around to the open player. This technique makes the slides short and quick. It requires good communication and anticipation on the defenders' parts, but is extremely effective. (See figure 7.4.)

Playing tenacious defense is critical in the modern game. More and more attention is being given to this aspect of the game. Coaches can set the bar high for their team by focusing on developing a solid defensive unit. Finding ways to celebrate great defensive play is important to team culture and ultimately to ensuring that a team plays a complete game. Tracking individual and team defensive statistics can help make playing defense fun. Addressing the defense first can be effective too. Let's face it, most players enjoy recognition. Offensive players get in-

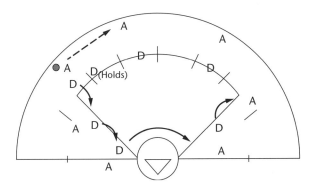

Figure 7.4 The defense slides and resets *opposite* the path of the ball.

stant gratification when a goal is scored. Often ignored is the hard work that defenders do just prior to goals. Many coaches play their best athletes on defense, and these players often dictate the outcomes of games. Remind your defense: "Offense wins games, defense wins championships."

DRILLS, DRILLS, DRILLS

3 v 3 in Half of the 8-Meter Drill

Set up the drill using cones to cut the 8-meter in half. Extend the cones behind to keep players from going across the midpoint. (See figure 7.5.) Encourage the attack to make one move and go to goal to draw the double. Once the ball moves,

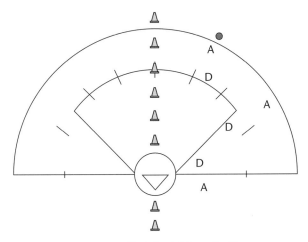

Figure 7.5 3 v 3 in Half of the 8-Meter Drill

the defense will have to reset quickly. Encourage your defenders to go for back side doubles and to come up with the ball. The attack must stay inside the boundary on one half of the field; the defense gets a point if the attack steps outside the cones. This will teach the defense to hold good body position 1 v 1 and in their doubles. The attack gets a point for scoring; the defense gets a point for causing a turnover or forcing an off angle shot.

Defensive Box Drill

This drill is a foundation for players who are learning how to play proper defense. There are many options to this drill. Coaches are encouraged to increase the difficulty and enhance learning.

Two players per group are needed for this drill. The whole field can be used to set these grids up for team practice. (See figure 7.6.)

Players are set up in a 10-yard by 10-yard grid. The defender begins without a stick. The offensive player has a stick and a ball. The offensive player sets up at the top of the box in the middle of the two cones. The defender is one stick-length away. On the whistle, the offensive player attempts to get to the opposite side of the box (H) without turning over the ball. The fender wants to step up, forcing the ball carrier to cradle on her weak side, and drive her out of the box before she reaches the opposite side of the box. The defenders are allowed to use their forearms or knuckles to direct the attackers.

The progressions on this drill are as follows:

1. Both players execute drill without sticks.
2. Attacker uses stick (no ball); defender has no stick.
3. Attacker has stick and ball; defender holds stick reversed, upside down, and can turn it around if the attacker drops the ball.
4. Attacker and defender use sticks in the normal fashion.

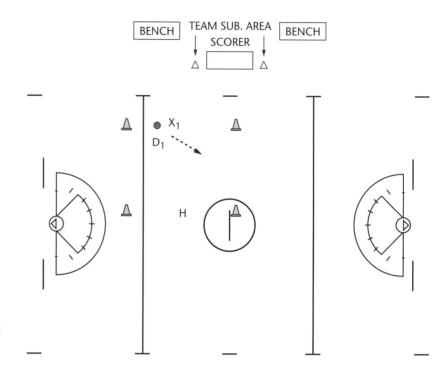

Figure 7.6   Defensive Box Drill

It is key that defenders understand proper foot-work and defensive body position. The defender does not want to end up chasing the offensive player; she wants to be directing the offensive player. The defender gets a point for a ball that is dropped, a point for forcing the offensive player out on her weak side, and a point if the offensive player has to cradle on the weak side. The offensive player gets two points if she reaches the opposite side of the grid and a bonus point if she switched to her weak side and cradled without turning over the ball.

Key Drill Aspects

1. Defender must use good footwork and stay balanced.
2. Defender sets up on the offensive player's strong side.
3. Defender must lead/direct her player out of the grid.
4. Offensive player must keep moving and cradling.
5. Offensive player must be creative to get by defender.

World Cup Drill (One Ball)

Set up four feeders (one each in the 1, 2, 4, and 5 spots). Set up a 1 v 1 or a 2 v 2 inside the 8-meter. (See figure 7.7.) There is one ball that moves around the outside, and feeders are look-ing for the inside attack player(s) to get open. The attack player(s) inside works to get open, using each other if there is more than one in-side, using picks, screens, pops, and so on. The defender(s) focuses on communicating, zoning up the cutters, switching on picks, STAYING BALL SIDE, to deny the pass inside. You can also control the drill by not allowing the ball to move. Each feeder takes a turn feeding the ball into the middle.

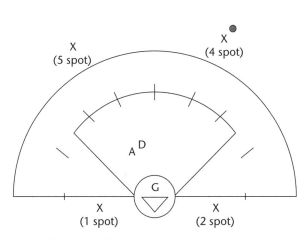

Figure 7.7 World Cup Drill

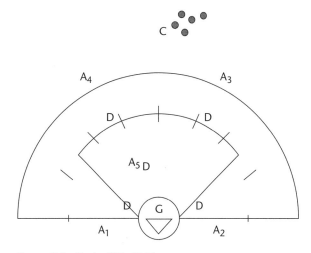

Figure 7.8 Early Slide Drill

Early Slide Drill

Set up with five attackers and five defenders (four pairs in a box around the 8-meter and one pair in the middle of the 8-meter; see figure 7.8). The balls are up top with a coach, who lobs a ball in to the attack player in the 2 spot (A_2), who dodges right away looking to draw the double. The attackers are encouraged to stay in their box and one, while the defense is encouraged to slide aggressively, looking to double hard and get the ball. Once the attacker moves the ball, the defense must work to reset quickly backside.

This drill works offensively on:

• Dodging hard to draw double teams
• Backing out of double teams
• Moving the ball quickly to find the open player on the back side
• Reading defenses

This drill works defensively on:

• 1 v 1 defense
• Sliding
• Closing double teams
• Re-setting out of double teams
• Defensive communication

8

The Art of Checking

This defender is ready to check on the ground ball pickup.

Checking is not just another defensive skill to be learned; it is an art to be practiced and perfected. In addition to the physical aspects of this skill, there's a particular mindset that distinguishes great take-away defenders.

A take-away defender is a supreme strategist. She's a seizer of moments: a rattlesnake waiting to strike. Keenly perceptive, she sizes up opponents, watching and waiting until she knows what they will do even before they themselves know it. Then—CHECK!—she shuts them down. Her calculated risk pays off. A whopping 90 percent of the time, a good take-away defender gets the ball. A great take-away defender steals balls—and more. She chips away at her opponents' composure and self-confidence. A great take-away defender exercises incredible mental toughness. She asserts herself, maintaining control and dominance even when she's a step behind the ball carrier—especially when she's a step behind.

PRINCIPLES OF CHECKING

As a defensive strategy, checking must be taught precisely and practiced carefully. Too many sloppy swipes and dangerous swings attempt to pass for checks because coaches and players are satisfied with poor technique or a lack of discipline. Women's lacrosse is best served by short, precise check-and-releases, by a snapping motion with no backswing or follow-through. Female athletes need to be vigilant about learning and practicing checking within the parameters of our game. One of the best ways to harness and streamline the lovely aggressiveness of today's female lacrosse players (who happen to be quicker, stronger, faster, and tougher than ever before), is by appreciating and fine-tuning the art of stick checking. Checking has a tremendous impact not only on the outcome of individual games, but also on the whole future of women's lacrosse. Out-of-control checking is unsportsmanlike and

dangerous, and it will land the women's game on a fast track to mandatory helmets.

Think about it: If a defender's main objective is to dislodge the ball from an opponent's stick and make away with it, fast, then it's actually counterproductive for her to come out waving a weapon in her opponent's face. It's impossible to be stealthy and efficient while swiping and swinging. The take-away defender holds a revered position on any team. She, better than anyone, understands that a fine line separates the great player from the goon. She knows that a check must be executed correctly, precisely, or not at all. It's that simple: Check the right way, or don't check. It's much smarter to concentrate on maintaining good body position than to throw a haphazard check.

Players and coaches have long recognized the advantages of being proficient with both hands while cradling, throwing, and catching; the same can be said for checking. Among the cutting-edge developments in the sport at the higher levels is that players are learning not only to check equally well with right and left hands but also to effectively contain opponents with their sticks in either hand.

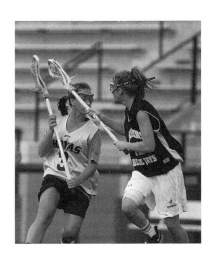  

Left: The defender sets up the check. Notice that her top hand is slid halfway down the stick to increase her reach. *Center:* The defender makes contact. Notice that her hips could be a little more square to her opponent to assure control and balance. *Right:* Success! The defender dislodges the ball with a controlled check.

THE SKILL OF CHECKING

First things first: Defensive body positioning, patience, and balance are the three fundamentals of stick checking. These concepts need to be understood before any specific method of checking can be mastered. They need to be reviewed again (and again!) with every new check that you want to add to your defensive arsenal. Key details are:

- Grip and positioning of hands
- "Snap" motion—working the wrists, NOT the arms

Grip and Hand Positions

Checking does not require a white-knuckled death grip. Soften your grip by allowing your fingertips to control the check. The bottom hand controls the motion and the top guides it. Place the bottom hand at the very end of the stick, resting the butt on the top of the inside of the little finger. Extend the thumb so it's pointing up the stick. Curl the remaining fingers around the pole.

The top hand is no higher than two-thirds of the way down the stick; it's not right next to the bottom hand because if they're too close, you give up control. It's no higher than two-thirds of the way down because you don't want to limit your reach, throw yourself off-balance, or inhibit the range of motion of your top arm. Here's how to arrange your fingers: Keep your thumb in line with the bottom-hand thumb: It will anchor your top hand onto the stick. Now, there's a bit of room for personal preference: The other four fingers can all be wrapped around the stick, or the top finger can point up the shaft. Try both styles and use whichever feels right to you. With this grip, you'll find yourself staring straight at the sidewall, with the open part of the stick head facing to your left. Many defenders like to check with their sticks in this position—

they aim for the corner of their opponents' sticks; the ball pops out as the stick turns.

Here's a slight variation on the theme: Keep the open stick head facing toward you while trying to connect with the top corner of your opponent's stick to dislodge the ball. With the stick head already open, you'll be able drop it immediately into a position to pick up a ground ball. This technique also gives you more surface area from your stick to connect with your opponent's stick and complete the check.

Snap Motion

Essentially, the stick check is a snapping motion: Snap down to make contact and a quick snap back to release. The wrists, not the arms, are most important in executing an effective check. Wrists, YES; arms, NO.

Arm Position

- Arms away
- Elbows locked at an angle

To maintain good body position, keep the arms away from the body, not in tight. You need to put space between the chest and arms: Think about hugging a tree. Now, keep the elbows locked and at an angle—not sticking out. Holding the arms away from the body and keeping the elbows locked at an angle are keys for maintaining balance and proper body positioning for checking.

Body Position

- Knees slightly bent
- Balanced body weight
- Sitting position
- Maintain body position in relation to each check

Here are some thoughts to keep in mind before you check, during the check, and after you dislodge the ball. (You will dislodge the ball on the vast majority of your checks if you execute these techniques.)

BEFORE THE CHECK

On-Ball Body Position

Good defensive body positioning depends on maintaining balance. If you're off balance, don't throw a check. Keep your knees slightly bent, as if sitting in a chair. Your back is straight up and down, as if sitting in a chair, with your butt tucked in and feet shoulder-width apart and directly underneath your shoulders. If the shoulders are thrust forward, the defender is not in a strong and balanced position. Feet can be square, or one can be slightly in front of another; that's personal preference.

Mentally, the checker is sizing up her opponent, assessing her speed and style of cradle. If she cradles close to her head and doesn't present her stick often, you are going to defer to maintaining good body positioning, holding the check until a more opportune moment. If the checker is up against someone who's protecting her stick, she doesn't force something that isn't there. (There are ways to bait opponents into hanging their sticks, but more on that later.) Self-control is what separates great from good defenders. Waiting for the right check is a smart defensive strategy; this way, you'll not hang your team out to dry by sacrificing good body position and forcing a check, risking a player-down situation because you've been beat.

Midfield Body Position

The midfield position mirrors the on-ball body position. If you're running with an opponent, slightly angle your hips and shoulders upfield; keep your feet under your shoulders, as this helps you keep your balance. Balance is always key. The same mental strategies and decisions apply here as with on-ball body position.

DURING THE CHECK

Midfield Checks

Quick Strike—Snap and Release

Elegantly simple, this is an excellent check to throw while moving at top speed alongside your opponent. Do not attempt this check if you are behind your opponent; you'll foul by reaching across her body. Catch up first. This check is driven by the wrists. Aim for the corner of your opponent's stick, ultimately turning her stick; as the stick turns, the ball will dislodge. Make sure to stay alongside or slightly in front of your opponent; this requires patience and timing. Always check away from the head, NEVER toward the head or body. Before the check, make sure your stick is perpendicular to the ground, at about 10 or 2 o'clock. Do not hold your stick across your opponent's body.

Handle Check

This is a tempting check to take while running alongside your opponent. Don't do it. This check involves checking in toward your opponent's body and making contact with the handle of her stick. It is not safe and most of the time results in a foul. This check is not recommended.

Butt-of-the-Stick Check

Players these days don't expose the butts of their stick very often, so the opportunities to use this check are waning. Hooking or checking the butt ends of sticks generally is unsafe and not recommended. Most times, these checks result in a defender sacrificing her body positioning and fouling.

Poke Check

The poke check often comes from behind, when a defender is trailing her opponent in the midfield. It's a sneak attack. Follow an attacker with your stick extended in front of you. Your top hand grips the stick loosely as a guide hand. Your bottom hand is for control; use a tighter grip here. While timing your opponent's cradle, choose an opportune moment to poke—extend your bottom arm so your stick slides smoothly and accurately through the top hand; the open stick head is facing down. Best timing tip: When an opponent cradles back, behind her, you poke forward.

The poke check also can be used when the defender is facing her attacker, as in a settled defensive situation. The defender will time the poke check to the ball carrier's cradles. As the cradle comes forward, the defender drops her stick slightly and pushes her stick through her top hand looking to poke the ball out of her opponent's stick. Remember to maintain your balance, poke away from the head, bring the stick back immediately, and be ready to pick up the ground ball.

Trail Check (from Behind)

The trajectory of your stick needs to stay in a limited range—from the top of your head to your belly button. It's a disciplined snap; if your stick starts above your head or ends up down by your feet, that's unacceptable and unsafe. Don't swing or swipe. Catch up with your opponent first, as with the poke check. Get as close to your opponent as you possibly can from behind. Your top hand is two-thirds of the way down on your stick; that's where it stays to execute this check. Snap and release (keeping well away from your opponent's head) without sliding your stick through the top hand. Remember, catch up first, wait for the right time to check, snap down and back, checking away from your

The defender extends her stick to execute a clean and controlled trail check.

opponent's head, aim for the corner of her stick to dislodge the ball. Be ready when she slows down to establish body position!

Bait and Check

This is a favorite of takeaway defenders. You're flying down the field defending the ball carrier, who is well aware of your presence, and she knows you want the ball. Use your bottom arm and the butt end of the stick to fake a check toward the front. Your opponent's natural reaction will be to pull her stick back behind her head and, possibly, her shoulder. Because your stick head is in good position—essentially angled back as you fake your bottom hand forward—you're ready to throw a quick and tight circular check as she brings her stick back, making contact with your opponent's stick in the first part of a counterclockwise rotation. The completion of the check is to finish the counterclockwise rotation, returning your stick back to where it started. The ball likely will dislodge behind your opponent. Be ready to stop and immediately step between ball and opponent for a ground ball pickup.

Ground Ball Pickups

Checking fouls are all too common during ground ball pickups. Timing, patience, and a quick release will lead to a successful check on a ground ball.

The "Out and Away" Check

This is a simple but sophisticated advanced-level check that's both safe and effective. The key is to make contact underneath your opponent's stick by snapping out and away as she attempts to pick up the ground ball. Focus on keeping the momentum of the check away from your body, instead of checking up, down, or toward your opponent. This check will immediately propel the ball out in front of you—be ready to cut off your opponent to recover the loose ball.

The "Up" Check

This check is commonly used and often draws fouls; it's considered dangerous when the follow-through brings your and your opponent's sticks toward her head and into her face as she attempts to pick up the ground ball. We do not recommend checking "up" on a ground ball pickup.

The "Down" Check

Even more common than the up check, this fundamental technique often results in a hold situation and draws a foul. If you plan to use this check, practice checking down when the ball is in your opponent's stick and releasing quickly. Also, make sure the downward motion is not a big swipe or swing starting from above

the head, but a quick, precise snap-and-release starting from eye level or lower. Remember to aim for the corner of your opponent's stick to try to turn the stick and dislodge the ball.

AFTER THE CHECK

A defender who executes good checking technique and pays close attention to the outcomes of her actions asks herself: Did I make contact? Have I dislodged the ball? Where did the ball go? What's my body position in relation to my opponent?

Having dislodged the ball, your first priority is to cut off your opponent's path to the ball by using your body as a barrier. This may be the moment when you simply have to take one for the team: Stepping into the path of a sprinting opponent requires guts, and a sturdy backside. Put your back and butt in between the ball and your opponent and maintain that position as if your life depends on it. Boxing out your opponent can determine possession of the ground ball.

Once you've stepped into an opponent's path, effectively inserting yourself between her and the ball, immediately slide your top hand to the top of your stick. This simple but often neglected action helps to protect your stick and the ball when you pick it up. It helps keep your stick (and the ball) between your shoulders, not exposed to your opponent. When you slide your top hand up, you tend to cradle between your shoulders and not leave your stick exposed, vulnerable to attack by an opponent who's coming to get her ball back. A key fundamental: Once your top hand is at the top of the stick, be sure to bend your knees to get low enough while picking up the ground ball. A critical fundamental: As soon as you pick up the ground ball—RUN FAST! Get out of pressure and look to move the ball to a teammate.

If you throw a check and miss your mark, regroup before throwing another one. Don't be tempted to keep attacking, piranha-like. Your first priority, before attempting a subsequent check, is to reestablish good defensive body position. Wait for another opportune moment. Patience is key to minimizing checking fouls.

THE DOS AND DON'T-EVERS OF CHECKING

Do

- Establish and maintain good body position.
- Stay balanced.
- Be patient.
- Check with purpose.
- Check and release with short, quick strokes.
- Check under control.
- Check when you're 90 percent sure you can come up with the ball.

Don't Ever

- Check toward the head.
- Check toward the body.
- Check with a big swing.
- Check out of desperation.
- Sacrifice body position for a check.
- Check and hold your opponent's stick.
- Check out of control.
- Check unless you are 90 percent certain you can come up with the ball.

DRILLS, DRILLS, DRILLS

Check-If-You-Can Drill

This drill emphasizes staying balanced while checking and the importance of a quick check-and-release with no backswing. Players are encouraged to be patient and wait for the best opportunity to check, which develops control and good decision making.

Partners face each other. One partner has a ball.

The player with the ball holds the stick parallel to the ground and with the stick head pointing toward her partner (with her top hand slid halfway down the stick), and cradles from side to side trying to avoid the defender's check. She wants to bait the defender into checking and then move her stick quickly out of the way.

The defender is timing the ball carrier's cradle and patiently waits to check. She has her top hand slid about two-thirds of the way down the stick and her feet are offset for balance. When she does check, she snaps her stick down and back immediately, aiming for the corner of the ball carrier's stick to dislodge the ball.

Emphasize:

- Checking with mostly wrist and only some arm.
- Staying balanced and maintaining good defensive position.

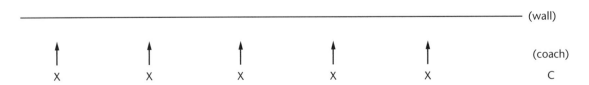

Figure 8.1   Defend the Wall Drill

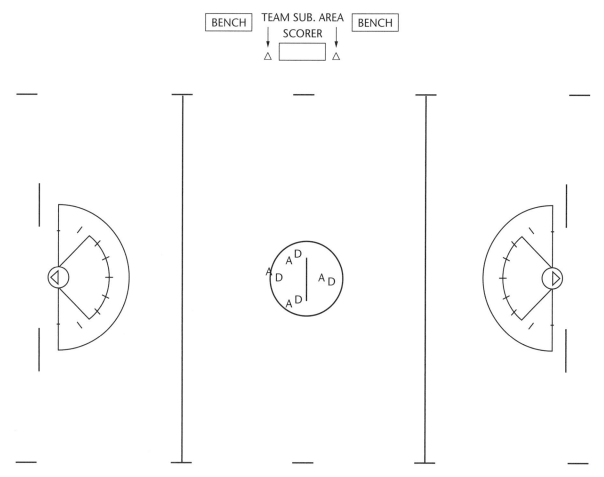

Figure 8.2   Center Circle Checking Drill

- No lunging, no backswing, no follow-through to the ground.
- Patience and timing.
- Variation—have the checker use a circular check-and-release motion.

Defend the Wall Drill

This is an excellent drill that teaches correct defensive stance, proper stick positioning, how to break down players' steps on their approach as well as stay balanced, and the importance of keeping arms away and elbows locked—all things critical to checking.

Have players line up (with their sticks) in groups of five, about 10 yards away from a wall, facing that wall (see figure 8.1).

Ask players to show you their defensive stance:

- Knees slightly bent—sit
- Feet and hips under the shoulders, butt tucked in
- Arms away, elbows locked at an angle (have someone push on them to emphasize locking the elbows), stick up

On the whistle, players sprint to the wall, make contact (with knuckles or forearm to the wall), all the while maintaining good defensive position with sticks up and flat against the wall. If players don't break their steps down correctly, they will smash into the wall (and that will hurt!). This drill teaches players how to keep their bodies under control and break down their steps while moving at top speed.

Players must keep their feet moving (fast feet) as they "defend the wall." After 15 to 20 seconds on the wall, whistle and the next group steps up.

Corrections to Make

Players must keep their sticks up, not at their waists.

Do not allow players to break their arms and have them too close to their bodies.

Maintaining balance is key—no leaning!

Encourage players to break their steps down quickly and maintain fast feet.

Center Circle Checking Drill

This drill works on checking technique in a confined area. It forces the defender to establish body position first and then check. It also works on closing double teams.

Set up the drill at the center circle (see figure 8.2).

Put the team inside the center circle and designate four players to be defenders. The remaining players all have balls.

On the whistle, the ball carriers are moving and cradling to avoid the defenders, and the defenders are trying to check the balls out of their sticks. Have the defenders work alone to start—then allow them to work in pairs in order to double team.

The last player left with a ball "wins."

Defenders who foul when they check have to step out of the drill and do pushups. Coaches, call them out! Remember to encourage checking, not swinging.

Checking Box Drill

Set up a box with four cones 10 yards by 10 yards. (See figure 8.3.)

Two defenders are in the box along with one attacker.

The goal of the drill is to have the defenders create a turnover by double-teaming and checking, or force the attacker out of the box through good body positioning within 10 to 15 seconds.

The defenders have to be smart, patient, and able to close the double team. They must communicate and check with patient control.

The attack player wants to work on protecting her stick, handling the pressure of a double team and reading where to beat the double.

Set up several of these boxes and rotate the entire team through them. Each box can have different rules and variations.

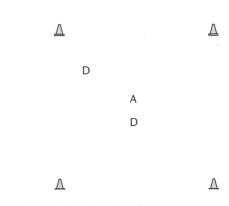

Figure 8.3 Checking Box Drill

9

The Draw

A center draw specialist sets up for the draw.

Every great team needs at least one player—several, ideally—to become a center draw specialist. That specialist is usually a midfielder, but not necessarily; she can be an attacker or a defender. No matter who, she consistently controls the ball at the center draw.

THE BASICS

A center draw takes place at the midfield on the centerline and is used to start each half of a game and any overtime periods. After a goal is scored, the game is restarted with a center draw at the centerline. Possession is paramount. Each team member, not just each center draw specialist, is vying for possession off the center draw. Each is anticipating, moving, and "boxing out."

Boxing Out

Center draw specialists, as well as the players around the center circle, should be proficient at being able to box out their opponents. Just as in basketball, this skill involves putting your body in between the opponent and the ball in order to come up with possession. For players around the center circle, when the whistle blows, the first step you want to take is across the body of an opponent, using your back, hips, and backside to maintain your position between an opponent and the ball. When the opponent moves to get around you, move to box her out or restrict her movement toward the ball.

If the ball is drawn short, step across your opponent's path toward the ball to establish your position. However, if the ball is drawn long—if it sails over your head—drop step and swing your hips open, pivoting on one foot, to position yourself in between your opponent and the ball, so your opponent is squarely at your back; your job is to stay in the path between your opponent and the ball.

Moving the Ball

As gratifying as it is for a team to "win the draw," it's just as deflating to have it taken away 5 seconds later. Therefore, the real mission is twofold: winning the draw and moving the ball into your offensive end. In moving the ball, that first pass is critical. The longer a player carries the ball, the more risk she takes of being swarmed. Once a player has the ball in her stick, she keeps her eyes up and feet moving to avoid being collapsed upon. Make the first pass toward the outside of the field and think deep! If a player is under lots of pressure, she can always pass the ball *back* and her teammate can send the ball *over* to the opposite side of the field away from the defensive pressure. Remember to use the concepts practiced in the Pass Back Weave Drill!

MECHANICS OF THE DRAW

Setting Up

The official is responsible for setting up the center draw, but players need to be vigilant. Heads up: If you see or sense that an opponent is even ever-so-slightly tilting her stick head after the ball has been placed by the official between the two sticks, it's up to you to alert the official. An opponent might attempt to tilt her stick because she will clearly gain an advantage if, at the start of the center draw, the ball is resting in the pocket of her stick. Here's the rule:

 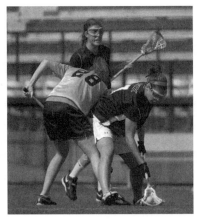 

Left: As soon as the ball hits the ground, the opponents fight to establish position. *Center:* Notice how the player in the dark jersey uses her back and legs to protect the ball. *Right:* After a clean pickup with the ball protected, the ball carrier accelerates.

After gaining possession, the ball carrier has her eyes up, scanning the field for a teammate to receive a pass.

In order for the ball to stay put until the whistle, the players taking the center draw must keep their sticks aligned together and remain motionless until the whistle. Adjusting (i.e., tilting) your stick after the official moves away is a foul; the official may choose to come back and reset the draw, or will award possession and a free position in the event of an illegal draw.

—NCAA Women's Lacrosse Rules and Interpretations

Once the official places the ball in the upper third of each stickhead at its widest point, both players must apply equal pressure to keep the ball in place between their sticks. Sometimes, an opponent will soften her hands or may not apply much pressure in an attempt to gain illegal advantage. Again, it's wise to call an official's attention to these tactics.

Assertiveness is one quality of a great center draw specialist. Here are some others:

Brute physical strength, in order to direct or place the ball

Quick hands and wrist movement; the ability to get the edge by getting under the ball first

Ability to communicate, not only with words, but also with eyes and subtle body language

Ability to read opponents

Ability to see open space and determine how to best use it

Ability to think on one's feet; knowing how to get the ball into her or his teammate's stick

Being tall is a bonus, not a requirement; an extra inch or two might allow you to outreach an opponent and pluck the ball out of the air.

Lining Up

When lining up to take the draw, a center draw specialist has lots of freedom and can be creative about the grip on her stick, where she positions herself, and her stance. However, one aspect of the draw always remains consistent no matter who's doing it and what she hopes to achieve: The back of your stick head will always face your goal.

The Grip

For strength and control, most center draw specialists tend to hold their sticks as high up on the neck and as close to the stick head as possible.

Two center draw specialists are ready to take the draw.

Note: A new rule prohibits centers from touching the sidewalls or the pocket of their sticks during the draw. An option for the bottom hand is to curl the pinkie around the bottom of the stick and, with the left hand gripping the top of the stick, curl the wrist forward as far as it will flex (to the point of discomfort). The top hand is as close to the stick head as the rules allow.

Stance and Positioning

Center draw specialists can and should experiment with (and adjust) the positions of their feet and bodies during the draw. Whether you are facing the goal cage or your back is to it, or whether your left foot or your right is toeing the line, your stance and positioning are critically important in terms of controlling and directing the ball.

Hand position and grip on the draw. Notice the pinkie finger at the bottom of the stick.

There are two general techniques; one involves pulling and the other pushing.

Pulling: The specialist's back is to her goal with the back of her stick facing her.

Pushing: The specialist is facing her goal and the open face of the stick is facing her.

"I'd always push three or four in a row, then I'd maybe switch to pulling; you should be good at both, but obviously you will have a preference," says Kerri O'Day, head coach of Loyola women's lacrosse and a notable center draw specialist in her playing days at Loyola College in Maryland. Kerri made it a habit to keep her options open. Her top three options, in order of preference, were

- Draw to herself
- Send a long draw to the offensive side of the circle
- Lose the draw on purpose after communicating with teammates about her plan

Toeing the Line

A center can "toe the centerline" with her right foot, left foot, or both feet. Each center involved in the draw has to have a foot toeing (or next to) the centerline. It's the placement of the feet and the pulling or pushing motion (this will depend on which side of the stick you're on) that help dictate where the ball will go.

Drawing for Distance: Pulling

When drawing for distance, use the rotation of hips and shoulders to power the ball up, out, and away to a teammate.

Stance: The center draw specialist's back is to her goal cage and the back of her stick is to the cage. The right foot is toeing the line, and the left foot is positioned back (a 45- to a 90-degree angle) with knees bent (anywhere from slightly, to sitting really low).

Hands: The right hand is at the bottom of the stick (option: curl the pinkie around the bottom). The left hand is gripping the stick, with the wrist curled forward as far as it will flex, to the point of discomfort. The top hand is close to the stick head, possibly on the throat but not on the sidewall or pocket. Some centers may grip a bit lower but may sacrifice strength and control.

Left: The center draw specialist in the dark jersey is lined up with her back to her cage, ready to take the draw with a pulling motion. *Right:* The center draw specialist in the dark jersey is lined up with her chest facing her cage, ready to take the draw with a pushing motion.

The Objective: To get under the ball with the stick by quickly rotating the wrists and pull for height and distance over the left shoulder.

Secret weapon: An advanced technique is the "tilt and seal." Using the pulling technique, center draw specialists tilt their sticks on the whistle with the rotation of their wrists—like "revving" a motorcycle to get under the ball. After tilting, push the bottom hand away from the body to "seal" the ball in the stick and then complete the follow-through.

Drawing to Self

The best way to possess the draw, says Kerri O'Day, is to perfect the ability to draw to yourself. You can draw to yourself from two different stances: with your back to the goal cage (pulling) or facing the goal cage (pushing). Try this one, and then reverse your stance and hand position for the alternate (pushing) technique.

Top: The center draw specialists are toeing the centerline and ready to take the draw with a *pulling* motion.
Bottom: The center draw specialists are toeing the centerline and ready to take the draw with a *pushing* motion.

Stance: The center draw specialist's back is to her goal cage and the back of her stick is to the cage. Both the right and left foot toe the line. Knees are bent with hips square.

Hands: In the same position as drawing for distance. The top hand is the guide hand.

Once the whistle blows, mirror your opponent's stick as she draws up and out, but only to the point where the ball stays up and over your head. During the draw, your top hand slides as your stick rises straight up; at the end of the draw, your left arm is fully extended as the ball pops above your head. Mirror the opponent's stick as she draws. Following through straight up will direct the ball up, instead of out, so the center can make a play on the ball.

Variation: Practice trying to guide the ball over your right shoulder.

Box out your opponent and take the ball out of the air with a quick turn of your wrist.

Down-the-Line

A center draw specialist can stand on either side of her stick for two different techniques (pulling or pushing) with the same objective: to send the ball sailing along the 50-yard line. Try this one (pulling), and then reverse your stance and hand position for the alternate (pushing) technique.

Stance: The center draw specialist's back is to the goal cage and the back of her stick is to her goal cage. Her left foot toes the line and right foot is behind, at a 45- to 90-degree angle. Knees are bent.

Hands: Curl the wrist of the left hand to get under the ball so the ball is resting in the stick as you're pulling out of the draw; remember to tilt with the revving motion and seal by pushing the bottom of the stick away from your body. As the stick extends above your head, push the ball

down the 50-yard line, or direct the ball to sail along the 50-yard line.

Tips

Here are a series of tips that apply to all of the center draw techniques:

- **Be Whistle Savvy:** Pay attention to the rhythm of the official's whistle so you can get a "jump" on the draw. Officials are supposed to try to vary the timing of their whistles for the draw, but chances are it's fairly consistent. Some players watch the umpire inhale and time the whistle. After a few draws, they can anticipate the whistle and gain a split-second advantage on their opponent.
- **Have a Quick Wrist:** The player who anticipates the whistle and gets "under the ball" first is likely to win the draw; her objective is to rotate her wrist quickly to trap the ball with the lip of the sidewall of the stick.
- **Punch the Pocket:** Some players like to punch the pocket of their stick before taking the draw to allow the ball to rest in their stick when the umpire sets up the draw.
- **Tilt and Seal:** The secret weapon. This technique can be used for both pulling and pushing. When pulling the draw, tilt with a rev and seal with a push of the bottom hand *away* from the body. When pushing the draw, tilt with a rev and seal by pulling your bottom hand *in toward* your body. This movement creates a better angle for you to push the ball over your shoulder. "Once I have pulled with the bottom hand and sealed, I still have a chance to come up with the ball even if I'm not quick enough with the tilt," Kerri explains.

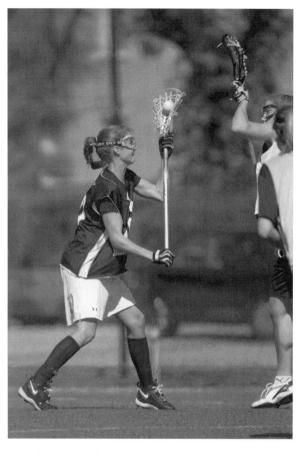

A quick rotation of the wrist results in a perfect draw possession.

- **Rotate:** The draw isn't so much about arm strength as it is about the power derived by rotating the legs, hips, and shoulders.
- **Feet and Follow-Through**
  - The position of a center draw specialist's feet, as well as the steps she takes during and after the draw, directly affect where the ball will go.
  - The follow-through is just as important as the positioning of the feet in directing and controlling the ball.
- Center draw specialists must practice Feet and Follow-through, Pushing and Pulling,

and Tilting and Sealing in order to consistently control the draw.
- Versatility and repetition are the keys to perfecting this important skill.

STRATEGY

Now that you know the mechanics of the draw, let's talk strategy. A player or coach would be remiss not to be aware of what's going on at the draw and make necessary adjustments. Coaches need to address the center draw during time out and halftime discussions by asking for feedback from their center draw specialists. However, well before this, effective coaches make it a point to observe their opponents' center draw techniques as a part of the scouting process. A well-planned strategy to disrupt an opponent's center draw plan can be game changing. Coach Tucker says, "There have been games when we've gone through three or four players taking the center draw, even a couple who weren't center draw specialists, just to mix it up, to try to slow down our opponent." When a coach changes the player who's taking the draw, this can bring a whole new dynamic to a game.

When does a coach decide to make an adjustment? Coach Tucker assesses what's going on after three or four draws: "My rule is, if a team scores, we have to answer. The same is true on center draws. If you're winning consistently, keep an eye on what's working. If you string a couple losses on draws together, on that third or fourth draw, something needs to be done differently."

Whenever an adjustment is made, it's vital to communicate it to the entire team. It could be a head nod or eye contact or discussion during a team huddle. Great center draw specialists make it a habit of approaching their teammates

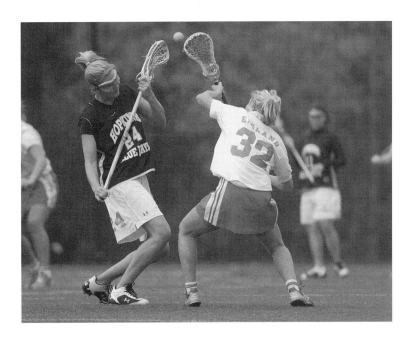

Up and away!

to discuss center draw strategies: "Hey, on this next draw, I'm going to change my stance and send the ball down the 50, make sure you get there."

Have adjustment options at the ready. Coaches can use a formula or plan about what to do when things aren't going well with the draw. Here are four adjustments that can make a big difference:

- Change the player taking the draw.
- Shift and move players on the center circle.
- Instruct the center draw specialist to "lose on purpose" if she's consistently winning the draw but the team is not coming up with the ball; make sure to give the team a heads-up about this plan.
- Adjust the stance of the center draw specialist; go from a "push" to a "pull," for example.

PLAYERS ON THE CIRCLE

At the collegiate level, only three pairs of players are allowed to set up at the center circle, one pair taking the draw and two pairs around the circle. At the high school level, four pairs are allowed to position themselves around, but outside of, the center circle. Three pairs are usually behind the offensive and defensive restraining lines. (If a team is giving up a lot of fast breaks off the draw, it might be beneficial to position one of its attack players behind the opposite restraining line; this added extra body in the defensive end may thwart a fast break.) It is a foul to cross the center circle line, or the restraining line, before the whistle is blown and the ball is in play.

Usually, the pairs line up at angles behind the center draw players, under the assumption that the ball often sails over one shoulder, or the other, of the center draw specialists (figure 9.1).

Players lined up on the circle explode toward the ball as the whistle blows.

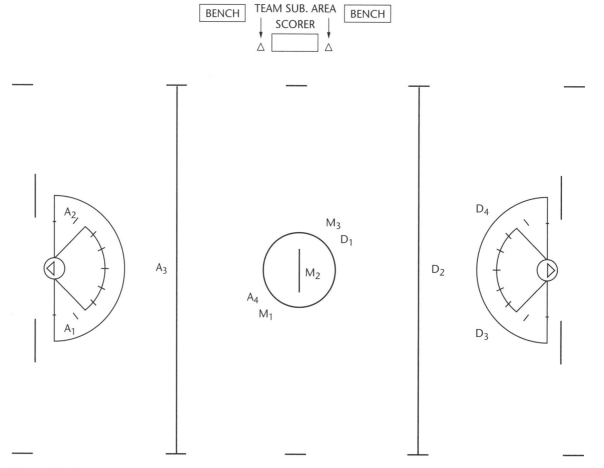

Figure 9.1   Center Draw Set Up—Over the Shoulder

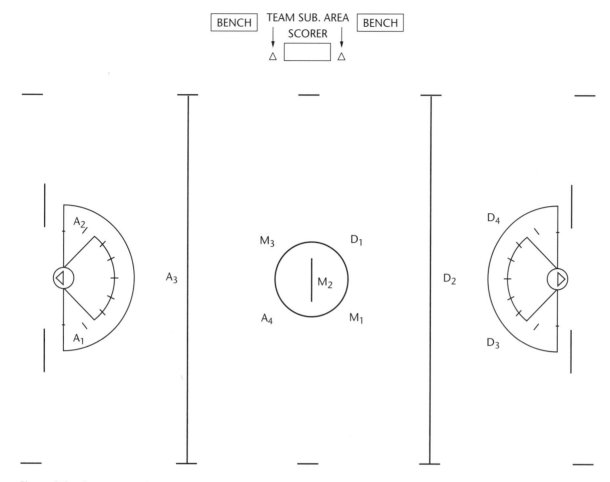

Figure 9.2 Center Draw Set Up—Square

A team may set up around the center circle in the shape of a square, covering each quadrant of the circle (figure 9.2).

The rules allow players to move outside of the center circle before and during the draw. Most teams don't take advantage of this. Most players line up toeing the center circle line, waiting for the whistle. Movement allows for short and long coverage and, more importantly, catches others off guard and helps teams gain an advantage.

Communication is key when trying to gain possession at the draw. One player goes for the short ball while the other goes for the long ball off of the draw. Once a player gains possession,

she immediately gets her "eyes up" to find a teammate to move the ball to and push the fast break. Coach Tucker's defensive secret weapon: One or two middies who are on the opposite side of the field from the draw as the ball sails up into play sprint to the defensive side of the field to take away any fast-break opportunity that the opponent may have off of the draw. "Our rationale is, that if we do come up with the ball, the middies can easily recut and reposition themselves for our offensive push. The priority is to take away our opponent's fast-break opportunity and allow us to be settled defensively, and not be in a pressure situation."

EXERCISES

Specific exercises will enhance any player's ability to become a center draw specialist. Here's some guidance from Chris Endlich, professional strength and conditioning trainer for the Johns Hopkins women's lacrosse team.

Developing Wrist Strength

One of the best ways to strengthen your wrists is to use a wrist roller. There are companies that make these rollers that you can find on the Internet if you do a search on "wrist roller."

Start by holding the roller shoulder level with your arms straight out in front of you and the weight by the floor; your hands should be face down. Start rolling the weight up by turning your hands forward one at a time. Once the weight has reached the top, start lowering the weight by turning your hands backward. When the weight reaches the bottom, repeat the exercise by turning your hands backward on the way up and forward on the way down. You can complete three or four sets of each direction two or three times per week.

Developing Quickness of Wrist Rotation

A fitness band, preferably with a handle, is used to develop quick wrist rotation. Resistance bands can be found on the Internet or in fitness stores. You will be completing two exercises with the band: wrist extension and wrist flexion. Wrist extension involves moving your hand at the wrist so that the top of your hand moves toward your forearm, back and forth. Wrist flexion is just the opposite; you will be moving your hand at the wrist so that your palm moves toward your forearm. Both should be done as quickly as possible so that the exercise is explosive. You should perform 10 to 15 repetitions for two or three sets for each exercise and each arm. Stand on the resistance band at the midpoint, and work your wrists equally.

Developing Strength for the Center Draw

There are a number of exercises you can do to help you with the center draw, many of which can be found in the workout section of this book. The one exercise that may help you the most is a squat with a shoulder press while holding a pair of dumbbells.

To do this exercise, you need a pair of dumbbells that will challenge you on a shoulder press. Start with the weights in your hands at shoulder level, with your palms facing each other, and your elbows directly under your hands. Squat down then stand up and press the dumbbells straight up over your head. This should be done quickly and should result in you leaving your feet slightly. Return the weight to your shoulder level and repeat. Because of the explosive nature of this exercise, you should do no more than 10 repetitions per set for about three sets.

10

Team Offense

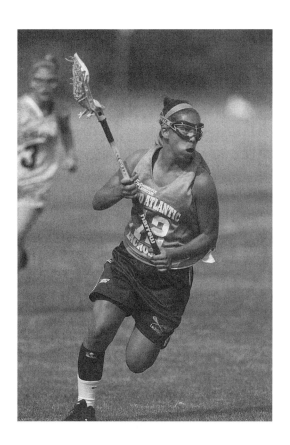

Offensive players always have their eyes up looking to move the ball or shoot! Courtesy US Lacrosse.

This chapter teaches hot spots, break-outs, clears, fast-break situations, settled offensive sets, and situational play. Specially featured are two effective offensive set plays that will put your team in a position to score.

- The defense starts the offense.
- The offense is a unit.
- A team offense will never happen if the defense doesn't accept full responsibility for being integral to the offense.
- Offense starts when your team gains possession of the ball, whether after a save, recovered ground ball, successful ride, or at the center draw; each loose-ball situation creates an offensive opportunity for your team.

• As soon as a team has possession of the ball, no matter where the ball carrier is on the field, that team is on offense, and every player is an attack player.

Coach Tucker says, "We want to play an exciting up-tempo style of offense that puts a tremendous amount of pressure on our opponents. We will choose when to slow the ball down, but until that time, we are playing an in-your-face, stop-us-if-you-can style of offense. The objective is to score often."

A disciplined team is consistent about its decision making on the field. The purpose of an offensive system is to provide a framework that describes where everyone needs to be, why they need to be there, and when. The priorities of an offensive system are as follows, in this order: Breakout, Clear, Fast Break, Slow Break, Settled Play.

THE BREAKOUT

This is the beginning of transition play. Once a team gains possession, no matter where on the field, all teammates break out into good passing lanes to begin transitioning the ball into the offensive end of the field. Running randomly is not effective. Each one of a team's 12 players is responsible for creating offensive opportunities every time her team gains possession. As a positioning guide, think of the field in four zones.

Zone One extends from your team's defensive goal line to the defensive 30-yard line (restraining line).

Zone Two extends from the defensive restraining line to the 50-yard line.

Zone Three extends from the 50-yard line to the offensive restraining line.

Zone Four extends from the offensive restraining line to the offensive goal line extended.

For every breakout, a specific number of players need to position themselves in each of the four zones to maintain balance and proper spacing in the field (figure 10.1). Coaches can be creative with breakout guidelines. Here is Coach Tucker's suggestion:

Zone One: Generally five players, including the goalie

Zone Two: Generally three players

Zones Three and Four: Generally two players each

Notice in the diagram that the attackers are set up in a diamond shape; this allows for options on either sideline as well as an open middle of the field. Be creative with positioning. One of the most important things for players to remember is to maintain proper spacing as they slip into open passing lanes.

During an effective breakout, players need to break at full speed, see the ball, and maintain good spacing. The ideal scenario is to pass the ball first to the sidelines, drawing defensive pressure away from the middle of the field, then move the ball toward the center to push a fast break. However, the ball carrier on the sideline is often pressured and has no option in the center of the field. She needs passing options behind her as well as on the back side (opposite side of the field).

Once the ball carrier draws defensive pressure, she moves the ball BACK and OVER to the opposite side of the field where there is not as much pressure. The pass-back-weave drill will help a team practice moving the ball away from defensive pressure and to the opposite side of the field to clear the ball effectively.

Once the ball crosses the 50, attack the cage from the middle of the field, pushing the fast break. Otherwise, move the ball down the side of the field and behind the goal to prepare for a slow break.

If the ball carrier has one player to beat, she should beat her by keeping the ball moving

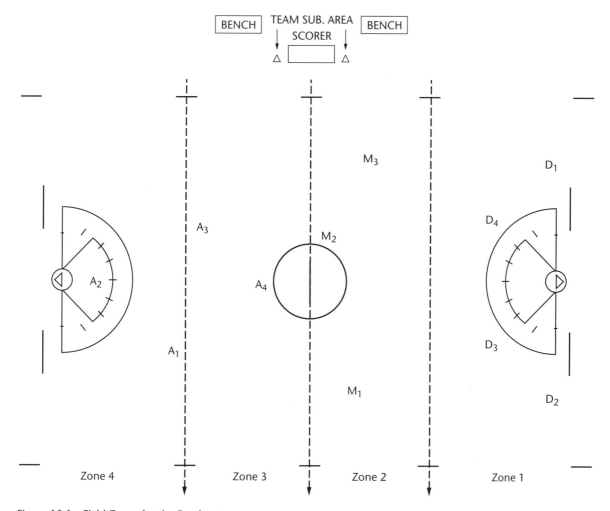

Figure 10.1   Field Zones for the Breakout

forward and dodging hard past her. She needs to lead with her stick, keep her eyes up, and quickly move the ball to an open teammate. Off-ball players: NEVER turn your backs to the ball carrier and run away. ALWAYS keep the ball carrier in your line of sight so you can give her help. (*Coach's tip*: Remember to use the bounce pass and the ground ball pass if pressured; never stop your feet.) Off-ball players are responsible for watching the ball carrier's back, literally, letting her know when pressure is coming, especially checks from behind.

The ability to effectively break out is a critical component of clearing.

CLEARING THE BALL

A clear takes place after a goalkeeper makes a save. It involves players breaking out to specific areas so the goalie can put the ball back into play. Teams can specifically design their clears based on how their opponent is riding. Clearing the ball is the all-important beginning of a team's offensive push. The clear sets into motion a full-field offense. The defense starts the offense. The team that's clearing is technically a player up on offense if they know how to effectively use their goalie. *Note*: A goalkeeper who thinks of herself as a field player will put her team a player up on offense if she's comfortable handling the ball outside of the crease. If the goalkeeper acts as a quarterback, seeing the field, she can quickly read what is available, react, and deliver the ball, putting the offense into motion.

Clearing occurs whenever there is a change of possession in the defensive end of the field. Settled clearing situations occur when there are stoppages of play—after a pass or shot goes out-of-bounds and after a foul is called. Unsettled clearing situations occur when there's a quick change of possession, a loose ground ball, or a save. Each involves the same basic principles. However, teams can develop and practice specific clears that will help to spark their transition game and beat an opponent's ride.

First, it's important for a team to recognize it's in a clearing situation, whether a midfielder has just picked up a loose ground ball or the goalie has made a save. Clearing means effectively getting the ball out of the defensive end of the field. Off of a save, the goalie usually gives direction to the defenders in her area and they,

in turn, relay the information to the remaining field players. A goalie will generally yell, "Break!", "Get Out!" or "Clear!" to alert her defense. However, she could also call a custom-designed clear. If the goalie has the ball inside the crease, she may hold it for up to 10 seconds and then must put the ball into play. Once a team gains possession of the ball in the goal circle and the ball is cleared, the team may not intentionally return the ball to the goal circle until the ball has been played by another player.

A key component to clearing successfully is to maintain quality space between players throughout the entire clear. Once players bunch up, it is easy for opponents to defend them; if the ball carrier doesn't have sufficient space and passing options, she will be double- or triple-teamed.

Clearing Options

Standard Clear

The low defender should cut below the goal line extended and angle back for the ball, allowing her to see pressure coming (figure 10.2). The

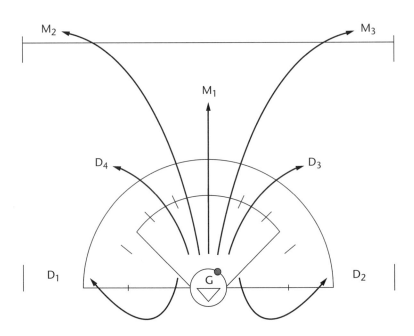

Figure 10.2   Standard Clear

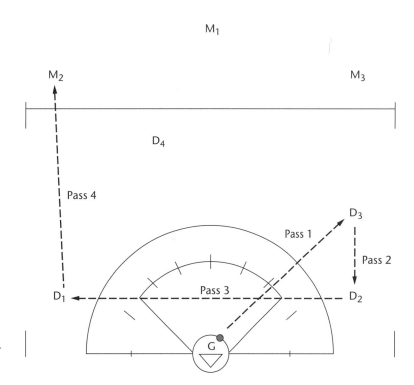

Figure 10.3   Pass-Back Clear

players break out in a balanced pattern, seeing the ball, maintaining good spacing, and giving the goalie a number of passing options. Discourage low defenders from breaking along the goal line extended; encourage them to dip below the goal line extended and angle back to receive passes. This allows players to keep any oncoming pressure in their line of vision.

Pass-Back Clear

The goalie moves the ball to the sideline first, avoiding the middle of the field. The ball carrier moves forward just enough to draw her opponents' pressure; she'll then put on the brakes and turn to the outside of the field, protecting her stick from pressure, sprint away from the pressure, and pass the ball backward to a waiting teammate, who's at least 15 yards away (figure 10.3). Once this player receives the ball, she immediately passes across the field to a waiting teammate, who looks to run or pass the ball upfield.

Long Clear

The goalie quickly clears the ball deep to a player on one side of the field, at about the 50-yard line, initiating a fast-break opportunity. This is a great opportunity to incorporate a designated attack player. Remember: The ball moves faster in the air than with a player carrying it.

Settled Clear—"50"

The middies and defenders break out high and away, half of them clustered on the right side of the field at the 50-yard line, and half of them on the opposite side, all occupying their opponents (figure 10.4). A designated player, M_1, will position herself in the middle of the field, between the 40- and 50-yard lines. Meanwhile, the goalie walks the ball to about the restraining line. The player in the middle of the field sprints toward her goalie, asking for the ball, bringing her defender with her. She puts on the brakes in order to back-door her opponent and curls out,

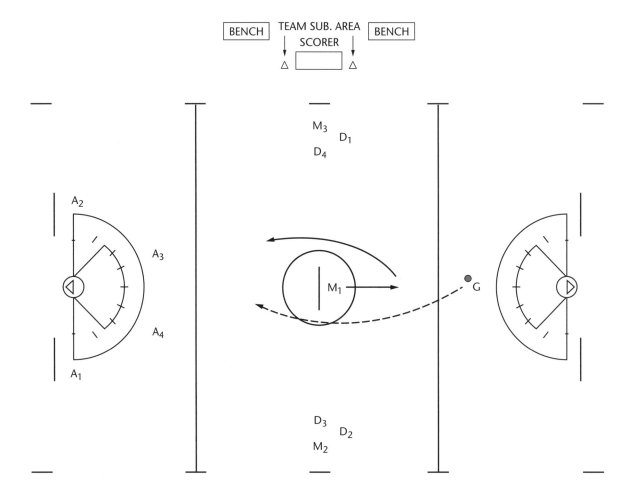

Figure 10.4   Settled Clear—"50"

asking for the ball over her shoulder. The goalie loops a leading pass over the defender and into her teammate's stick, starting a fast break.

Settled Clear—"12"

This clear opens up the middle of the field for a middie to receive the ball. Once she has the ball, her team has a fast-break opportunity. When a save is made, the defensive players break out low and away; a rule of thumb is to head 10 yards above the crease while cutting hard toward the sidelines and looking for the ball (figure 10.5). If opponents are in a player-to-player ride, they will go with their girls.

At the same time, a designated midfielder, M_1, on the defensive end of the field, will hover around the top of the 12-meter fan, looking "lost." She will then burst upfield in a "C" cut, looking for the ball over her shoulder and leading with her stick. The goalie will clear the ball over the cutter's shoulder, starting a fast break.

An attack player will be ball-side at the opposite 40-yard line, ready to pick up an overthrown ball. The remaining attackers are positioned low and toward the goal in a triangle ready to execute a fast break as the ball moves down the field.

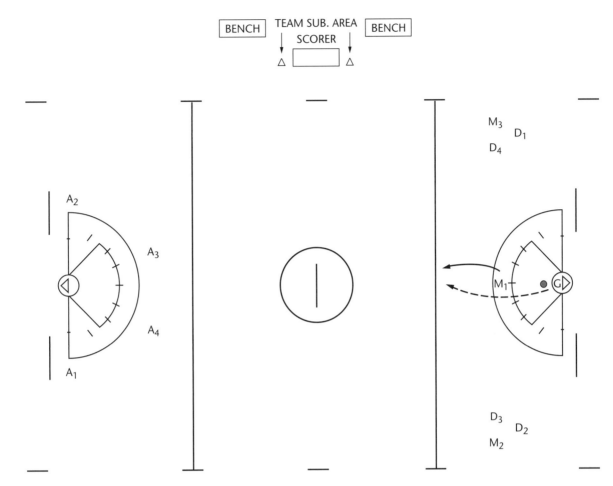

Figure 10.5   Settled Clear—"12"

THE FAST BREAK

Once a team has possession of the ball, it attacks the goal quickly and aggressively, placing its opponents under extreme physical and psychological pressure. The fast break often results in a player-up advantage if the ball is moved quickly enough upfield. It's important to recognize when a fast-break situation occurs. A team has a fast break if, at any time during the transition of the ball, it gains a player-up advantage, for example, a 3 v 2, 4 v 3, 5 v 4, or 6 v 5. If the ball carrier is one step ahead of her opponent, consider that a player-up advantage and push the fast break.

3 v 2 Fast Break

The player bringing the ball down the field initially must decide by the 12-meter whether to pass or shoot (figure 10.6). Look to force the ball-side defender to slide to stop the ball. The two lowest attackers must get to the crease while seeing the ball. This maximizes the space the ball carrier has to work with and makes the slides longer for the defense. Remember, a ball carrier who's coming down the field ahead of her defender does not need help! Avoid cutting toward her and bringing your defense with you; instead, cut to the goal line extended to give the ball carrier space and lengthen the slides for the defense. As the ball-side defender slides to

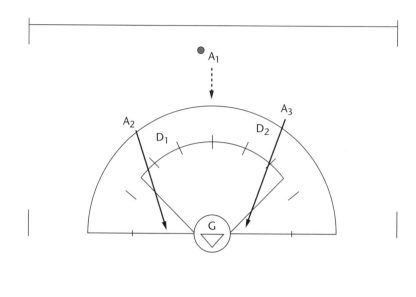

Figure 10.6   3 v 2 Fast Break I

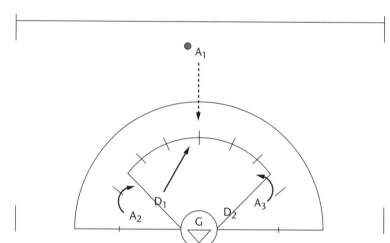

Figure 10.7   3 v 2 Fast Break II

the ball, the attack player whose defender left must curl into the passing lane in good position to catch and shoot (figure 10.7). The opposite attack player should mirror her in an open passing lane and be ready to retrieve the rebound or missed shot or be prepared to receive the second pass and shoot. The ball carrier must read the diagonal defender who's not sliding to the ball; she dictates which attacker is open.

4 v 3 Fast Break

The two lowest attackers must get to the crease while seeing the ball. This maximizes the space the ball carrier has to work with and makes the slides longer for the defense. The ball carrier maintains possession until she is picked up (staying on her original side). She forces the ball-side defender (D_1) to commit (figure 10.8). Once D_1 starts to slide, she passes the ball to the

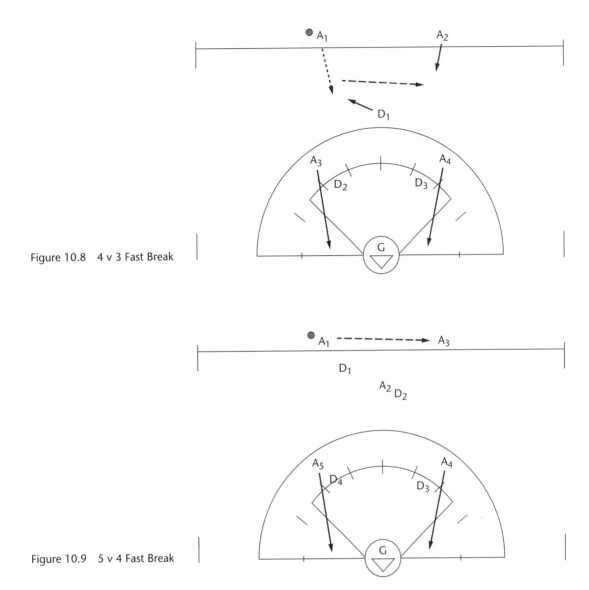

Figure 10.8   4 v 3 Fast Break

Figure 10.9   5 v 4 Fast Break

open player (A_2). Think square: If the attackers stay in the shape of a square, they will maintain good spacing and make sliding longer and harder for the defense. If the defense doesn't slide, shoot!

Force defensive players to commit. Move the ball as the defense moves. Back up the shot. Spacing is key. The ball carrier must read the diagonal defender; it is she who dictates which attacker is open. Do not force the ball; make smart decisions. Read the defense and quickly move the ball to the open player.

5 v 4 Fast Break

The two lowest attackers must get to the crease while seeing the ball. This maximizes the space the ball carrier has to work with and makes the slides longer for the defense. The ball carrier forces a defender to commit and passes to the open player (figure 10.9). The middle offensive player (A_2) must get below the ball and not stay on the same plane as the ball carrier. Look to pass to the middle player if she gets a step on her defender. Maintain spacing and move the ball to the open players.

Another option is for the low attack player on the same side as the ball to pop out and receive a pass; she can dodge or move the ball quickly to the opposite side, which dodges right away or looks for cutters from up top. The middle attack player should look to set picks and/or pop to the ball.

In every player-up situation, remember to back up the cage.

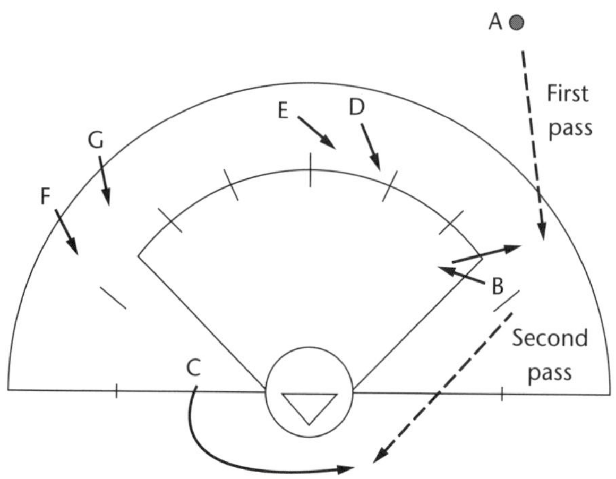

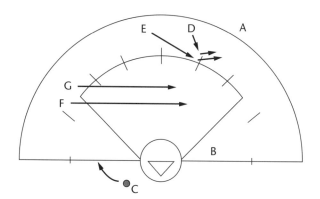

Figure 10.10   Slow Break I

THE SLOW BREAK

If the fast break is not there, or not seen—if a team has missed the advantage—consider running a slow break. Just when the defense thinks it's safe because they've thwarted your fast break and now everyone's matched up, this is when they're vulnerable to a slow break. Now's the time to run a quick strike dictated by the position of the ball and the off-ball defenders.

A slow break can hinge on a quick give-and-go or a double pick, for instance. There are lots of different options; as you develop your own slow-break opportunities, be creative. Here's a secret slow-break weapon from Coach Tucker: "If the ball is cleared to the offensive end, and a fast break is nonexistent or not recognized, run a slow break. Spacing and timing are essential."

The ball carrier, A, passes to the attack player on her side, B, as soon as she is open (figure 10.10). B immediately puts pressure on the defense by challenging to the cage. If she is not open on the dodge, she passes to C behind the goal. As the ball is in the air, F and G cut across the 8-meter. C carries the ball strong, as if she is

Figure 10.11 Slow Break II

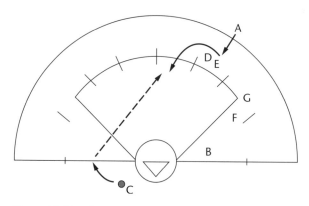

Figure 10.12   Slow Break III

dodging, while D and E set a double pick on A's defender (figure 10.11).

A cuts off of the double pick, and heads down the pipes looking for the feed from C. B plays her defender on the backside. E and D roll around for the second look, balancing the field and ready to intercept overthrown or missed passes. A continues cutting out of the 8-meter if she is not used (figure 10.12).

If a quality scoring opportunity is not available off the slow break, simply maintain possession and set up a settled offense.

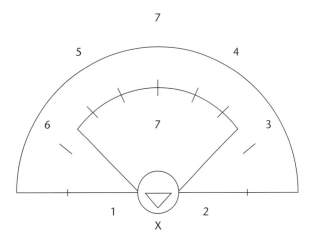

Figure 10.13   The Hot Spots

SETTLED OFFENSE

To recap: A team breaks out; clears the ball; pushes the fast break or, if the fast break isn't there, runs a slow break; and, if the slow break doesn't result in a high-quality scoring opportunity, then a team runs its settled offense.

The offensive unit needs a solid understanding of offensive concepts and sets. The defense is a unit, and so is the offense: Seven players need to work together to give a teammate the best opportunity to score. An effective offensive unit creates high-percentage scoring opportunities.

The team in possession of the ball has one main objective: to score goals. Maintaining possession of the ball will also prevent the other team from scoring. The offensive team wants to use its passing, dodging, and shooting abilities to beat the defense. Offensive success comes from having players who execute fundamental skills consistently, make quality decisions with and without the ball, communicate well with each other, and understand their roles in relation to the ball.

The "Hot Spots"

When you are first teaching or learning settled-attack concepts, it is helpful to designate the "hot spots"—areas on the field from which

your team attacks. Giving numbers to these areas around the goal makes it easier to explain and understand positions and areas on the field. "X," or "point behind," designates the area directly behind the center of the goal (figure 10.13). Having offensive players in these spots around the goal balances the field. The seventh offensive player has the option of playing on the inside of the 8-meter or can take the "top center" position to balance the attack outside of the 8-meter.

With numbered areas designated on the field, players will clearly understand where to dodge from, pick to, clear out of, and move toward; for example, "Jane, clear out of the 4 spot because we want Sarah to dodge from the 3 spot," or, "Offense, we need to balance the field. Let's get everyone to a hot spot so we are not so congested around the ball."

The Restraining Line

The restraining line limits the numbers of both offensive and defensive players in front of goal at any given time. Seven offensive players and seven defensive players—plus the goalie—are allowed to be inside the 30-yard line on each end of the field. Any seven attackers and any seven defenders can venture over the restraining line to play in a settled situation. It is important in transitioning the ball from one end of the field to the other to communicate who is going over and who is staying back to avoid an off-sides foul. Offensively, many teams designate four attackers and three midfielders who go over; defensively, four designated defenders and three midfielders stay back. As you can tell, the midfielders are responsible for playing both offense and defense and are usually the fastest and most fit players on the team. "Complete players" will feel comfortable inside the restraining line on both offense and defense. For example, if one of your attackers beats one of your defenders down the field and finds herself on defense, inside the restraining line, she will have no problem fitting into the defensive unit if she has been in that situation at practice. Attackers should know how to play defense, and defenders should know how to play offense. This strategy pays off in the short- and long-term, as it will serve players throughout their lacrosse careers.

The Ball Carrier

The player with the ball recognizes, as well as anticipates, what is happening off-ball and reacts accordingly. She first recognizes if there is a fast-break opportunity as she is bringing the ball upfield. Once the ball is settled, she can dodge, draw a double team, run a give-and-go, feed, or shoot. The ball carrier "checks the cage" whenever there is an opportunity and challenges her defender in a one-on-one situation. As she challenges, she is aware of what her teammates are doing off-ball and where the defense is. If she draws a double team, the ball carrier back outs of pressure (drawing the defense with her) and passes the ball to an open teammate. If the defense does not slide and double-team, she takes the one-on-one to the cage and shoots the ball around the goalkeeper. Tip: The ball carrier wants to always be a threat to the defenders.

Having the attitude "I can score any time on your defense" goes a long way toward wearing defenders down. Develop the look, moves, and attitude to keep defenders on their toes.

Off-Ball Players

Only one person at a time can have the ball, so the other six offensive players are moving to do one of three things: cutting hard to create space for the ball carrier, being an outlet for the ball carrier, or occupying their defenders. Being an outlet for the ball carrier means providing an option for her to pass. Occupying a defender means moving so that your defender pays attention to you and not the ball carrier. This is known as "playing the defender." Offensive players without the ball need to play their defenders in one of the following ways:

Cut to Create Space

If a player is adjacent to the ball carrier, and the ball carrier has a good opportunity to dodge, the adjacent player must "play her defender" by cutting hard at her defender and then behind her, away from the ball carrier. This type of cut forces her defender to look at her, not the ball carrier. This will create space for her teammate to dodge. Whenever a player cuts away from or to the ball, she asks for the ball with the "correct hand." It could be either the right or left hand, but make sure it's the one away from the defender so as not to pull back into the defender to pass or shoot.

Provide an Outlet

The player with the ball needs someone to pass to if she is being pressured or does not have a lane to dodge to the goal. Give her an outlet or a passing option by executing a "V" cut: The offensive player cuts in toward her defender and then cuts hard away from her defender in the shape of a "V." Then, she moves toward the ball

Left: Cutting with the correct hand is critical. Keep your stick away from your defender.
Right: Cutting with the stick in the wrong hand—the defender is easily able to impede the pass to this cutter.

to gain the needed space to receive the ball without defensive pressure. Out of a "V" cut, remember to square up to the defender to put her on her heels if you are going to challenge the cage.

Set a Pick

Picks are used in many sports to create offensive opportunities. To set a pick, player X assumes a legal defensive position. Her stick is straight up and down and not parallel to the ground; she's the one setting a pick for her teammate, player Y. Player Y directs her defender toward the pick that has been set by player X. Player X blocks the path of player Y's defender, forcing that defender to stop, or change direction, and allowing player Y to gain an advantage into open space. In the game of lacrosse, a pick can be set both off the ball and on the ball to free teammates for shots on goal or to produce uneven situations favoring the offense. Effective picks require legal defensive positioning and an element of surprise. The player setting the pick is trying to get the defender to take a couple of extra steps to get around her, subsequently

allowing her offensive teammate to get a step ahead of the defender being picked. When setting a pick for a teammate who has the ball, the picker must be prepared for physical contact, because she'll likely get bumped into. After the pick is set, the picker always wants to pop or flash opposite the direction that her teammate has cut into, giving the ball carrier two options: She can pass either to the cutter or to the picker, who has now popped into open space. This will negate the defensive strategy of switching.

One of the major mistakes players make when setting a pick is holding their sticks parallel to the ground, at their waists. This results in holding the defender, which is a foul. It is also a foul to set blind picks. To avoid setting a blind pick (a pick that the defender doesn't have time to react to), the pick should be set off to one side of a defender. Coach Tucker encourages her pickers to remain stationary until their teammates run off of the pick. A moving pick is a foul. The complete offensive player sets the pick, allows her teammates to run off the pick, and then moves to be an outlet and offensive threat!

Cut Off of a Pick

A player on the off-ball side should anticipate picks being set for her and be ready to use them effectively. She must play her defender first by making a move away from where she wants to go (to get the defender to turn toward her) and then, as the pick is set, cut back into the pick and run off the shoulder of her teammate, making close enough contact so that she seals off her defender. Remember to cut off of the pick with your stick in the "correct hand" and away from your defender so you can catch, shoot, or pass effectively.

Make Backdoor Cuts

If a defender is "ball watching," simply cut behind her to the goal and look for a feed. Offensive players position themselves so defenders are forced to turn their heads to find the ball. In the split second that a defender turns her head, the offensive player bursts behind her asking for the ball with her stick in the correct hand. So many lacrosse players wear ponytails in their hair that Coach Tucker's players have named this backdoor move "cutting to the ponytail."

Switch Positions

Rarely do smart offensive players stand still on attack. Standing still makes defense easy and doesn't benefit fellow offensive players. One way to keep moving is to play the defender (forcing her to look at you) and then switch positions with the player next to you who has done the same. Playing your defender and then switching with an adjacent teammate forces the defense to pay attention to off-ball players and may give the ball carrier the time she needs to get to the goal without added defensive pressure.

Balance the Field

Off-ball attackers are responsible for balancing the field. As they move to create space and scoring opportunities for the ball carrier, they are aware of exactly where they are on the field and realize how their position (or lack thereof) affects the ball carrier. If the attackers are all bunched together, it is easy for the defense to guard them. If they are too close to the ball, the ball carrier has nowhere to go and lots of defenders ready to play her. Balancing the field and timing cuts to the ball (both have to be done simultaneously) are two of the most challenging concepts for lacrosse players to understand and execute. The "hot spots" help players to balance the field.

Settled Offensive Sets

Once the offense has transitioned the ball and there is no fast- or slow-break opportunity, it must try to score in a settled offensive situation or "set." In settled offense, the attack unit is maintaining possession, passing the ball around the 8-meter arc, and cutting, setting picks, and creating space in an attempt to create quality scoring opportunities. The focus should be on finding a rhythm, maintaining space for the ball carrier (not all cutting to the ball at once), and creating one-on-one situations to challenge defenders to the cage. Very often, you'll see a group of players get the ball down on offense but take so long making a move to the cage that they end up losing possession. A quick transition to the offensive end of the field is critical. Attack players need to keep their eyes up, anticipate opportunities to the cage, and keep the ball moving.

There are a number of "sets" or formations an attack can develop, depending on its strengths as a unit. Some teams need lots of structure; other teams, often the more seasoned ones, need very little. No matter which kind of team you're on, there's a time for running set plays and a time to improvise. Even in the context of a set, players have opportunities to be creative by executing picks, creating space, drawing double teams, and dodging. It's all about reading the defense. Assessing an opponent's defensive strengths and weaknesses is key to any game plan. They will dictate whether set plays will work or if a freelance offense will be more effective.

The following offensive sets are described from the top center of the 12-meter fan to X, or point behind. Within each set, the ball carrier is looking either for a lane to the cage, a give-and-go opportunity, or a teammate popping for a feed. She can also look to draw a double team, and when she does, back out of the pressure and move the ball quickly to an adjacent player who will find the open player on the back side. The off-ball attackers are creating space for the ball carrier in any number of ways: by "playing their defenders" (moving in such a way that their defenders focus on them rather than the ball carrier), being an outlet, setting picks, cutting off of picks, cutting back door, or switching positions.

When developing a team offense, try practicing first without a lot of defensive pressure, until the attack is familiar with the formations. Gradually increase the amount of defensive pressure to simulate game conditions. The bottom line: Whether the offense is highly structured or loose, success comes with the ability to read defenders and exploit their weaknesses.

The 3-2-2 Set

The 3-2-2 circle formation maintains a balanced attack and keeps the middle of the 8-meter clear for cutters (figure 10.14). This is a basic offensive set. It offers good support for the ball and an open 8-meter to cut through, and it supports the pass-and-pick-away concept as well as the give-and-go concept.

Players use the circle formation (hot spots) to keep the field balanced and to lend strong support to the ball carrier. After a player passes, she cuts at her defender (to draw attention to her and away from the ball) and sprints to the opposite side of the field to set a pick (pass and cut away). The player who received the pass challenges the cage into the space that was va-

cated by the passer and then shoots or feeds a teammate who is cutting off of a pick that was set for her by the passer. The remaining off-ball players are moving to support the ball carrier by playing their defenders, balancing the field, and anticipating the movement of the ball and the development of the next scoring opportunity. At least one attack player must back up the cage. Another option in this set is the "give-and-go." After the ball carrier passes to a teammate, she immediately cuts behind her defender, to the goal, asking for the ball back. Her teammate feeds her quickly, and she catches and shoots on cage.

The 2-4-1 Set

The 2-4-1 formation is ideal for teams that can set effective picks and whose attack players can handle the ball under pressure inside the 8-meter (figure 10.15). This offensive formation is effective for an offense with strong dodgers and players who are good at setting and using picks.

The outside players have lots of space to dodge while the two inside players work off of each other, setting picks and screens and creating space for the ball carrier. The players on the outside and inside of the 8-meter are interchangeable. If a player on the inside sets a pick

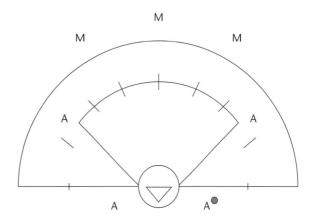

Figure 10.14   The 3-2-2 Offensive Set

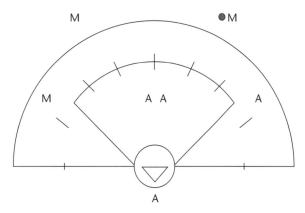

Figure 10.15   The 2-4-1 Offensive Set

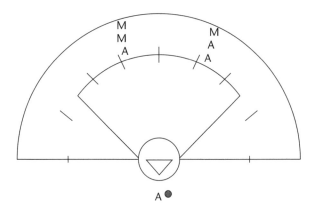

Figure 10.16   The "Stack" Offensive Set

and finds herself on the outside of the 8-meter, she then directs the attack to "balance the set" by sending the closest player to the inside. The attack player who works behind the cage is in an ideal spot to roll the crease and dodge, draw a sliding defender from an inside player, and feed the ball to her teammate, who catches and shoots immediately.

The "Stack" Set

The stack set lulls defenders into ball watching or "girl watching" and allows attack players to exploit defenders who aren't in position to see both girl and ball. If defenders in a stack are girl watching, the ball carrier has an opportunity to roll the crease with no slides. If they are ball watching, the players in the stack have an opportunity to get a step on cutting to the cage.

In this set, one or two feeders are behind the goal with the ball while the remaining attack players "stack" themselves in a line or cluster, usually at the top of the 8-meter arc (figure 10.16). The attack players cut, one at a time, out of the stack toward the goal, trying to get a quick step on their defenders. Once a player cuts to goal and the feeder does not use her, she fills back into the stack and waits to cut again.

The feeder must be patient and accurate with her passes and, every so often, should move the ball back and forth behind the cage or challenge to the goal herself. Teams can set up one or two stacks. The stack(s) may be moved to either side of the 8-meter, and the feeders can feed from the wings (either side of the 8-meter) as well as from up top. *Coach's Tip:* When in the stack or muddle, avoid being predictable by only cutting from the outside of the stack or muddle. Encourage offensive players to cut and pop to the ball from the middle of the stack. This makes defending the stack or muddle much harder, and it gives the offense more opportunities to beat the defense.

Each of these offensive sets relies on the attacker's abilities to read the defense and utilize solid offensive skills: cutting, picking, popping, dodging, and shooting.

OFFENSIVE PLAYS

Described next are a couple of structured offensive plays that will give a team some good looks to the cage. Even though there are specific components to execute in a set play, always read the defense and be ready to feed when you have an open player. Don't simply go through the motions of the play by just looking for only one option.

Pick-and-Pop

The attack is in a 3-2-2 formation. Timing is critical; every move happens within a second or two of each other. Whenever there's an open feed, take it. Work the ball around, maintaining positions.

The play starts when B gets the ball (see figure 10.17). B passes to A, while G and C set picks for F and D. B cuts to the opposite pipe, while E cuts over the top behind F and then curls back to the top of the 8-meter. F and D cut to the outside of the picks (figure 10.18). The feeder is looking for C to roll and pop to the ball, after C sets the pick for D.

The Cut and Curl

The attack is in a 3-2-2 formation and works the ball around the 8-meter. The play starts when G moves the ball to A. As the ball is heading to A, F and D cut and crisscross in the middle of the 8-meter. If either F or D is open, A can feed one of them (figure 10.19). If not, A moves the ball to B, as G and C curl around the picks set

by D and F (figure 10.20). The best opportunity should be when D pops to the ball as G curls around. However, if at any time a teammate is open, feed her.

Free Position Shots

The free position shot isn't commonly thought of as a team offensive opportunity, but it is. It's not just about the player taking the shot; the entire offensive unit needs to be a part of it. Teammates need to be ready to back up the cage to regain possession as well as for rebounds.

A free position shot in women's lacrosse is similar to a foul shot in basketball. A free position shot is awarded to an offensive player when a defender commits a major foul (3 seconds, shooting space, etc.) inside the 8-meter arc. The offensive player is placed 8 meters from the goal on one of the seven hash marks that are evenly placed around the 8-meter arc, the one that is closest to where the foul occurred. Any players inside the arc must clear out of the arc at the closest point and be at least 4 meters from the fouled player. The player who committed the foul is positioned on the 12-meter fan directly behind the player with the ball. On the official's whistle to restart play, the offensive

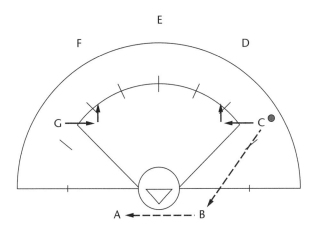

Figure 10.17 The Pick-and-Pop I

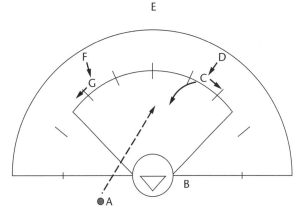

Figure 10.18 The Pick-and-Pop II

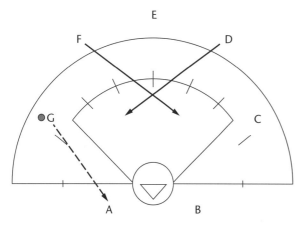

Figure 10.19   The Cut and Curl I

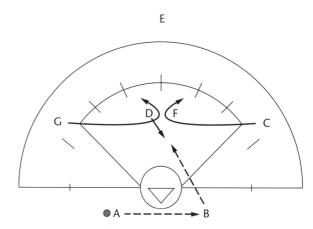

Figure 10.20   The Cut and Curl II

player tries to score while the defensive players try to gain good defensive position to prevent or block the shot.

Coach Tucker's secret weapon: The defender who committed the foul and is placed 4 meters behind the player with the ball can be a secret weapon. Instead of encouraging this player to check on the shot, which is usually pointless, encourage her to break out, upfield. Now, in the event of a save, the goalie has an immediate outlet upfield in a position to start a fast break. If the shooter misses the cage, or there's a rebound, the defender who breaks upfield needs to get herself back in on defense.

Backing Up the Cage

The offense needs a player committed to backing up the cage on an 8-meter shot. A missed shot can present another opportunity to score if your team can gain possession. If an offensive player is not already behind the cage on an 8-meter shot, the players must communicate who will back up the cage and be ready to run for the ball once the shot is taken. A rule of thumb: All offensive players positioned in front of the goal and not backing up the cage are ready for a rebound.

Ready Position

When the offensive player is positioned on the hash mark, she needs to assess her offensive options.

1. Are defenders on either side of her, or is one side freed up for her to move into that space?
2. Is there an open teammate on the crease ready for a feed, and can she communicate with her?
3. Is there an open teammate anywhere on the 8-meter with a better opportunity to score?
4. The ball carrier needs to assess her strength and energy levels. For example, midfielders might find themselves exhausted after running the field, and the best decision for them would be to not force the 8-meter shot, but rather to maintain possession by pulling the ball out and allowing the offense to work for a good scoring opportunity.

The player assumes a "ready position" so that she is prepared to shoot as soon as the whistle blows. Which foot a player leads with while setting up is a matter of personal preference.

Coach Tucker encourages players to try taking free-position shots sometimes with the left foot in front on the hash, and sometimes the right. Whichever foot is on the hash, the opposite foot is back for balance, the knees are bent, and the player leans slightly forward on the balls of her feet. Her feet are not pointing directly at the cage, but are positioned at an angle that will allow her to cut off defenders. She is ready to explode toward the cage on the whistle. Once the whistle blows, *avoid* rocking back and then exploding forward. In the time it takes to rock back, the defense is already swarming. The stick position is also a matter of personal preference. The offensive player can be creative about setting up; for instance, she might have her stick

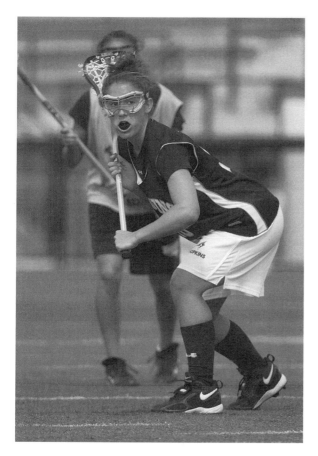

At the 8-meter, the attack player is ready to explode toward the cage on the whistle. Notice how she is looking at the official to anticipate the whistle.

in front of her, she can turn her shoulders to the side and place her stick behind her head, or she can start with the stick in one hand.

Take It In

The main offensive option on the 8-meter is to "take it in"—to release a shot from the middle of the 8-meter, a bit closer to the cage than the hash mark (figure 10.21). Taking the ball in, even for just a couple of steps, makes for a higher-percentage shot. The key is to burst into the 8-meter arc at enough of an angle to cut off one defender while drifting away from the defender on the stick side. Because the shooter has only a couple of seconds before the defense collapses on her, she must have a quick release. Coach Tucker tells a player to take between two-and-a-half to three-and-a-half steps inside the 8-meter before releasing her shot. Releasing quickly also serves another purpose: It gives the best angle for shooting. The closer the ball carrier gets to the cage and the goalie, the more her angle to score diminishes.

Eight Shooting Tips for the 8-Meter

1. Release the shot sooner rather than later.
2. In-tight-high does not work. Only shoot high if you have faked the goalie in the opposite direction.

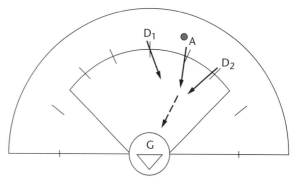

Figure 10.21 A right-handed player taking an 8-meter shot should veer away from the defender on her strong side so she can take a quality shot.

3. Faking high and shooting low works.

4. Shooting at the goalie's feet does not work. Shoot behind her feet or off hip.

5. Looking at where you're shooting does not work; keep your head and eyes up. Be deceptive.

6. Speaking of eyes up, always check around the 8-meter to see if there is an open teammate to pass the ball to who may have a better shot.

7. Assess whether defenders have taken your shot away and if it would be best to back out and maintain possession rather than force the shot.

8. Always cut off one defender as you "take it in." Look to move the goalkeeper before shooting!

The Outside Shot

Although taking it in is best, this is another option: to take an outside shot from the hash mark as soon as the official blows her whistle. This allows the offensive player, if she has a strong enough shot, to release the shot quickly and avoid defensive pressure. A well-placed, strong outside bounce shot might catch a goalie by surprise. The offensive player gets in her ready position on the 8-meter with her shoulders turned to the sideline and her stick back to shoot. On the whistle, she takes one shuffle step inside the 8-meter at an angle away from the defender on her stick side and then releases. She rotates her hips, shoulders, and arms while snapping through the shot with her wrist. Both bounce shots and risers are effective. Once the shot is taken, players inside the 8-meter arc are ready for a rebound; players outside of the arc are ready to break out in case of a save.

SITUATIONAL PLAY

The Last Two Minutes of the Game

Many lacrosse games are won or lost in the last two minutes. A team must be prepared to maintain a lead, or come from behind, successfully. This specific situational play must be practiced and perfected.

There are key considerations as the last two minutes of the game approach:

The score
Time left on the clock
The momentum and tempo of the game
Time outs available
Players available
Matchups

There are critical factors that come into play during the last two minutes:

Possession is essential.
Patience is fundamental.
Risk is integral.
Never stand with or without the ball.
Sticks must be up at all times when not in possession of the ball.
Keep the ball moving.
Get every ground ball.
Mental and physical toughness is a must.
Display constant intensity.
Maintain composure under pressure.
Believe.

Setting Up a Stall

A stall is called when a team wants to maintain possession of the ball and take time off the clock. A team can stall at any point in a game—at the end of the first half, in the middle of the second half, or at the end of the game. The priority is to take care of the ball and maintain possession. When stalling, do not go to the cage, do not force the ball into a crowded 8-meter area, and do not make poor passes or poor decisions with the ball. Discipline and patience are critical factors when stalling the ball, as well as spacing, throwing, and catching. Put your players in the mindset of dictating the tempo of the game and controlling the other team.

Set up a stall this way to maximize space inside the restraining line (see figure 10.22):

- To maintain space and remove a defender from pressuring the ball, set up a player at the TOP of the 8-meter to be an outlet.
- If the ball handler has only one defensive player on her, she keeps possession of the ball by protecting her stick and constantly moving to the open areas until the defense commits to a double team. She maintains confidence in her ball-handling ability.
- Be aware of where the double teams are coming from (adjacent or farthest player from the ball) and give the ball handler help accordingly.
- Be aware of players on the 30-yard line (restraining line) who are waiting to check.
- Be aware of running out of bounds.
- Do not stop your feet if you have the ball and are being pressured. Keep moving and protect your stick. Remember: shoulder, shoulder, stick.
- Always look to the back side for an open teammate. Defenses tend to leave from the farthest player from the ball.
- NEVER go to the goal in a stall. In the event of a save or missed shot, you risk a

change of possession that could cost your team the game.
- Coaches must clearly outline their "rules" regarding their stall plays. Some coaches have a call that will allow their players to go to the goal when a certain amount of time is left on the clock. Others never allow the ball carrier to shoot.
- Off-ball players are ready to clear space for the ball carrier and take their defenders away from the ball to avoid double teams.
- Stay calm, no need to panic; do the easy.

DRILLS, DRILLS, DRILLS!

Pressure Box Drill

Ten players: Five in Black and five in White. The Black team sets up with a player at each cone and one in the middle (figure 10.23).

The Black team starts with the ball and can move only in a small area around their cone (no cutting allowed). The player in the middle pops to the ball to get open but must stay in the middle of the square.

After the Black team passes the ball three times, a White defender is allowed inside the box, with her stick up and playing the ball. After another three passes, another White defender is allowed into the box (so now it's a 5 v 2). The five Black players are moving the ball quickly, using fakes and look-away passes, and finding the open player. As long as the Black team continues to complete three passes, the White team can keep sending in defenders until it is a 5 v 5. If the Black team drops the ball, the White team sets up in the next box and the Black team becomes the defense, and the drill continues.

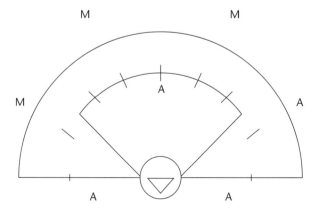

Figure 10.22   Spacing on a Stall

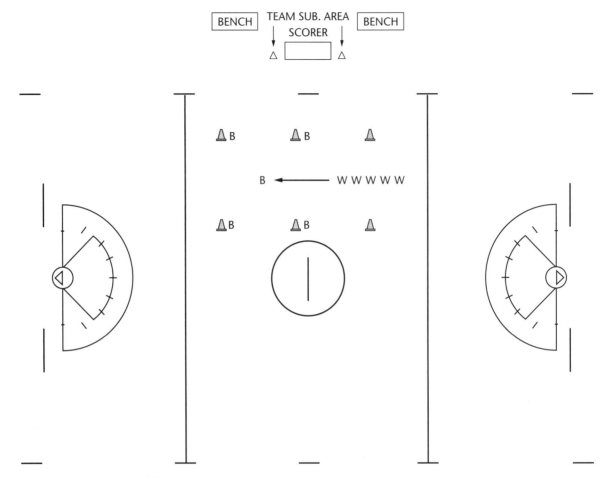

Figure 10.23   Pressure Box Drill

Offense working on:	Defense working on:
Handling the ball	Sticks up
Quick, accurate passes	Approach to play the ball (stay balanced, break steps down)
Look-away passes	Communication
Fakes	Anticipating passes
Protecting the ball	Angles to see both ball and girl

A Variation: Have the defender playing the ball work on throwing quick checks once she establishes position. Focus on patience, staying balanced, timing, quick striking, and gaining possession if the ball is dislodged.

Marked Shuttle Drill

Set up by splitting the team in half (White and Black), and then split those two groups in half again. Send a group of white and black to one end of the field and the remaining groups to the other end. Designate how many points will win the game; 21, for instance. One point is awarded for each completed pass and two points for interceptions.

The first White player in line starts with the ball and she is defended by the first Black player in line. The ball carrier's job is to pass the ball

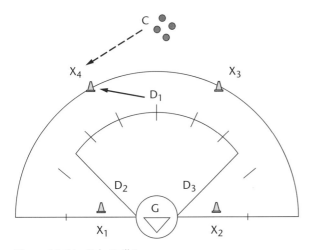

Figure 10.24 Yale Drill I

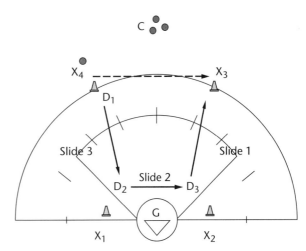

Figure 10.25 Yale Drill II

safely to her teammate who is cutting toward her from the opposite line. Players on defense must focus on seeing ball and girl, marking cutters tightly, and anticipating the passes to intercept. Players on offense must focus on accurate passing, cutting *to* the ball, deliberate back-door cuts, faking before passing, and running through their catches. No flat cuts!

Yale Drill

The Yale Drill is essentially a stationary 4 v 3. Set up four cones in a good-sized box in front of the goal cage. The lower cones are slightly above the goal line extended, and the top cones are outside of the 12-meter. One attack player is at each cone (see figure 10.24). There are three defenders, one at each of the lower cones and one at the top of the 8-meter in between the top two attack players. Balls are at the 20-yard line with the coach.

The drill starts when the coach feeds a ball in to one of the top attack players. The defender slides to play the ball (figure 10.25). As that happens, the attack moves the ball to the open player and the defense slides to play the ball.

Defense stays in a triangle, attack stays in a box. Attack looks to get off a quality shot by keeping the ball moving quickly and one step ahead of the slides.

World Cup Drill with 3 v 3

Set up four feeders; one each in the 1, 2, 4, and 5 spots. Set up a 3 v 3 inside the 8-meter (figure 10.26). There is one ball at each of the outside feeder positions; feeders are looking for the inside attack players to get open. The attack players inside work to get open using picks, screens, and pops. The defenders focus on communicating, zoning up the cutters, switching on picks, STAYING BALL-SIDE, and denying the pass inside.

5-Point Passing Drill

- Set up 5 points around the goal cage, as shown in figure 10.27.
- The ball starts in the middle line.
- There are five passes, not everyone has to touch the ball.
- After you pass, you must move to "productive space"—or space that is not crowding another teammate.

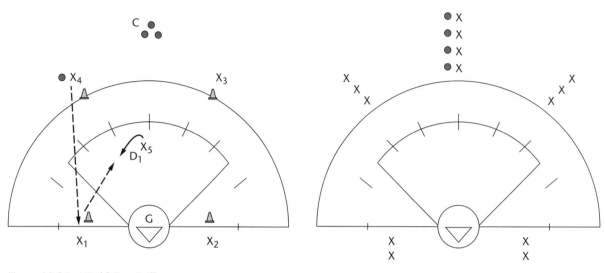

Figure 10.26   World Cup Drill   Figure 10.27   5-Point Passing Drill

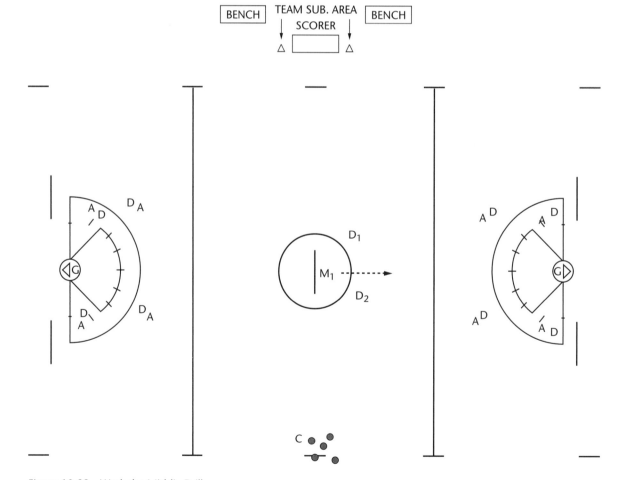

Figure 10.28   Work the Middie Drill

- Movement, spacing, and timing are key.
- Shoot on the fifth pass.
- Variation: Can go from five passes, to four passes, and so on; can add quick-stick passes, etc.

Work the Middie Drill

This drill pressures middies and defenders as they beat or get out of double teams, move the ball into the offensive end of the field, and make good decisions with the ball when they are tired.

Set up as shown in figure 10.28, using the full field. A coach is at the 50-yard line with lots of balls. The coach sends a ball in to M_1, who has to get past D_1 and D_2 (who are working on double teams) and move the ball over the 30-yard line. The ball carrier is now in a 5 v 4 and has to make good decisions with the ball so the attack can score. Play it out and, if a goal is scored, the goalie clears the ball (free clear) to M_1, who is breaking upfield. M_1 then has to get past D_1 and D_2 again and carry the ball safely to the opposite end of the field for another 5 v 4. If the defense comes up with the ball in the 5 v 4, they must clear it to M_1, who is breaking upfield.

After two full-field runs, M_1 comes out and is replaced with another middie or defender. This is an exhausting drill, so two to three runs are usually plenty. Remember to rotate the double-teamers.

11

Team Defense

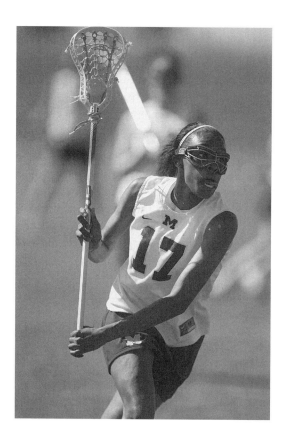

This defender is looking for a teammate to pass to on the clear. Courtesy US Lacrosse.

The defense has two main objectives: to stop an opponent from scoring, and to start the offense. Successful team defense comes from fundamentally sound individual defense and solid communication skills incorporated into a defensive unit. There are two basic styles of defense: player-to-player and zone. Within these two styles are five types of defensive systems, three player-to-player systems and two zone systems: force weak all over the field, force away from the line of center, force to help, a passive or sagging-zone defense, and a pressure-zone defense. Each of these defensive systems has strengths and weaknesses. As a coach, it is important to determine which defensive system your players will best understand and execute. As a player, it is important to have a solid understanding of, and appreciation for, each defensive system. Teams usually have one-word names for their team defenses so they can easily call in the defense they're running, such as "Protect" for a sagging, player-to-player, force-to-help defense.

DEFENSIVE TERMINOLOGY

As mentioned, the single most important thing defenders can do for each other is to communicate. Everything else will fall into place if defenders are able to direct each other and have an understanding of what the others are doing or about to do. Coaches and players can create their own list of defensive terms that the team can use consistently on the field to keep everyone on the same page. Remember to keep it simple—defenders don't have a lot of time to speak in sentences when attackers are driving to the cage. Here is a sample of the defensive terminology used at Hopkins:

Ball's in the 2
I have the ball and the location is the 2 spot.

Hot
I'm the First Slide.

2nd
I'm the Second Slide.

3rd
I'm the Third Slide.

Bring her
I'm waiting to double; bring the ball carrier to me.

Double
I'm doubling the ball.

Step right
Step upfield with your RIGHT foot on a 45-degree angle.

Step left
Step upfield with your LEFT foot on a 45-degree angle.

Hold
Hold your player where she is, or I don't need help.

No slide
I'm in good positioning on ball and don't need a slide.

Blue jay
Look for a check from behind on dodges/challenges.

Feed
Ball has just been fed into the 8-meter.

SOAP
Shut Off Adjacent Player.

Turn her
Turn your player back toward your teammate waiting to close the double.

Ball side
Position yourself between the player you are marking and the ball.

Goal side
Position yourself between the player you are marking and the goal.

Jump
Look to double the ball off of a screen or a criss-cross move by the offense.

Get in
Get to the top/middle of the 8-meter as fast as possible.

PLAYER-TO-PLAYER DEFENSES

The general concept behind player-to-player defense is that each defensive player is responsible for a player on the opposing team. The on-ball defender must be able to contain her player when she is challenging to the cage until a defensive teammate can slide to help. Off-ball defenders must position themselves at appropriate angles so they can see both the ball and their players. All defenders must communicate clearly and consistently.

Within team defense, the individual defenders position themselves ball-side (between their opponent and the ball) (figure 11.1) and/ or goal-side (between their opponent and the goal). This allows the defenders to cover both the passing lanes as well as the lanes to the goal. Defenders should always keep their sticks up and in the passing lanes. Defenders position their top hands at least two-thirds of the way down their sticks so they can cover as much space as possible and use their sticks to direct the path of the offensive player. Off-ball defenders can take one hand off of their sticks as they keep their sticks straight up and in the passing lanes. This makes the defender seem bigger and allows her to better cover the passing lanes.

Force Weak All over the Field

This defensive system relies on establishing defensive body position that will force the ball carrier to her weak hand no matter where she is on the offensive end of the field. Off-ball defenders also establish defensive body position, taking away the strong hand cuts to the ball and forcing the attack players to use their weaker hand to catch, pass, and shoot. This is a more advanced defensive system that requires quick, aggressive defenders and the ability to determine your opponent's strong hand.

Force Away from the Line of Center

This defensive system forces the ball carrier away from the middle of the field and, if executed well, forces her to take off-angle shots. Draw an imaginary line down the middle of the field

through both goals. Depending on what side the ball is on, the on-ball defender steps up and takes away the middle of the field, forcing the ball carrier down and away from the goal, minimizing the angle with which the attack player can shoot.

Force to Help

This defensive system relies on the on-ball defender's ability to force the ball carrier "to help," that is, forces the ball carrier toward her fellow defenders, who can then look to double-team. The "help" may be over the top of the 8-meter into the center, or it may be down the side away from the line of center. At Hopkins, a sagging, man-to-man, "force-to-help" defense is called "Protect." This defense is designed to protect the 8-meter and pack it in, not extend out past the 12-meter. Here's how it works:

- Defenders crowd the 8-meter and do not allow the offense clear lanes to the cage.
- In Protect, defenders pressure on-ball (out to the 12-meter) and sag into the 8-meter off-ball.
- Off-ball, defenders maintain a triangle so they can see both ball and girls. Defenders constantly move in and out of the 8-meter with sticks up to take away passing and dodging lanes.

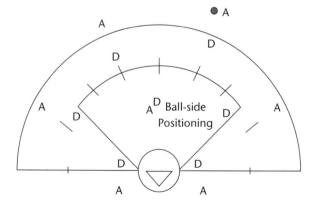

Figure 11.1   Ball-side Defense in the 8-meter

- If defenders maintain good angles, they won't get beat on backdoor cuts.
- Off-ball, defenders hedge (drift into the 8-meter to shorten the slide to the ball) into the 8-meter, not toward the ball. They keep sticks UP and to the INSIDE of the 8-meter. They are mindful of the 3-second violation, so they hedge in and out of the 8-meter.
- On-ball defenders pressure the ball and step up left or right to force the ball carrier to the double team. They play the ball between the 8-meter arc and the 12-meter fan.
- Defenders double-team the ball carrier if she gets anywhere near the 8-meter.
- When marking an opponent inside the 8-meter, defenders play ball-side.

Communication is key; defenders keep their ears open, listening for the double team, as that's where there's help. They play solid one-on-one defense while moving and sliding as a unit.

Double Teams

In settled defense, never allow an offensive player to dodge to the cage without a double team. The purpose of a double team is to gain possession of the ball. The on-ball defender steps up to one side of the ball carrier at an angle and drives her toward another defender, who is calling, "Bring her, bring her," or "Double, double." The second defender will step up to the other side of the ball carrier at an angle, which "closes" the double team.

The defenders position themselves as if they are making a "V" with their feet and trapping the ball carrier between them. It is critical for defenders to be on either side of the ball carrier, always remaining on the side they started on, so as not to cut each other off. Each defender has a specific responsibility when she's in a double team. One defender holds solid body position while the other defender tries

to stick check and dislodge the ball. Throughout the double team the defenders are communicating: "I've got hold . . . I'm holding," and "I've got check . . . I'm checking." The pressure alone may force the attack player to drop the ball, make a bad pass, or hang her stick enough for a solid stick check. The defenders on the double team stay with the double team until they gain possession or the attack player passes the ball. Once the ball is passed, one defender must stay on the opponent while the other defender "resets" back into the settled defensive system looking for the open player. Her defensive teammates should be telling her where the open player is; most likely, she's on the backside, or side of the field opposite the ball.

Backside Doubles

The backside double, an advanced type of double team, is a sneak attack extraordinaire. Instead of a traditional double, which happens in front of the attacker, a backside double comes from behind the attacker, virtually blindsiding her. A defender forces the attacker with the ball toward the sideline. Then, she steps in front of her path to turn the attacker back to a defender who is approaching behind her to close the double.

Role of the On-Ball Defender

Force the ball carrier outside toward the sideline.
Force the ball to keep going in the same direction; allow no flip-flopping by the attack.
Be patient.
Listen for the "doubler" to give the step-up-and-turn-her command.
Turn the ball back toward the middle of the field when you hear "turn her."
Establish good double-team position first, and then go for check.

Two defenders initiate a double team. Notice that they are balanced in a seated position and their sticks are up.

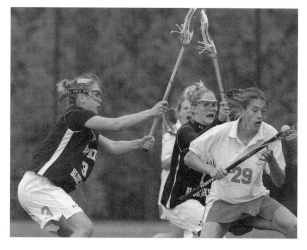

As the attacker tries to turn out of the double team, the defenders pursue her and close the double team.

Role of the "Doubler"

Be patient and wait until the ball carrier has her back to you and your teammate is ready to turn her toward you.

Communicate your intent to the rest of the defense.

Communicate to the on-ball defender: "I'm coming, get ready to turn her, step-up, step-up!"

Don't hesitate. If you are going, GO!

Be aggressive and take a risk; close the double.

GET THE BALL. You might be the "checker" in this situation, but be sure to establish body position first. Don't go in swinging.

Resetting Out of a Double Team

On many teams, once a double is over, the defenders pull off and run around until they find an open player. Often, this leaves opponents wide open, sometimes next to the ball or inside the 8-meter. These players are dangerous and need to be marked. Instead of running around haphazardly, defenders need to reset backside. This will cover all the players closest to the ball and force the opposing team to

As the attacker turns to run away from defensive pressure, she is surprised by the aggressive backside double team.

find the open player on the opposite side of the field.

"Should I stay or should I go?" Each team has established guidelines about when to pull off of a double team. Coach Tucker instructs her players to stay in the double until the ball gets passed or until her players come up with the ball.

"Now what?" Once the attacker passes the ball, the defenders who are in the double team need to reset. The backside/weak-side player (she's furthest from the point where the ball now is) releases and triggers the reset while the ball-side/strong-side player holds.

Communication: "Hold!" means the defender is holding on the player who just passed the ball and is continuing to mark her. "Release!" means the defender is pulling off the player she was just doubling and is resetting backside.

The keys to resetting out of a double team are the following:

- **Bumping:** Go to the closest attacker and BUMP a teammate toward the next player until everyone is covered. Push each other in the right direction.
- **Resetting inside out:** Always go into the 8-meter first and then out toward your player. The 8-meter is the hot zone and the most dangerous area; protect it at all times.
- **Keeping your sticks, heads, and eyes up:** You might have the chance to knock down or intercept passes during the reset.
- **Doing the easy:** The reset doesn't always go as planned. No matter. Players should run the shortest distance to an opponent, protect the 8-meter, and take away the most dangerous passes. And always, always play the ball and play it hard. Never leave the ball carrier without pressure.

ZONE DEFENSES

Zone defenses can be very effective if your players have a solid understanding of zone concepts. Zone defenses are designed so that defenders cover areas (zones) on the field and not individual players. Defenders will cover an attack player if the attack player moves into their zone but will release the attack player to another teammate once she moves out of that defender's area or zone. When running a zone defense, players must be aware of the 3-second rule, which states that "a defender may not be in the 8-meter arc more than 3 seconds unless she is marking an opponent within a stick's length."

Hopkins plays an active and aggressive pressure-zone defense that it calls "Backer." It requires each defensive player (whether she's the backer, on-ball defender, or one of the two "generals"; see figure 11.2) to be trusting of the others and extremely focused and aware. Here's how it works.

The on-ball defender:

- Pressures the ball at all times, even outside the 12-meter
- Steps up and dictates which direction the ball carrier moves, forcing her to the weak side

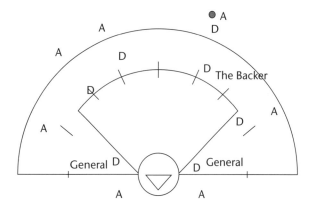

Figure 11.2   Backer Zone Defense I

- Dictates which direction the ball goes and keeps it going in one direction
- Doesn't worry about getting beat; she knows there's a "backer" behind who will cover her
- Recovers quickly if beat and attempts to check from behind
- Has an active stick, attempting to block and intercept
- Releases and sprints back to the 8-meter, in the opposite direction of the ball when it's passed

Off-ball defenders:

- Cover an area and any player in that area
- Do not worry about backing up the ball
- Stay with cutters as they move through the arc
- Rotate opposite the direction of the ball once an area is vacated
- Stay on the 8-meter, and do not extend past it
- Keep sticks up and active, ready for interceptions

The backer:

- Follows the ball to back up the on-ball defender
- Stays between the 8- and 12-meter
- Communicates constantly and loudly with the defender on-ball: "Increase pressure! Keep stick active! Step up right (or left)! Close the distance!"
- Positions herself at an angle in relation to the ball carrier and the on-ball defender to avoid shooting-space and 3-second fouls
- Steps up to slow down the ball carrier if the on-ball defender gets beat
- Anticipates where the ball is going and communicates that to the defense

The "generals":

- Occupy the low defensive spots at either side of the goal cage
- See the field and constantly communicate what they see
- Direct the rotation
- Protect the high-percentage shooting areas
- Call for a replacement as she vacates

THE RIDE

When Coach Tucker first started at Hopkins, she began to assimilate concepts and tactics from other sports into her lacrosse program. One of the first tactics she stole was from men's lacrosse, where "riding," or redefending, had always been taught and implemented. She and her assistant developed several rides to fit the women's game. These rides have become Hopkins' signature strategy. Coach Tucker instills in each of her players Ride with Attitude!

The two main reasons to ride are: to get the ball back, and to slow down your opponent's clear so as not to give up a fast break. Here's what makes a ride unique:

- All 12 players on the field are involved and working together.
- It takes away the "individual" focus and gives structure to the group.

There are a few types of rides: passive, aggressive, and a combination of both. When deciding which to use, coaches should ask themselves: Is my team trying to take the ball away? Trying to prevent a fast break? Will my team force the ball carrier into the middle of the field toward a double team? Will my team force the ball carrier to the sidelines and try to trap her there (now that there are hard boundaries)? Will we pressure the goalie? Will we allow a certain player to get the ball? Will we deny a certain player the ball?

Coaches can set up a ride, but each and every player must buy into the concepts, structure, philosophy, and rules of a particular ride. Patience is key for both players and coaches. Here's what players involved in a ride need to know:

1. You are responsible for areas, NOT individual opponents.
2. If an opponent moves into your area, then you must mark her.
3. Communication is CRITICAL to the success of the ride (talk through double teams and shifts in the ride, for instance).
4. You must deny passes on the ball-side and force your opponent to throw long, cross-field passes.
5. When shifting in the ride, go the shortest route (again, communication is key).
6. Be ready to close double teams.
7. Refrain from swinging your stick—no dangerous checks!

Lots of variables help determine what kinds of rides coaches can implement: one is team speed, another is the mindset of the players (are they passive, aggressive, and do they have conceptual understanding?).

Following is a description of a ride that Hopkins uses to take away opponents' fast breaks. When the opportunity presents, Hopkins will snag the ball, of course, but the primary focus of this ride is slowing down opponents and forcing them to play a half-field game. This allows Hopkins to play a settled defense if the ball is cleared.

Zone Ride to Take Away the Fast Break, aka "PEARLS"

Coach Tucker admits this ride is named for Francine Brennan, class of 1996, who, even though she wore a pearl necklace to every practice, epitomized the hard-core role of the attacker whose job it is to pressure the goalie during a ride.

Set up in a 1-4-3-2-1 (see figure 11.3). Once the ball is saved by the opponent's goalie, an aggressive and relentless attack player, A_1 (think Francine!), immediately pressures the goalie. The other three attackers and one midfielder drop back to the 30-yard-line and form the first line of the ride. (The 30 is a default position, where Hopkins generally sets up the ride. However, when playing a weaker opponent, for instance, they'll set up outside of the 12-meter. When riding a stronger and speedier opponent, they'll set up with the first line at the 50, with all successive lines adjusting accordingly.) Two middies and one defender form the second line of the ride at the 40. Two defenders position themselves at the opposite 40-yard-line, and the final defender is deep at the opposite 30. Players in successive lines stagger themselves so that they are filling in the gaps of the line in front of them. The goalie stays in goal.

A_1 forces the goalie to pass to a designated side of the field (X). When the ball is on the designated side and at an established area on the field (inside the 30), A_2 and A_1 double-team the ball carrier. Everyone else adjusts to mark a player in her area; the priority is to take away any ball-side passes. Don't worry if the ball carrier passes back to the goalie; as long as they're not moving forward, the ride is working. Never slide low to high. Otherwise, the ball carrier will just pass over your head. As the ball is passed, shift *back* and then *over* to adjust to the ball side of the field. Always have a player on the ball, slowing it down. As defenders get "in" to their defensive end, they need to keep the ball in their line of sight. The ride is successful if the ball is slowed down enough to prevent a fast break, and defenders are able to mark up easily.

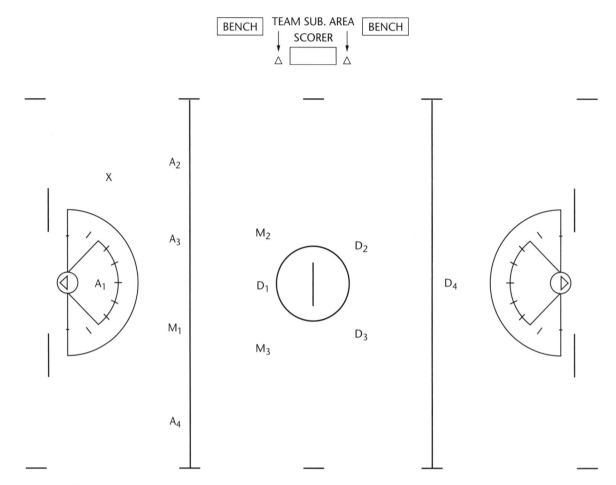

Figure 11.3   "PEARLS" Zone Ride

Key Points for PEARLS Zone Ride

- Set up in 1-4-3-2-1.
- A goalie's save prompts A_1 to exert relentless pressure.
- Attack, middies, and defense SPRINT OUT to designated areas while seeing the ball.
- The riding team's goalie stays in the cage.
- A_1 forces the opponent's goalie to pass to a certain side of the field.
- The deeper attack player, A_2, slows the ball down and turns the ball carrier back to A_1, who is chasing to close the double.
- Everyone ball-side must be tightly marked.

- Keep the ball in the riding team's offensive end of the field.
- Never slide low to high.
- Take away the fast break.
- Allow the riding team's defense to get into settled play.
- As the ball is passed, shift back, then over.
- Always have a player on the ball, slowing it down.
- When the ball reaches the 50, get into the 8-meter defensively while seeing the ball and drifting toward a player to mark.
- Call out opponents' uniform numbers to make sure everyone is marked.
- Ride with attitude!

Coaches need to encourage sensible risk taking on defense. By doing this you build a defensive culture on your team that allows defenders to take risks, buy into their role, and contribute to the total game. Find a way to celebrate defensive performance, especially in the ride.

DRILLS, DRILLS, DRILLS!

Early Slide Drill

Set up with five attackers and five defenders (four pairs in a box around the 8-meter and one pair on the inside of the 8-meter). The balls are up top with a coach. The coach lobs a ball to the attack player in the 2 spot (X_2) who dodges hard and looks to draw the double (see figure 11.4).

The adjacent attack player cuts through to create space for the dodge forcing the defense to stay with her, or slide. The attack stays in the shape of the box in order to keep the defenders spread out. The defense slides aggressively, looking to double hard and take the ball (figure 11.5). Once an attacker moves the ball, the defense must work to reset quickly backside. When you receive the ball, look to dodge, draw the double and move the ball—working for a good shot on cage.

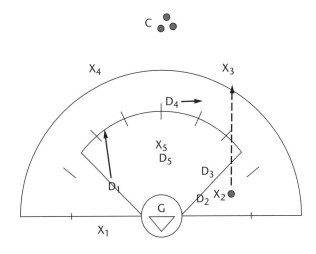

Figure 11.5　Early Slide Drill II

The coach goes around the box, next sending the ball to X_1, then X_3 and X_4. Then a new group of 10 players comes in and the drill starts again.

Pentagon Drill

The Pentagon Drill forces the defense to communicate, play solid 1 v 1 defense, slide (or hedge) to teammates, and double-team. It forces the attack to move the ball quickly, dodge hard, pass accurately, draw, and dump. The attack's objective is to make it to the center cone, earning a point.

Set up with five cones arranged in the shape of a pentagon about 10 yards apart. Have a sixth cone in the center of the drill (figure 11.6). An offensive player and a defensive player stand at each of the five outside cones. (The attack and defense can switch when possession changes.) On the whistle, play for 3 minutes.

Attack players:

- Stay spread out at the cones.
- Move the ball around the outside of the pentagon, dodge, and feed teammates who are trying to catch and touch the middle cone.

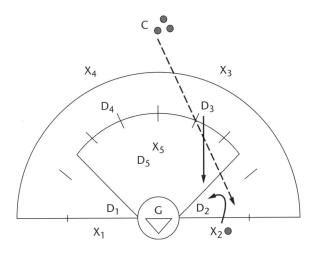

Figure 11.4　Early Slide Drill I

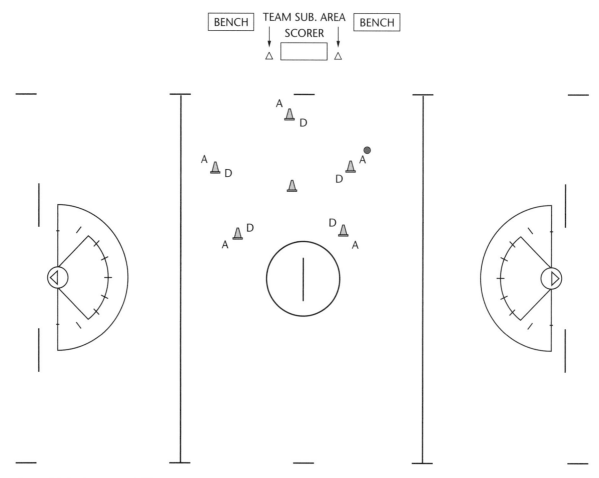

Figure 11.6   Pentagon Drill

- Use fakes, quick passing, and strong dodges.
- Look for backdoor cuts.
- The object is to beat your defender on a cut or a dodge to get to the middle cone with the ball.

Defensive players:

- Communicate who has the ball and who is help.
- Keep sticks up and maintain strong defensive positioning—no shopping-cart defense.
- Maintain angles to see both ball and girl.

- Hedge, slide to help, close double teams.
- Reset out of double teams; talk.
- Pressure attack players; try to intercept.
- Keep attack player between the shoulders.
- Stay low and balanced.

You are ultimately trying to prevent the offense from getting to the middle cone with the ball.

Lane Drills to the Goal

Lane drills help teach attack players to make quick, explosive, and concise moves to the cage, and defenders to play at angles that force attack

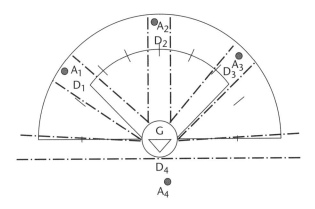

Figure 11.7   Lane Drills to the Goal

players off-course. Set up cones in three lanes to the goal, each about 5 to 7 yards apart. Play ends when an attack player is forced outside of her lane (figure 11.7).

Defense players should not check, but should work on locking onto attackers using balanced, defensive positioning and forcing them outside of the lanes to the goal, containing attackers for 5 seconds or longer, and forcing in one direction.

Attack players should work on quick, explosive moves and quick releases of shots, forcing the defense off-balance, dodging by leading with their sticks, and accurate shooting.

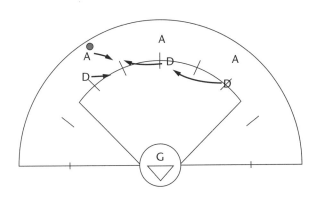

Figure 11.8   Double-Team Drill

Double-Team Drill

Set up the double-team drill going to goal. Three attackers and three defenders line up at the top of the 12-meter as they would in a game (see figure 11.8). One pair starts with the ball. The attacker dodges and the defender forces her to help. The adjacent defender doubles, and the next defender slides. (If the ball starts in the middle, try to incorporate the backside double.) The third defender is the second slide. All three sets of players are involved in the drill. Defenders are working on stepping up and directing the ball carrier to the double team, closing the double team and communicating. Attackers are working on drawing the double, protecting their stick, backing out, and moving the ball. Coaches can blow their whistles to stop play, make adjustments, and highlight key points.

Halt the Footrace Drill

This drill works on slowing down a fast player in the midfield and disrupting her path to the goal. Being able to slow down a key opponent who likes to run the ball in the midfield can be a valuable tool in controlling an opponent's offense. (See figure 11.9.)

Split the field down the middle with cones until about 15 meters away from the goal cage. There are several progressions to this drill that eventually drop into a live 2 v 2 or 3 v 3.

Two defenders, D_1 and D_2, are attempting to slow down X_1 and prevent the foot race to the cage. They do this by:

- stepping across the ball carrier's path to slow her down
- doubling the attacker in the midfield and moving her east-west
- using the sideline as a third defender
- being patient looking for the check and a turnover.

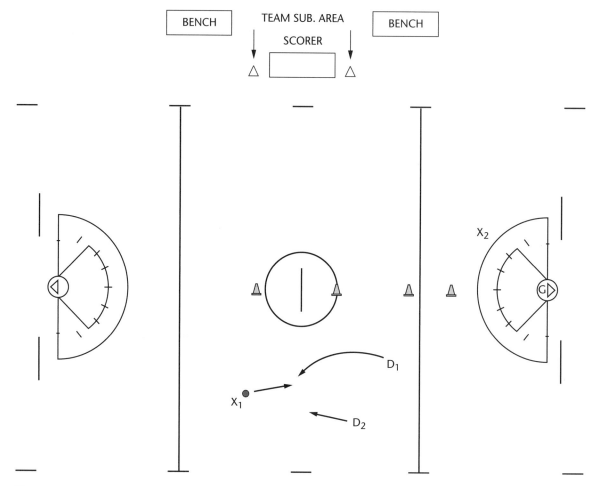

Figure 11.9   Halt the Footrace Drill

The drill begins with the attacker receiving an over the shoulder pass from her goalkeeper or the coach. Once she receives the ball, the two defenders are released and they try to double her and slow her down. The key is to HALT the attacker's north-south progression.

Defenders need to break down their steps as they approach the attacker. D_1 wants to turn the ball carrier toward the sideline and D_2. D_2 needs to close the double team, maintain her balance, and not foul. Sticks are up and limiting options for the attacker. Call the double team tightly. Do not allow the defenders to swing, push, or foul in the double team.

Remember

- Don't wait for the attacker to come to you
- Break down your steps
- Keep your feet moving
- Limit passing options with sticks up
- Communicate!
- Hold the double and turn toward sideline
- Only go for the check if you have a 90 percent chance of getting it
- At all costs halt the north-south progress—slow down the ball carrier

Drill Progressions

If the attacker gets through the double team, she can go to goal and use X_2 as an option if she cannot get a quality shot. The defenders never quit; they must communicate, recover, and reset.

The coach can have defenders begin this drill at different points on the field. One defender can be a trail defender recovering and coming in on the double. The drill can be run on both sides of the field going in opposite directions.

This readies your midfielders and defenders to perform at a high level in the Work the Middie Drill described in chapter 10.

12

Goalkeeping

"Some days it's a golf ball, some days, a beach ball."
—Trish Dabrowski describing a lacrosse ball, relative to whether
she was having a good or bad day in goal.

> Trish Dabrowski, NCAA Division I Goalkeeper of the Year in 2002
> and former assistant coach at Johns Hopkins University, is a guest
> contributor to this chapter. A graduate of Loyola College in Mary-
> land, Dabrowski is a three-time Brine All-American.
>
> Also contributing is Laurie Tortorelli, a former All-American goal-
> keeper at the University of Delaware and former assistant coach at
> Cornell University.

Awesome save!

One of the biggest challenges facing the majority of goalies, and prospective goalies, is not having goalie coaches associated with their teams. Likewise, one of the biggest challenges coaches face is knowing what to do with their goalies; most are at a disadvantage because they weren't goalies themselves. This chapter is for both players and coaches.

WHO'S RIGHT FOR THE JOB?

Goalkeeping is 90 percent mental and 10 percent physical. A player needs mental toughness that borders on arrogance when she puts on goalie pads and steps onto the field. It is the mental game that takes the most time, and effort, to learn. Who wouldn't be intimidated by getting hit with the ball and getting scored on? A goalie, that's who. Successful goalies keep their heads up and spirits intact no matter what.

Like it or not, goalkeepers get scored on. It's important to accept this simple fact of goalie life. How do top goalkeepers stay calm and focused at critical times? One way is to concentrate on the simple things. If a goalie's having a bad day and not making saves for any given stretch of time, she keeps herself in the game by doing what she can to help her team: getting ground balls and making interceptions as well as directing, motivating, and inspiring her defense.

Mental toughness, important as it is, isn't enough. The all-important traits of a goalie include:

- Quick hands and feet in order to save the ball and recover for second or third shots
- Hand-eye coordination for successful reaction to oncoming shots
- An all-over agility that allows a goalkeeper to be mobile outside the crease, whether it's running down ground balls or making interceptions

- An ability to communicate, loudly, always verbalizing the position of the ball to help the defensive unit to work as one; in addition, a goalie wants to emote high energy

Some Criteria for Success between the Pipes

1. Goalkeepers are quick, have game sense, and often are multisport athletes with excellent reaction times. Ideally, a goalkeeper is one of the most athletic players on the team.
2. Goalkeepers pay keen attention to detail: "Lacrosse is a game of inches," Coach Tortorelli insists, "and every inch counts."
3. Goalkeepers are students of the game; they watch films and attend camps/clinics in order to perfect their saving techniques. They're prone to self-reflection and welcome constructive criticism.
4. Goalkeepers embody "persistence for perfection." Perhaps nowhere on the field is repetition of the basics more important than in goal.
5. Goalkeepers have a work ethic second to none when it comes to extra conditioning, training, and repetition. "To be the best you must beat the best," Coach Tortorelli says. "What is the competition doing right now?"

TECHNIQUES

Stance and Hand Positioning

A goalkeeper's stance and hand positioning are critical to her success in the cage. Both should feel comfortable, relaxed, and balanced.

In the stance, the goalkeeper needs to be on the balls of her feet (not on the toes) with her knees slightly bent. Feet should be shoulder-width apart, and most of her weight should be felt in her feet. Her back should be upright and both arms away from the body, yet inside the goalkeeper's body frame. "Inside the body frame" means that the stick, elbows, arms, and feet are within your shoulders. On some occasions, a goalkeeper may have to reach outside her frame for a wide or high shot.

The arms should be slightly bent so there is significant space between the body and the stick. The goalkeeper's top hand should be at the top of the stick; the thumb should be lined up with her eyes ("thumb-to-eye"). Her bottom

The goalkeeper's stance is strong and balanced.

hand should be in the middle of the shaft and aligned with her belly button.

Moving in the Crease/Aligning Angles

A goalie has to be always on the move, depending on the position of the ball, to cut down the angle of the shot, make herself as big as possible, and remain balanced while making a save. Traditionally, goalkeepers played either a "house" or a "semicircle" style of positioning. But when changes in stick technology increased the speed, accuracy, and placement of shots, goalkeepers adopted a "semiflat," or the triangle, method.

To play the semiflat style, a goalie's initial step coming off of the pipe from the goal line extended should not be up and out. This is the old style of play and does not allow as much reaction time as the newer method. The semiflat style keeps the goalie more square to the shooter and closer to the goal line extended, which allows for greater reaction time after a shot is taken. Goalkeepers should practice moving from pipe to pipe while staying deep and flat to the goal line extended.

It's vital to stay square to the ball. "Staying square" means to keep the hips, shoulders, and feet balanced and lined up directly with the ball. A goalie's hips should be balanced and parallel with the shooter. She should never open her hips, or drop step back into the cage while she's moving to stay aligned with the shooter because this opens up the surface area of the goal. Staying square to the ball and shooter allows a goalkeeper to make saves with her body even if her stick happens to miss.

Keeping the correct angle in goal requires patience and discipline; those who don't have it tend to creep out toward the top of the crease, where it becomes possible for a good field player to fake and shoot around them. One way to stay back and patient is for the goalkeeper to verbally remind herself to "hold, hold, hold" until she sees the release of the ball from the stick.

Making the Save

When goalkeepers drop their upper bodies and bend forward at their waists, they seem smaller in the goal. That's why a goalkeeper needs to "stay big"—maintain an athletic vertical stance and use whatever height she has to her advantage.

A goalkeeper's stick, arms, elbows, and feet need to stay within her body frame as she steps square to the ball. The initial step should be UP AND OUT to the ball. Coach Dabrowski reminds Hopkins goalies to "keep the ball between your shoulders." This ensures that goalkeepers stay square and aligned with shooters. Just as important is Coach Dabrowski's instruction to "keep your nose to ball." When the goalkeeper's nose follows the ball, her eyes have no choice but to watch the ball into her stick. This helps the goalkeeper stay focused until she makes the save.

One of the most important things for goalies to practice is to take their hands to the ball with force. Coach Dabrowski recommends overexaggerating this move to the point where a goalie actually falls forward to catch herself as she extends her hands. Goalkeepers commonly make the mistake of stepping first, before moving their hands, which leaves the hands too close to the body and makes it difficult to save and control the ball. Goalkeepers should explode and power to the ball FIRST with their hands and SECOND with their step.

The step to make a save should be on a 45-degree angle in order to effectively cut down the angle of the shot. This step is neither a lunge nor a hop, but actually is two quick steps, with one foot trailing for balance. Some goalkeepers explode to the ball so powerfully that their momentum causes them to hop-step. This is fine so long as they do not bring their feet together in the end. Here's how Coach Dabrowski suggests a goalie can check her 45-degree angle: If she

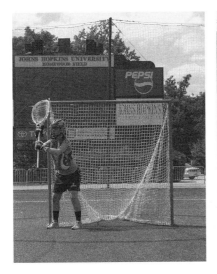

Notice the semiflat movement from one goal post to the other.

can walk in a straight line backward and touch her backside to the pipe, she's right on.

If the ball is shot anywhere toward the right side of a goalie, she needs to step with her right foot first. If the ball is shot anywhere toward the left, then she needs to step with her left foot first. However, before stepping anywhere, she first takes her hands to the ball. Watch the ball all the way into the stick; give with the ball, and keep the body square and behind the ball. A good check for correct positioning is to have the goalkeeper line up her belly button to the ball. This applies to all shots. Always line up with the ball as opposed to the player who's shooting.

The goalkeeper should never take her eyes off the ball. She must watch it all the way into her stick. Goalkeepers should not punch at the ball or catch and cradle the ball. The goalkeep-

On a save, the goalkeeper first takes her hands to the ball, even before moving her feet.

er's job is to save it. This requires soft hands. As the goalkeeper reaches out to save the ball, she should pretend that the ball is an egg. As the goalkeeper watches the ball into her stick, she gives with it in front of her body, all the while keeping her eyes on it.

A Breakdown of Goalie Saves

Here are some of Coach Dabrowski's tried-and-true techniques.

Goalkeeper's Right-Side High: From the stance position, the goalkeeper's top hand extends out to the ball while she steps with the right foot and follows with the left. Her feet are shoulder-width apart. The goalkeeper extends her hands toward the ball while keeping her stick directly in front of her body. The ideal is to save the ball directly in front of her face, not off to the side or at her shoulder. Once the ball is in the stick head, she punches out her bottom hand (in order to "give"), which helps the ball rest in the pocket of her stick. Her bottom arm is fully extended. If the goalkeeper's stick remains vertical during a save, the ball will pop out.

Goalkeeper's Left-Side High: From the stance position, the goalkeeper needs to bring her stick "out and over" to the opposite side of her body. The incorrect way is what we call a "windshield-wiper motion." The arms will cross and form an X. In this case, the goalkeeper did not take her hands out to the ball. The correct way is to explode to the ball with the hands first; then the left foot steps to the ball, and the right foot trails. As always, the motion is give-and-step.

Goalkeeper's Right-Side Mid: From the stance position, the goalkeeper bends her knees and saves the ball at her hip. Her body is behind the ball. Most times when making this save, goalkeepers do a good job of taking their hands to the ball but often forget to move their bodies.

Make sure the ball is still "between the shoulders" and "in front of the belly button," and that the stick is not outside the body frame on the save. The goalkeeper steps with her right foot first and left foot trailing.

Goalkeeper's Left-Side Mid: This is a difficult save that calls for either dipping one's body or flipping one's stick. Here's an easy-to-recite rhyme that reminds goalkeepers to react to the ball in the correct way: "From your shoulder to your hip, you dip to the ball; and from your hip to your knee, you flip to the ball."

The time to dip is when the ball is shot between the shoulder and the hip. From the stance position, the goalkeeper reacts to this ball almost as if it's a left-side-high shot. However, she will have to bend her knees to get under the ball. Some can hunker low enough to save this shot at their left knee. At the end of the save, the stick should be out in front of the body and the goalkeeper's body should be underneath and behind the ball.

The flip is used when the ball is shot between the hip and the knee. From the stance position, the goalkeeper needs to drop her stick head low while keeping the stick out in front of her body. A common mistake is to bring the stick in and then back out, which takes a lot of time. Once a goalie drops the stick in front, she simply flips the stick head out to the ball, making sure it stays within her body frame as she steps to the ball with her left foot, right foot trailing. Her body is behind her stick, and the stick is behind the ball. Having made the save, the goalie controls the ball by bringing the stick head back above her shoulder while looking for a quick clear. On this save, beware of these tendencies:

- Turning the hips and opening up the body
- Moving the stick outside the body frame in a "windmill motion"

Bounce Shots: The best bet is to save the ball before it bounces. The goalkeeper needs to get her hands out in front and explode to the ball.

There are two different types of bounce shots: low ones that are shot close to the goalie's feet and bounce no higher than knee level, and high ones that are shot just inside the top of the crease and ricochet above the goalie's shoulder. Low bounce shots can be played just like low shots. Get the hands out in front while bending at the knees (not hips) to get low and over the top of the ball. Watch the ball all the way into the stick.

High bounce shots require goalies to track the ball carefully. Quick hand-eye coordination is key. Some goalkeepers play on grass where there rarely is a true bounce. On a turf field, high bounce shots can be truer and a little easier to save. ("True" means the ball does not take a bad bounce or get misdirected.) The best way to test any field surface for possible divots in the crease is to ask for a lot of high bounce shots during warm-up. In response to the high bounce shot, a goalie's hands are far out in front of her, almost pulling her body along. Her body is behind the ball so that if she misses with her stick, there's a good chance she'll save it with her body. Ideally, a goalkeeper saves the ball before it bounces up high, over her shoulder.

Close Shots: Goalies need to be prepared for lots of shots in close to the crease. The key to saving these shots is for the goalkeeper to mirror the shooter's stick with her own stick. Take a small step out toward the shooter to cut off the angle of the shot. The goalkeeper should not rush out because a good shooter will see the goalie coming, throw a fake, and put the ball right around her into the goal. Instead, a goalie needs to resist the urge to creep out to the shooter. Goalkeepers need to say "hold" until they see the shooter break her cradle and notice the ball rolling up toward the shooting strings. This is the moment when the goalkeeper takes her step out and mirrors the attack player's stick.

8-Meter Shots: As the umpire sets up the 8-meter-shot, the goalie lines up belly button to the ball. This alignment puts her on the correct angle to make a save. She remains patient until the shot is released and then attacks it. More advanced goalkeepers may try to fade a bit by inching to the offside to bait a shooter to aim toward her strong stick side. This tactic sometimes entices shooters to take the bait and shoot exactly where the goalkeeper wants them to. Goalies can use the 8-meter hashes to help visualize their positioning on the field as well as the shooter's.

Crease Rolls: When an attack player is rolling the crease, she starts her move from behind the goal cage. As soon as the attacker reaches the goal line extended, the goalkeeper should be on the pipe. If the attacker starts making her way to the center of the cage, the goalkeeper must be patient and stay square with the ball instead of lunging or moving ahead of the attacker. Her belly button is to the ball and she is balanced on the balls of her feet. She keeps her hands out in front and attacks the ball at the moment when the attacker releases it. She is careful not to get ahead of the ball. (Remember: A goalie has less ground to cover; her one or two tiny steps will equal a handful of steps by a player outside the crease.) The worst thing a goalkeeper can do is take herself out of position by creeping out too high. The keys to commit to memory are stay patient, and watch the ball.

Intercepting the Ball from Behind: A goalie's job when the ball is behind is to intercept or get a piece of the ball to knock it down. Foot positioning is most important when playing the ball

behind. A goalkeeper never should be caught standing on the goal line or out at the top of the crease. She should be in the middle of the goal, between the goal line and the top of the crease. That way, if she misses the interception, she is in the correct position to make the save. If the ball is "behind low right" (also referred to as the 2 spot), the goalkeeper wants to place her right foot a little closer to the goal line at an angle. Her feet are shoulder-width apart and still positioned in the middle of the crease. Ditto for when the ball is "behind low left," or in the 1 spot. This time, however, the goalkeeper's left foot is slightly closer to the goal line and at an angle, because the foot that is closer to the goal line is the foot she will pivot with. As always, she's balanced on the balls of her feet with her knees slightly bent.

The goalie's bottom hand is all the way at the bottom of the stick. The pinkie should hang off the bottom of the shaft and wrap underneath the stopper. The top hand is in the middle of the shaft. A cagey goalkeeper doesn't wave her stick above or along the top pipe, as this lets the attacker know her intent. Nor is her stick at her waist, lazily out of position to make a save. The stick head should be at shoulder-height.

When intercepting the ball, the goalkeeper uses her bottom hand and pinkie to power up and reach for the ball. The goalkeeper wants a piece of anything that goes over the top pipe or is remotely close to the side pipes. She reaches, but doesn't jump or hop for the ball. On the reach, her stick is tilted back a bit so the ball will sit nicely in her pocket. She doesn't attempt to cradle the ball into the stick; rather, she gives to let it fall in.

If the goalkeeper misses the interception, which may happen, she should watch the ball and follow the feed, first with her head and hands, and then with her body. A goalkeeper

A successful save is a job only half done; the clear is just as critical. Notice the goalie steps and rotates her hips and shoulders on the release.

should never turn her back to the ball. The goalkeeper drops her stick into her normal stance positioning, but not so low that she has to bring it back up again on her turn. She wants to stay big as she makes the turn to find the ball.

Clearing/Throwing

A big save is a job only half done. Equally important as the save is a goalie's ability to clear the ball. When a goalie makes a big save, it could be momentum changing for her team, but it could be just as devastating if she throws it away on the clear. Practice is key—and easy. All a goalie needs is her stick, a ball, and a wall.

The technique of clearing is similar to pitching a baseball. Just as a right-handed pitcher steps with her left foot and points that foot toward the intended target, a lacrosse goalie moves in a similar way to clear the ball. After she steps with her lead foot, she rotates her hips and shoulders into the pass, releases the ball, and follows through toward her target.

During clears, the hand positioning on the shaft of the stick differs from the standard-stance hand positioning. The top hand slides down to the middle of the stick; the bottom hand is all the way at the bottom. This allows the goalkeeper to throw the ball far with accuracy. IT IS IMPORTANT TO KEEP THE ARMS OUT AND AWAY FROM THE BODY. When the arms are close to the body, a goalie will tend to push the ball off of her shoulders and the ball won't go very far. On the release, the goalkeeper's arms should be up and away from her body and the stick should be behind her head. Step with the opposite foot, turn the hips square, and follow through to the intended target. The follow-through should be across the body—not under the armpit or into the stomach.

Throwing a lacrosse ball requires a push-pull motion. This applies to goalies and field players: Pushing with the top hand and pulling the stick with the bottom hand ensures power and distance. If the ball goes directly to the ground, either a player is pulling too much or her follow-through is toward the ground. If she sails the ball over the head of the intended target, she is pushing too much. Crisp passes require balancing the push-pull motion. Like field players, goalies need to be proficient at throwing the ball with both hands.

A goalkeeper has 10 seconds in the crease with the ball before she needs to clear. There's no real need to rush to make a clear. Relax and be confident with the ball. Possession, control, and good decision making take only a few seconds. An umpire counts out loud, indicating how much time a goalkeeper has left in the crease. If an opposing attacker is pressuring the ball, a goalkeeper can create space by walking to the back of the goal cage within the crease to clear the ball. If she hasn't already cleared the ball by the time the umpire counts to about 8, the goalkeeper should step outside the crease and look for an open teammate.

Outside the crease, goalkeepers have an unlimited amount of time to clear. A rule limits goalkeepers from reentering the crease with the ball to one time during each possession. This means that if the goalkeeper saves the ball in the crease and walks out of the crease with the ball, she CANNOT roll the ball back into the crease again.

After the ball is cleared, a goalkeeper wants to position herself as a trail pass. If the teammate who recovered the clear gets pressured or needs help, she can throw back to the goalkeeper, who is outside of the cage. The goalie looks to move the ball to the opposite side of the field or holds the ball until a teammate is open.

Most goalkeepers are told not to clear to the middle of the field. This is because if there is a turnover, the opposing team is in perfect position to score. If there is an open teammate in the middle of the field, the goalkeeper should clear to her as long as the pass is on her stick. However, the sidelines are the safest areas for clears.

Goalkeepers should never force passes. They must exude confidence when clearing the ball. Tensing up can cause them to throw bad passes. When a goalkeeper has the ball, her team has possession and the opposing team cannot score. A goalkeeper's poise and versatility is dependent upon her practicing cradling at different levels on the move as well as various throwing techniques—overarm, sidearm, and underarm passes.

COMMUNICATION

As the "quarterback" of the defense, a good goalkeeper talks nonstop to the defenders. Because a goalkeeper can see the entire field, her team relies on her direction and leadership. She's their eyes on the field. A goalkeeper does most of her talking when the opposing goalkeeper or team has the ball. She yells "Goalie ball!" to let her team and defense know that the opposing team is preparing to clear the ball. When the opposing goalie releases the ball, she calls "Ball out!" Most talking is done in the defensive 30, below the restraining line.

When the ball is in the defensive end of the field, a goalie announces various hot spots to communicate the specific position of the ball. To effectively communicate with her defense, a goalie can refer to the hot spots: numbered areas surrounding the 8-meter used to designate areas on the field. The 1 spot is at the goalie's back left while the 2 spot is at her back right. X is the spot directly behind the goal (see figure 12.1). This talk helps not only the defense but also forces the goalkeeper to stay focused.

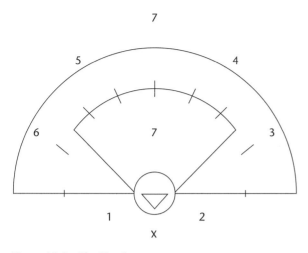

Figure 12.1 The Hot Spots

Goalie Talk

"Ball's High" or "Top Left" corresponds to hot spots 5 and 6.

"Ball's High" or "Top Center" corresponds to hot spot 7.

"Ball's High" or "Top Right" corresponds to hot spots 3 and 4.

"Ball's Behind" or "Low Left" corresponds to hot spot 1.

"Ball's Behind" or "Back Center" is X, or point behind.

"Ball's Behind" or "Low Right" corresponds to hot spot 2.

"Check": When the ball is fed anywhere into the 8-meter, this term alerts the defense to close the defensive space on the ball carrier to prevent her from taking a good shot.

"Crash": When a player effectively dodges into the 8-meter, or is fed the ball, this term alerts players anywhere near that player to collapse on her.

"Ball Down": This phrase alerts teammates that the ball is on the ground.

"Break" or "Clear": As soon as the goalkeeper makes a save or gains possession, she instructs her teammates to move into passing lanes to receive the ball.

OUTSIDE-THE-CREASE PLAY

A favorite pastime of world-class goalkeepers like Coach Dabrowski was to intercept lazy passes from the attack around the crease, intercept feeds in the middle, or come up with possession for her team by running down ground balls or missed shots behind the cage. Big plays like these can change the momentum of a game.

When playing outside of the crease, a goalie wants to be aggressive and not worry about making mistakes. Once a goalkeeper makes the decision to go, she should "GO," with no hesitations. Timing is critical. Goalkeepers should take risks during practices in order to determine when it's appropriate for them to go outside of the crease in games.

EQUIPMENT IN GENERAL

Make sure that the equipment neither weighs down the athlete nor inhibits mobility. Properly fitting equipment won't impede a goalie's athleticism. Here's a hint: A goalkeeper should wear more protection than is necessary in practice; during games she should shed everything that's not absolutely required. The rationale is that she'll feel freer, but still be safe. A goalkeeper is bound to get hit more in practice because she'll see more shots then than in a game. All goalkeepers must wear an NCAA-approved helmet, mouthguard, separate throatguard, chest protector, and padded gloves. Thigh and shin pads are highly recommended.

Helmet

The helmet should fit comfortably and not be too tight when the chinstrap is secured. The goalkeeper should be able to see through the top bar of the helmet. If she is looking anywhere else, then she may need another size.

Throatguard

Specific lacrosse throat protectors are made of either foam or plastic. These should attach easily to the bottom of a helmet by ties or snaps. The foam pad stretches the length of the helmet and covers the entire throat area. The plastic protector hangs from string and is not as wide as the foam guard. This particular model moves around a lot more and does not cover all of the throat area. Field hockey and ice hockey throat protectors are not approved for lacrosse.

Chest Protector

There are dozens of styles of chest protectors for goalies. Consider purchasing a chest protector that includes side and/or rib protection. The top of the chest protector should be fitted at the neck and cover that area where the neck and collarbone begin, including the entire chest and stomach. Make sure it's not too big, too loose, or too tight, and that it allows for mobility.

Gloves

Gloves made specifically for goalkeepers have metal bits in the fingers and thumb area. The gloves should be padded and not too big. The goalkeeper needs a full range of motion for the hands and wrists. Field player gloves are not allowed.

Thigh and Shin Pads

Thigh pads have been designed specifically for women's lacrosse goalkeepers. Most are made of spandex and have padding and a pelvic protector. If a pelvic protector is not already provided in the pads, purchase one separately. Ice hockey pads are not allowed; they are too thick and limit mobility.

Custom-fitted shin guards, also used for field hockey, will protect the entire shin. Shin guards used by baseball catchers are too big and can limit mobility. Soccer shin guards are adequate, but most do not protect the entire shin area.

Sticks

There are a variety of goalie sticks and shafts. It is a matter of personal preference which style of stick a goalie chooses.

Hard vs. Soft Mesh

A hard mesh pocket takes time to break in. Still, most goalkeepers today prefer the hard mesh because it allows them to create pockets. The ball tends to stick to the hard mesh and this allows for better possession in the pocket. However, when hard mesh gets wet, it tends to shrink and the pocket gets smaller; when it dries, it expands again and the pocket gets bigger. This can adversely affect one's ability to clear. Soft mesh tends to create a very low pocket close to the stopper. When this happens, the ball can get stuck there, making it more difficult to clear the ball.

Shafts

The three main types of shafts are titanium, aluminum, and alloy. There are a number of different styles, widths, and textures. Shafts range in price, weight, and color.

DRILLS, DRILLS, DRILLS!

Note: Using a small (field player) stick adds an element of challenge to any drill. It also forces the goalkeeper to watch the ball all the way in, give with her stick and get her body behind the ball.

Coach Tortorelli's Goalie Warm-Up Routine

- Ladder drills (minimum two different sets).
- Plyometrics: Lateral slides, carioca, high knees, butt kicks, sprints.

- 8-meter arc movement: muscle memory for quickness in the crease.
- Jump rope every other day.
- Line drills: jumping over lines (ski jumps, front-to-back, etc.) and stepping over lines while incorporating lateral movement.
- Step-and-follow: focus on the explosive; step with lead foot and follow with trail, finishing in proper stance.

Coach Tortorelli's Goalkeeper Routine for Prepractice and Game Day

- Lap run
- Stretch
- Plyo routine

High knees × 10 yards up and back
Butt kicks × 10 yards up and back
Carioca × 10 yards up and back
Sprint at 100% × 10 yards up and back

Step across from the intersection of the crease and goal line extended, alternating the lead foot × 2

Jump rope × 50 standard jumping, × 50 alternating feet, × 25 side-to-side over a line

Visualization

Three saves each spot: make save, hold (3-second count), and finish save by stepping with second foot to regain balance and control. Return to arc and set for next save.

Steps on your arc: quick steps R to L, L to R, × 2

Shots

- Receive shots around arc from 6–7 meters out: high, mid, low/bounce.
- Receive shots with shooter running in to 3 meters out.
- Receive shots with shooter running side-to-side.
- Receive shots around both sides of the crease.

Coach Dabrowski's Goalie Drills

Jump Rope

Jump rope for 10 minutes prior to every practice. This will warm you up before getting into the goal while it works on quick feet.

Quick Feet

Lay your stick parallel on the ground in front of you. Stand behind the stick and use the shaft for these speed drills. Get in a good stance: feet shoulder-width apart and balanced on the balls of the feet. Keep your hands up and away from your body as if you are in your ready stance. Keep your head up. Hop over the shaft of the stick with both feet. As soon as you land on the other side, hop back with both feet. **Variation:** Hop over right foot first and follow with the left. Hop back and forth for 30 seconds.

Juggling

Start with two balls. When you're comfortable juggling these, use a third. Hold the two balls in your dominant hand. Toss one up in the air, not too high, and as that ball is on its way down, toss the other ball that is in your hand up in the air. Repeat this same process until you become proficient.

Hand and Knee Slap Games

Both of these games work on your hand-eye coordination and peripheral vision.

The hand slap game is an oldie-but-goodie. Goalkeeper number 1 lays her hands on top of goalkeeper number 2's hand with palms touching. Goalkeeper number 2 tries to slap the top of goalkeeper number 1's hands. Once goalkeeper number 2 misses, her hands go on the bottom and goalkeeper number 1 attempts to slap her hands.

The knee slap game: Goalkeepers 1 and 2 try to slap each others' knees while trying to protect their own. This game helps them to remember to stay low and on the balls of the feet while making quick movements.

The Pressure Drill

A coach is in the middle of the 8-meter with a stick and a ball, positioned at the top of the crease looking at the goalkeeper. A field player is positioned at the top of the crease, facing the goalie. The goalkeeper is in ready stance preparing to save a shot. The coach rolls the ball behind the crease to either side. The goalkeeper chases the ball behind the cage with the field player pursuing her. The goalie clears to the coach, again under pressure. The goalkeeper stays relaxed and composed while clearing. This works on handling the pressure and using both the right and left hands to clear the ball.

Tennis/Lacrosse Ball Toss

This drill is done without sticks. The object is to practice 45-degree stepping. The goalie straddles either a line on a field or the shaft of her stick and is in good stance position with her hands away from her body. A partner tosses a ball in the air high to the goalkeeper's dominant side (low to the nondominant side, etc.). The goalkeeper takes both hands to the ball and steps up and out on a 45-degree angle. She takes her nose to the ball and her eyes will follow. Make each save 10 times.

Rapid-Fire with Tennis Balls

This is one of the best drills for hand-eye coordination. A coach/partner kneels or stands 10 yards from the goalie and uses a racquet to fire tennis balls at her. First, the goalie uses just her hands to make the save, then progresses to a field player's stick, and, finally, to her goalie stick. The goalkeeper focuses not only on the saves but also on quickly getting set for subsequent shots. She takes both hands to the ball and gets her body behind it.

Turning to Find the Shot

A coach stands on the perimeter of the 8-meter with a ball in her stick. The goalkeeper is facing the goal with her back to the shooter. The coach moves around the 8-meter; when she is ready to shoot, she yells "shot." The goalkeeper listens for the shooter's voice and turns around. It doesn't matter which way the goalkeeper turns as long as she gets herself set and in a good position to make the save. The coach shoots the ball when the goalkeeper looks set.

Clearing/Throwing: Both Right- and Left-Handed

This drill is for accuracy. It is done against a wall on which various sizes of boxes have been marked with athletic tape The goalie stands 7 to 8 yards back and throws the ball into each box.

For a variation of this drill, a goalie takes a bucket of lacrosse balls into the field. From the 50-yard-line and below, she clears/throws the balls into the cage, working to perfect accuracy at various distances.

Coach Tortorelli's Goalkeeping Tips

Footwork

Goalkeepers move in a relatively small space. They must be able to move quickly and efficiently, eliminating all unnecessary extra movements. For quickness, do the following:

Jump Rope: work on speed, switching feet and rhythm

Ladders: forward, backward, sideways, change direction

Eye Reaction and Hand Quickness

Eye drills are a combination of concentration, focusing on the ball, and watching the ball all the way in. The key is to see the ball all the way in and react as quick as possible. These drills will work on your hand quickness. Always keep your hands out to improve reaction time.

- **Tracking off a wall with colored/numbered balls:** Begin facing the wall with your eyes closed. Have a partner throw the ball and say "go" for you to open your eyes. Catch the ball with both hands. Call out the number/color as soon as you see it off the wall. Variation: Start with your back to the wall, eyes shut. When your partner says "go," open your eyes, turn, and catch the ball.
- **Deck of cards:** Have a partner flip through a deck of cards; call out the color (red or black), suit, or card.
- **Number reaction:** The object is a quick step, touch and reset. Place index cards numbered from 1 to 20 randomly on a wall in front of you. Place the cards in positions where low, mid, and high shots would take place. If you are by yourself, start at 1 and progress to 20, then change up the sequence: proceed from 20 to 1; proceed up by even numbers or down by odd numbers. If you're with a partner, have the partner call out random numbers as you step to touch the cards.
- **Juggling:** Learn to juggle off a wall for hand speed.

Making the Save

Making a good save requires patience, timing, positioning, and the ability to keep the ball in front of your body.

Spot Shooting: Work on technique. Don't get into a rhythm. Work on bringing your nose to the ball. To warm up, play the catch game with gloves on.

Bounce Shots: Trap the ball. This prohibits the ball from bouncing up into you and reduces the amount of rebounds. Keep the stick away from your feet. Drive your hands out away from your feet and explode to the shot. Push your stick out, then give. Don't bring your stick directly to your feet.

Fakes/Patience: Begin without a stick. Have a partner hold the ball in her hand and fake a throw. Stay balanced. If you get faked out, reset right away. A little shuffle step is OK if you are faked. Progress by having your partner use stick fakes to shoot randomly. Work on your patience. Then have the individual move with the ball. The goal now is for you to move on angle and not get faked.

Movement with Shots: Run-ins train you to be patient. There should be very little movement on your angle with this type of shot. The shooter begins at the 8-meter and stays in a straight line to goal.

Run-ins with a Change of Direction: The shooter veers hard before releasing her shot. You move on your angle BEFORE stepping to the shot.

Carry Left/Shoot Right: Stay on your angle longer, be patient and step to the ball when released. Have the shooter begin about 4 meters out and to the side.

The shooter runs flat across the goal cage and releases the ball after she crosses the line of center.

Carry Right/Shoot Left: Same principle as above.

Throwing/Clearing

Work on accuracy with movement. This is the final component of a great save.

Accuracy: Pick a spot on a wall (distinctly mark it) and work on hitting it with a pass/clear. Vary your distance to the wall to work on longer and shorter throws. Repeat with your nondominant hand.

Accuracy with Movement: Use a cage or find a partner. When by yourself: Place balls on the 8–12-meter; make a ground-ball pickup, give a quick cradle, and continue to run in the same direction and throw to your target (pick a spot in the cage). Always keep your feet moving; never stop to clear. Don't hesitate after you pick up the ball to sight your target. Sight your target while you are running.

Conditioning and Clears: Spread balls around the 12-meter. Begin in the cage, sprint out, pick up a ground ball, turn, and throw it in the cage. Sprint back, touch the crease, and go to the next ball.

Pressure: It's important to feel comfortable with the ball in your stick while outside of the goal cage. Work on stick fakes, dodges, and cradling with both hands. Also work on outmaneuvering your opponent with spins and pivots. Working with a partner: Place a ball outside the cage. Run out and pick up the ball while your partner is pressuring you. Don't stop to look at a target; keep your feet moving.

A Word about Conditioning

Concentrate on quickness, speed, and explosiveness. For instance, during sprints, focus on your first three steps as they are the most important and specific to your position. Being explosive and quick off the mark is your goal. Focus on sprints of relatively short distances: 10, 15, 20, and 25 yards. In addition, focus on pivoting and changing direction. During strength training, pay special attention to your abdominal and back muscles, also known as your core.

Final Thoughts

Practice and repetition are the keys to goalkeeping. The more shots a goalkeeper gets, the better she will become. Period. Whether a goalkeeper just made a big save or missed one, Coach Dabrowski advises her to always be thinking: "I've got the next one."

COACH TORTORELLI'S ASSESSMENT GUIDE FOR GOALIES

Strengths/Weaknesses

Knowing what you can and cannot do is an important step in defining goals. Once you understand your weaknesses, you are better able to focus your training. Everyone has weaknesses; choose one you want to work on.

Strengths:

Weakness:

Goals

A goal is something you wish for, desire, or dream about achieving in the future. Write your goals for the upcoming season.
Short-term goals: You can focus on these while training on your own, such as improved footwork and clearing ability.

1.
2.
3.

Long-term goals: Goals for the season, such as improving communication with my defense and saving 50 percent or better on free-position shots.

1.
2.
3.

A Relentlessly Positive Mindset

List the positive and negative things you say to or about yourself during competition or training. Try to turn the negative thoughts into positive thoughts. Write down the new positive thoughts.
Positive Thoughts: "I have a good clear."
Negative Thoughts: "I can't make the off-hip save!"
Review the negative thoughts and rework into:
New Positive Thoughts: "I'm having trouble right now making the off-hip save but if I quicken up my steps and anticipate the shot earlier, I'll get to the ball."

13

Effective Practices

One-on-ones are a great drill to do at practice.

What keeps practices fresh, even as coaches rely on repetition? This chapter lets you in on a number of secrets. First, successful practices are a direct result of a coach's ability to be organized and energetic. If coaches take the field without practice plans, their credibility is shot. Players disengage when a coach is not prepared.* A specific practice plan should be written for each practice. Many coaches like to plan four weeks out, keeping in mind the big-picture goals they want to accomplish; for example, focusing on the fundamentals during week 1; defense, week 2; offense, week 3; and the ride, week 4. Or, perhaps, focusing on teaching a few plays by game 1 and adding several more by game 5. With a master plan in hand, coaches can adjust daily plans based on how their teams are progressing. To help create a master plan, here are our

*Sometimes players tire of hearing the coach's voice throughout the season. Utilize your seniors or older players to serve as additional assistants. Allow your older players to take some ownership of practice, set up certain drills, teach specific skills—this will also help to develop respect, leadership, and camaraderie among your players. Buy-in by your oldest group makes for successful practice.

suggestions for the skills you want to touch on before your first game:

- Cradle—Right and Left Hands, Changing Levels, Stickwork Tricks
- Catching—Run through catch, In close to the body, Leading
- Passing—Overhand, Flip, Loop, Riser
- Pivot—Explode, Lead with stick
- Dodges—Face/Pull, Roll, Split, Sword, Dip, Rocker Step
- Ground Balls—Toward, Away, Under Pressure
- Interceptions/Blocks
- Give and Go's
- Cutting—Whole field and 8-meter
- Picks and Screens
- Shooting and Feeding
- 1 v 1 attack moves with and without the ball
- 1 v 1 defense on ball and off ball
- Player Up/Player Down Fast-Break Offense and Defense—3 v 2, 4 v 3, 5 v 4, etc.
- Settled Offense—7 v 7 and set offensive plays
- Settled Defense—7 v 7 aggressive and passive
- Zone Defense
- Clears and Full Field Passing
- Midfield Defense and Midfield Offense
- Rides—Pressure, Zone
- Redirecting the Ball
- Double Teams
- Center Draws and Circle Play
- 8-Meter Shots and 8-Meter Play
- Full Field Scrimmage
- Situational Play—Last two minutes, Stalling, Breaking a Stall, etc.
- Goaltending
- Conditioning

The primary objective of practice in any team sport is to prepare both the individual and the team for game-day situations. A team will have a tough time making adjustments if specific situations have not been addressed prior to games. "If circumstances arise that I have not prepared my team for, then I have failed," Coach Tucker says. "I cannot hold my team responsible. I also feel that the most important practice is the one after a loss."

GENERAL CONSIDERATIONS

The Plan

A good lacrosse practice flows instead of drags on; it adheres to a set time schedule. Varied and challenging drills are set up and executed crisply and efficiently. Keep in mind that practice does not make perfect. Practice makes permanent. Only *perfect* practice makes perfect. A coach must demand that players execute their skills and drills the *correct* way at practice; otherwise, you are fostering a climate of bad habits. Make your players DO IT RIGHT! Along with your plan, keep detailed track of drills, noting what is taught, and when, with comments for reference.

Some coaches may e-mail or post practice plans ahead of time; Coach Tucker simply announces her plan for the day at the start of each practice. Other coaches may want to keep their players guessing.

Length of Practice

The length of practice is an important decision. In the preseason, Hopkins typically practices for 2 hours plus an hour of conditioning. As the season unfolds, Hopkins shortens practices to about half that time. It's important to gauge a team's attention span and adjust your practice time accordingly. An efficiently run 90-minute practice can be much more effective than a poorly designed or managed 3-hour practice.

It's time well spent to explain the purpose of various drills to players. This helps them to become thinking players instead of robots; they'll begin to acquire a conceptual understanding when they realize how drills apply to game-day situations. If an individual or team seems distracted, take a moment to ask what's going on, recognizing that there are other stressors in your players' lives: tests, papers, sickness, exhaustion. Let them know you care. This is also a great way to foster effective communication between coaches and players.

Lacrosse is a year-round outdoor sport. Advise players to be prepared for the elements. Coaches need alternative practice plans and facilities in case the weather confines them to limited indoor spaces.

Practice Hints

- Maximize prepractice time. Get your players moving with stickwork tricks, jumping rope, shooting, and feeding as they are waiting for practice to begin. Expect players to show up early for practice.
- Stick to a structured warm-up and stretching routine (such as the ones included in chapter 14) to minimize injuries and wasted practice time.
- Get your goalies warmed up prior to or just at the beginning.
- Allow players to socialize during warm-ups, as long as they stay focused.
- There is a time during practice for positive reinforcement as well as for a swift kick in the pants—do whichever is needed.
- Keep explanations clear and concise; minimize standing-around time.
- Avoid having too many players in too few lines; utilize station work and keep drills moving quickly.
- Streamline practices, distinguishing Position Work (attack, midfield, defense, and goalie), and Team Work (rides, clears), from Group Work (midfielders and attack working on offense while defense and goalies work on breakouts).
- Jog from one drill to the next.
- Incorporate transition play into every practice: offense to defense and defense to offense.

Before the first game, teach your team exactly what to do in these "special" situations:

- Down a goal with 2 minutes left
- Up two goals with 4 minutes left
- Game is tied; need the draw
- Overtime

Try to incorporate center draw play and free positions in every other practice. These two areas are undercoached and underpracticed. Developing center draw specialists is a must, and they should be given time to practice their draw techniques often. Always incorporate lots and lots of shooting and stickwork. Run drills that build on, and complement, one another.

Practice Philosophies

Some questions that coaches should consider when designing practices are:

- When scrimmaging full-field or half-field, do you play your starters against starters or your starters against your support players?
- Do you save conditioning for the end of practice, and are you an "on-the-endline" coach? Or do you incorporate creative conditioning throughout practices/during drills?
- Do you play 12–14 players and rarely sub, or do you try to rotate players (especially midfielders) on a regular basis?
- Do you run midfield lines (two specific groups of three players)?

PLANNING PRACTICES

Start on Time

If practice is supposed to start at 4:00 p.m., then be ready to blow your whistle and have your players "bring it in" at 4:00 p.m. sharp. Discipline, structure, and consistency are critical. If you don't begin practice until the last of the teammates straggles in, a lackadaisical attitude will trickle down and infect the team. A routine of being organized and starting promptly promotes a positive and respectful environment as well as lends credibility to the authority of the coach. At Hopkins, the rule is "If you are early, you are on time . . . if you are on time, you are late . . . and if you are late, you're in trouble!"

The Best-Laid Plans

As important as structure is at practice, there needs to be a degree of flexibility built in. If you put a drill out there and notice that the players aren't getting it, or that key players are missing, by all means make a change. Improvise to keep practice flowing. You can revisit drills later.

No matter how organized you are, disruptions happen. The key to capably handling the countless unforeseens that inevitably crop up is to have back-up plans. At the very least, mentally walk yourself through the what-ifs, if only in a general sense. In the event of bad weather, is there an indoor site? In the event of an emergency, can you count on the cool-headedness of your assistant coach?

Practice Planner

Bring It In (5 min.):

_____

_____

Warm-up and Stretch (10 min.):

_____

_____

Stickwork, Shooting, Feeding Drills (up to 25 min.):

_____

_____

Offense-Defense Combinations/Game Concepts (20 min.):

_____

_____

Scrimmage Play/Game Concepts (25 min.):

_____

_____

Bring It In/Wrap-up/Stretch (5 min.):

_____

When presented with dilemmas, keep this simple question in mind as guidance: What would you, as a parent, expect or want a coach to do if it was your daughter in a similar situation?

GENERAL PRACTICE FORMAT

A practice routine provides structure and helps players (and coaches) to establish good practice habits. Follow the same basic routine for each practice, no matter what the levels of your players are, but vary the activities, difficulty of drills, number of players, player combinations, space, and concepts presented to keep everyone motivated and interested. A Practice Planner is an excellent way to keep on task and organized. A 90-minute practice is the maximum recommended for beginner- and intermediate-level players, and a 2-hour practice is the maximum recommended for advanced-level players. The goal is for players to learn, execute, and understand skills while they are focused and engaged. Coaches know when a practice is dragging on or is ineffective. Make it a habit of reading your players, and adjust accordingly.

Prepractice Routine

Coach makes sure each player has a ball in her stick and is moving—partner-passing, ground balls, and stickwork tricks, for instance. Take a little time to offer specific instruction or direction to individual players.

Bring It In (5 minutes)

Let players know about the format for practice; tell them the goals for the day. Let them know you'll call water breaks over the next hour and a half, at regular intervals. The coach does the talking during "Bring It In," emphasizing the focus of the practice. Make sure all eyes are on you, and do not allow side conversations.

Dynamic Warm-up (10 minutes)

This warm-up routine can be used before each practice, after a warm-up jog and stretch. Do each of the following in order for about 15 yards and then repeat on the return.

- Cocky Walk
- Foot Flutter
- Walking Knee Tucks
- Heel-to-Hamstring Run
- Russian Walk
- Butt Kicks
- Forward Monster Walk
- Backward Monster Walk
- Carioca
- Slide
- Backpedal—turn and jog

Cocky Walk: Start walking in a straight line, keeping the leg straight and placing the heel of the front foot on the ground. As you start to move forward, allow the toes of the foot in front to drop down, and when the foot is directly in line with the body, go up on the toes and hold for a moment. Repeat as you place each step: It should look like you're walking cocky or with confidence; allow the arms to swing big with the legs.

Foot Flutter: While on your toes, take tiny flutter steps. No long striding: you move your feet only slightly in front of your body while bouncing on your toes. Leaning forward slightly with your arms pumping as if sprinting.

Knee Tucks: Walking in a straight line, step forward with the left leg and lift the right leg so the thigh is parallel to the floor. While wrapping both hands around the right knee and tucking the leg, you go up on the toes with your balance foot (left). Repeat walking forward, switching from leg to leg.

Heel-to-Hamstring Run: Run forward with a high knee lift. Keep a slight lean forward, with arms pumping close to the body. Kick the leg out and finish with the knee coming up high and the heel touching the hamstring. Don't lean back; the knee should go only slightly higher than parallel to the ground.

Russian Walk: Start with both feet together; arms are straight out in front, parallel to the ground. Step forward with the right foot, kicking a straight left leg high into the air. Don't hunch while trying to touch the outstretched hands with your foot. Bring the left leg to a stop next to the right foot. Now step forward with the left foot and swing the right leg just as you did the left. Bring the right leg to a stop next to the left foot. Repeat sequence. Precision and technique, not speed, is important.

Butt Kicks: With a slight lean forward, jog forward pointing the knees straight down so your thighs are perpendicular to the ground and try to touch your heels to your butt. Each repetition should be fast. Don't worry about distance; the key is lots of repetitions completed with each leg.

Forward Monster Walk: Walk forward with the trail leg circling forward from the hip while the knee is bent in a 90-degree angle and the thigh is parallel to the ground. Pretend to lift the leg over a small hurdle as you walk forward.

Backward Monster Walk: The same as the Forward Monster Walk except in reverse.

Carioca: Move laterally with the right leg in the lead. The left leg crosses in front and then in back of the right leg as you move laterally. Keep the upper body square and bend your knees; arms are relaxed and bent for balance and moving out in front of the body. Repeat with the left leg in the lead.

Slides: Slide laterally—with the right leg leading—making sure the feet do not cross or touch. Don't pop up; keep shoulders and head on an even plane while sliding. Point the lead foot in the direction you are moving. Repeat with the left leg leading.

Backpedal: Jog backward while leaning slightly forward for balance. Kick each leg back as if trying to kick someone behind you. Arms are pumping at the side, elbows bent, for balance and propulsion.

Static Stretching Routine (5 minutes)

Do the following stretches in order. Hold each for 20 to 30 seconds.

Seated legs out wide, stretch to the middle.
Seated legs out wide, stretch to touch right foot.
Seated legs out wide, stretch to touch left foot.
Seated legs out wide, stretch to the middle.
Seated Butterfly: With the bottom of your feet together and holding onto the ankles, push down on your thighs with your elbows.
Leg Hug: Lying on your back, pull the right knee into the chest, hugging the leg. Repeat with left knee.
Hamstring Stretch: Lying on your back, raise the right leg until perpendicular with the ground and straighten for a hamstring stretch. Repeat with the left leg.
Glute Stretch: Lying on your back, move a straight right leg across your body at hip level, coming to rest on the opposite side for a lower back and glute stretch; keep both shoulders pinned to the ground. Repeat on the other side.
Lying on the left side, grab your right ankle and pull bent leg gently toward your back to stretch your quad.
Calf stretch: While standing with your left foot slightly in front of your right, flex your ankle with toes pointing up and lean

forward, into the stretch. Repeat with the other leg.

Stickwork Drills (25 minutes)

Devote a chunk of each practice to fundamental drills and skill building. Here are five secrets to keeping this part of practice energized and effective.

- Keep the players moving.
- Break players into small groups.
- Set up stations.
- Emphasize two key tactics (one offensive and one defensive) for each station.
- Insist on repetition.

The basis for any athlete's success is how well she executes the fundamentals. Of equal importance is understanding how to apply fundamental skills in game situations. Drills provide terrific opportunities for teaching, polishing, and correcting skills. Going through the motions simply won't cut it. Coaches who visit each station and make specific comments to players are making the most of prime teaching time.

Nobody likes to stand around at practice. Divvy players up into small-group situations as opposed to long lines. Run several stations for 7–8 minute segments with players rotating through.

A Sampling of Stations

Stickwork tricks
One-on-ones
Shooting with no pressure; shooting under
    pressure
Dodging
Double teams
Feeding drill
Yale drill (stationary 4 v 3)
Early slide (5 v 5)
Ground balls
Grub drill (works on ground balls in the 8-meter)

3 v 2, 4 v 3, and 5 v 4
Slow breaks

Offensive and Defensive Combinations/ Game Concepts (15–20 minutes)

It's critical for players to understand that the experience they gain every day at practice is what helps them to perform well in games. What an athlete does at practice defines her as a player and probably determines her playing time in games. It's of no use to players to master the fundamentals of lacrosse if they can't transfer these basics into game-like situations. Players need to be able to make decisions and execute skills in games and scrimmages.

Coaches: If you focus only on developing fundamental skills, your team will have trouble putting them into action on game day. How, as a coach, do you help players achieve a conceptual understanding of the game of lacrosse? The first step is to put them in small-sided, game-like situations.

One of the most important, and challenging, concepts to teach is creating space for the ball carrier. In a 3 v 3 or 4 v 4 station within your practice, begin to emphasize good field sense. Field players need to learn when to support the ball and how. They need to recognize when the ball carrier has a good opportunity to go to the cage and allow her to do so, and perhaps support her by going behind the cage to chase down a missed shot. The fewer people in this drill initially, the greater chance of more light bulbs being turned on: When you break down settled offensive and defensive situations and teach to small groups of players, then your team has the best chance to "get it." Once they do, then you can progress to 5 v 5, 6 v 6, and finally, 7 v 7.

Scrimmage (25+ minutes)

When a team scrimmages, it practices transferring offensive and defensive concepts into game situations. Scrimmaging is fun and competitive. Whether it's a half- or full-field scrimmage, players love to play. This is your chance, as a coach, to really assess your players.

Start them off with clear direction. Then stand back and let them play. It's especially important in the beginning of the season to simply observe during that first practice or two, to see what talents emerge. It'll become apparent in scrimmages who has a natural sense of the field and play. Individuals will show themselves to be impact players, support players, solid or poor decision makers, aggressive or reserved. You'll notice teammates forging connections. When you do offer direction, stress effort: Remind players to hustle after ground balls, to cut hard for the ball, to make their teammates look good.

Let one side win and the other lose. In practice, competition needs to be paramount, but sportsmanship must be prevalent. Players need to accept that they'll win some and lose some and they can learn to do both with dignity. Make sure your players shake hands after each full scrimmage. Both "teams" within your team need to demonstrate respect for each other. Focus on two to three key points for them to keep in mind when scrimmaging.

It's important for a team to realize that when a coach addresses an individual, she's really teaching everyone. At Hopkins, when Coach Tucker tells someone to keep her stick up while off-ball on defense, she follows it up by asking, "Ladies, who am I talking to?" The answer she demands: "Everyone." When a coach is giving instruction, players must recognize that it's not a time for conversation. When players are asked to do something, the responses should be limited to "Okay, coach" or "I don't understand, coach." NOT ACCEPTABLE RESPONSES: "I'm sorry." "I know." "I can't." (Spin the "I can't" into "I'm having a little trouble right now," and the "I know" into "Okay, coach.")

Avoid calling a full-field scrimmage at the end of every practice; mix it up, be creative. Set up little tournaments: Use four goal cages and break the team up into four smaller teams; play a 5 v 5 tournament with winners playing winners. Energy levels are usually highest at the beginnings of practices, of course. By midpractice, energy and enthusiasm may wane. Scrimmages and competitive drills are effective ways to infuse energy into the ends of practices, but they can be done at any time.

When you discuss the scrimmage, express constructive criticisms first; specify two things you want to see improved. Conclude with a positive comment, a compliment. When players hear the good stuff last, they walk away knowing what they have to work on, but bolstered with the feeling that the coach noticed that they did something well.

Bring It In Again—Wrapping Up Practice (5 minutes)

Encourage players to stretch on their own during this segment of practice; their muscles will appreciate it. Make sure they're in a circle with eyes on the coach.

Throughout practice, the coach is the authority. Coaches coach and players play. However, it's important that coaches are not always doing all the talking. Now is the time to ask players for feedback: "What did we do well as a team today? What did you like about today's practice? What did we achieve today as a team?" If coaches can elaborate on the players' answers, it helps to build rapport and trust between them. Also consider asking: "What do we need to improve? What could we have done better today?" This way, players take ownership of the parts of their game that need work.

Wrap up "Bring It In" by giving some idea about what the next practice will be like: "We spent a lot of time on offensive drills today. Tomorrow our emphasis will be on defense."

Just a reminder: Water breaks are a necessary component of practices. Keep your players hydrated. The rule of thumb is that if they're thirsty, they're already becoming dehydrated. Build regular water breaks into practices; two is usually sufficient except for when it's really hot. Encourage players to bring their own water bottles.

SPECIALTY PRACTICES

The Practice after a Tough Loss

It happens to the best of teams. You were moving along just fine, winning some games, losing some games, and then it happens: You suffer a demoralizing loss. Remember: You are not as good as you look when you win but are not as bad as you look when you lose. How do you handle the practice immediately after a team has beat you by 20 goals, or perhaps by 1 goal in the last 5 seconds? One thing's for sure: Don't dwell on it. Infuse the next practice with extra energy; don't allow coaches or players to rehash the experience time and again.

Assess the areas where your team needs to perform better and incorporate them into this practice. You might ask yourself: Was it a lack of possession? Did the defense slide to double-team? Was it poor shooting? Were we able to slow the ball down at all? Were we completely outmatched? When you "Bring It In," be decisive and firm about the things to be worked on at practice, let the team know what adjustments were necessary in the game, and assure them that with a lot of hard work, they will improve. Mention some positive accomplishments in the game to let the team know you noticed. Talk to them about inevitable stumbling blocks on the field and in life in general, and tell them that a tough loss is a learning experience. Enthusiastically send them out to start your warm-up.

Defensive drills should be the focus for the practice after a good drubbing. Set up drills to work on slowing down the ball in transition, sliding to double team, marking cutters in the 8-meter, and picking up ground balls.

The Practice after a Big Win

Well done. You beat your opponent by nine goals, the team played well, and everybody's feeling great. Let's keep up the good work. The practice following a big win is not the time to slack off. It's time to polish. Build on your offensive success by incorporating additional shooting drills. Continue to challenge your defense by putting them in player-down situations; tell them what a great job they did holding their opponents to a couple of goals. Remind your team that they can't afford to get comfortable after a big win. The focus still needs to be on consistent, daily improvement.

The Practice after a Poor Shooting Performance

Your offense couldn't hit the broad side of a barn during the last game, much less the inside of the goal cage. What to do? KEEP SHOOTING. NBA players say, "When you're hot, keep shooting. When you're not, keep shooting more." The practice after a poor shooting performance should be completely dedicated to shooting and offensive drills. Get your team back on track. Run drills that allow them to score. Start without a goalie so your team has no trouble finding the net. Give them targets to shoot at: Put a pinnie in each corner of the goal cage and have a contest to see who has the most accurate shot. Set up shooting stations so your entire team is getting lots of touches on the ball. Make sure many of your drills run continuously; when the defense gets the ball, they become offense, and vice versa. This will help to develop complete players. Set up a short field. Bring the goals in close to make a 40-yard field for a 3 v 3. The offensive team gives it their best shot. But when the ball turns over, the defense becomes attack.

This way, attack players will develop defensive skills and defensive players, attack skills. An attacker will be better able to beat a defender if she understands defensive concepts, if she can play defense. The converse is also true.

During these offensive and defensive combinations, coaches need to stop play occasionally to discuss possession, as well as throwing and catching skills; don't allow players to simply run the ball. Also address on- and off-ball defensive positioning. Get two short games going on at one time. One coach can focus on offensive concepts such as spacing, throwing and catching, and cutting; the other can concentrate on defensive positioning, double-teaming, and clearing. Then switch. This way, your players will get a variety of input.

Any switching of attack and defense will momentarily cost your team the finely tuned synergy that can develop among a core group of offensive or defensive players who practice together as a unit and therefore know each other's abilities and idiosyncrasies. But the benefit is that they're all developing into complete players who will have a comprehensive understanding of the game.

PRESEASON PRACTICE PLAN

WEEK 1—Emphasize stickwork and conditioning. Teach the hot spots.

Day 1	*3:00–5:00 p.m.*
3:00 p.m.	Teach hot spots, spacing and the importance of communication offensively and defensively
3:15 p.m.	Warm Up and Stretch
3:30 p.m.	Partner Passing (emphasize top hand slid, soft hands, protecting the stick, shoulders turned/roll, move feet)
3:40 p.m.	Line Drills—lots of touches on the ball
4:00 p.m.	Sprints—100, 75, 50, 25 × 3
4:10 p.m.	Star Drill (with 2 balls)
4:20 p.m.	Sprints—50 × 6
4:30 p.m.	Teach and practice Pass-Back-Weave
4:45 p.m.	Closing remarks; Stretch
Day 2	*3:00– 5:30 p.m.*
3:00 p.m.	Lift weights in the weight room
3:50 p.m.	Warm Up and Stretch
4:00 p.m.	Jazzy partner passing (emphasize top hand slid, drop steps, spins and turns, move feet)
4:10 p.m.	Pass-Back-Weave
4:20 p.m.	Stations (15 minutes each, then switch)
	Shooting and Feeding
	Yale Drill

4:50 p.m.	Teach and practice Early Slide Drill
5:10 p.m.	Teach Settled Defense—walk through angles, defending cutters
5:25 p.m.	Closing remarks; Stretch

Day 3	*1:00–3:30 p.m.*
1:00 p.m.	Conditioning—footwork and sprints
1:50 p.m.	Partner passing (emphasize top hand slid, soft hands, protecting the stick, move feet, spins and turns)
2:00 p.m.	Pressure Box Passing Drill (2 boxes)
2:15 p.m.	1 v 1's on the crease at 2 cages. (Coaches shoot video of players to be viewed by team during scheduled film session.)
2:30 p.m.	Split into 2 groups (10 min. each then switch): Station 1, Shooting; Station 2, Mirror Dodging Drill
2:50 p.m.	Half-field play—focus on Settled Defense
3:25 p.m.	Closing remarks; Stretch

Day 4	*1:00–3:30 p.m.*
1:00 p.m.	Lift weights
1:50 p.m.	Warm Up and Stretch
2:00 p.m.	Groups of 4 passing—move the ball quickly; add creative passes.
2:10 p.m.	Early Slide Drill—videotape.
2:25 p.m.	Midfielders and Defenders: Review Settled Defense in half-field setting; review backside (sneak attack) double team Attack: Give-and-Go Shooting Drill; teach beating a double team.
2:40 p.m.	Half-field scrimmage from the 50-yard line, starting with center draw. Emphasize attacking with speed, establishing a strong side and moving the ball quickly, finding the weak defense. Emphasize settled defense communication, slowing down the ball, protecting the 8-meter. Incorporate goalie clear long to start the drill. Rotate players often.
3:15 p.m.	Teach and practice 8-meters
3:25 p.m.	Closing remarks; Stretch

Day 5	*3:00–5:00 p.m.*
3:00 p.m.	Review hot spots, settled defense, primary offense and clearing
3:15 p.m.	Warm Up and Stretch
3:30 p.m.	Partner Passing (add drop steps and turns)
3:40 p.m.	Line Drills—lots of touches on the ball to 5-Point Passing Drill
4:00 p.m.	Sprints—100, 75, 50, 25 × 3
4:10 p.m.	Star Drill (2 balls), add quick sticks, add 2–3 defenders in the middle.
4:25 p.m.	Sprints—50 × 6
4:35 p.m.	Pass-Back-Weave
4:42 p.m.	Practice 8-meters
4:50 p.m.	Closing remarks; Stretch

WEEK 2

Day 6   *8:15–11:00 a.m.*

8:15 a.m.   Lift

9:10 a.m.   Warm Up and Stretch

9:20 a.m.   Partner passing—add bait and check

Videotape the remainder of practice:

9:30 a.m.   5-Point Passing Drill—lots of touches, add fakes, look away passes.

9:40 a.m.   2 Stations: (15 min each) Station 1, Shooting and Feeding; Station 2, Teaching general breakout/spacing/clears

10:10 a.m.   Half-field Play—focus on breakout, clears, and offensive movement

10:50 a.m.   Closing remarks; Stretch

Day 7   *8:15–11:00 a.m.*

8:15 a.m.   Conditioning

9:00 a.m.   Stretch and Warm Up

9:15 a.m.   Partner Passing to Defend the Wall Drill

Videotape the remainder of practice:

9:30 a.m.   2 Pass Weave with a Shot

9:40 a.m.   Pressure Box Drill (set up 2)

9:50 a.m.   Yale Drill

10:05 a.m.   Early Slide

10:20 a.m.   Teach and practice 3 v 2, 4 v 3, and 5 v 4's

10:50 a.m.   Closing remarks; Stretch

Day 8   *8:15–11:00 a.m.*

8:15 a.m.   Conditioning

9:10 a.m.   Warm Up and Stretch

9:20 a.m.   Star Drill (2 balls), then with 2 defenders, then 3 defenders to add pressure

9:30 a.m.   1 v 1's at two cages from the wings

9:45 a.m.   Teach "12" Clear and "50" Clear

10:00 a.m.   Full-field scrimmage—focus on center draw play, dropping in on defense, marking up, fast break, slow break, run clears. Call fouls tightly—no shopping-cart defense or poor stick position. (Two 20-minute halves with 5-minute halftime)

10:50 a.m.   Closing remarks; Stretch

Day 9   *1:00–3:30 p.m.*

1:00 p.m.   Conditioning

1:50 p.m.   Stretch

2:00 p.m.   4 Corners with a Shot Drill—quick ball movement

2:15 p.m.   Continuous long 1 v 1 on two fields widthwise (emphasize slowing down ball, driving the attack player off angle, catching up first then getting hands in front—forearm/knuckle D—sticks up)

2:30 p.m.	Teach double teams and set up competitive ground balls drill—focus on closing double teams, no swinging, attack backing out and running off of a shoulder to beat the double
2:45 p.m.	3 v 2, 4 v 3, 5 v 4 and slow break
3:15 p.m.	8-meter play—remind defenders to break out on save
3:30 p.m.	Closing remarks; Stretch

Day 10	*1:00–3:30 p.m.*
1:00 p.m.	Conditioning
1:50 p.m.	Warm Up and Stretch
2:00 p.m.	5-Point Passing Drill
2:10 p.m.	Pentagon Drill
2:25 p.m.	Pass-Back-Weave
2:35 p.m.	Beating-the-Double-Team Drill. Have everyone do both—closing the double and beating the double; run off of the shoulder, protect stick, and keep heads up
2:45 p.m.	Mirror Dodging Drill
2:55 p.m.	Scrimmage—call fouls, push the ball offensively, long clears; teach and work on specialty situations (last 2 minutes, stall, breaking a stall, etc.)
3:30 p.m.	Closing remarks; Stretch

WEEK 3

Day 11	*8:15–11:00 a.m.*
8:15 a.m.	Conditioning
9:00 a.m.	Partner passing—bait and check, fakes, drop steps, spins and turns
9:10 a.m.	Pass-Back-Weave and 2 Pass Weave with a shot
9:40 a.m.	Stations (10 minutes at each, then switch): Double-Team Drill; 1 v 1's
10:00 a.m.	Coach A: Teach/review settled offense with attack and middies
	Coach B: Teach/review defensive sets and clears with defense
10:20 a.m.	Controlled scrimmage—call the fouls, run slow breaks.
10:50 a.m.	8-meter play
11:00 a.m.	Closing remarks; Stretch

Day 12	*8:15–11:00 a.m.*
8:15 a.m.	Conditioning
9:00 a.m.	Pressure Box Drill
9:10 a.m.	Stations (10 minutes each then switch): Turn-and-shoot drill; World Cup Drill
9:30 a.m.	1 v 1 at 2 cages (cage 1 from the crease, cage 2 from the wings) once you go you sprint to the next cage
9:45 a.m.	Slow break
10:05 a.m.	Teach and practice zone defense (Backer)

| 10:25 a.m. | Half-field play |
| 10:55 a.m. | Closing remarks; Stretch |

Day 13	*8:15–11:00 a.m.*
8:15 a.m.	Conditioning
9:00 a.m.	Box Passing Drill—move ball quickly
9:10 a.m.	3 v 2, 4 v 3, 5 v 4's
9:25 a.m.	Slow break
9:40 a.m.	Black v White scrimmage
	(Two 30-minute halves with 5-minute halftime)
10:45 a.m.	8-meter
10:55 a.m.	Closing remarks; Stretch

Day 14	*1:00–3:30 p.m.*
1:00 p.m.	Conditioning
1:45 p.m.	Pressure Box Drill—add checking
2:00 p.m.	1 v 1 at 2 cages (cage 1 crease, cage 2 wings—sprint to next cage)
2:15 p.m.	Pass-Back-Weave
2:25 p.m.	Teach/review checking—no swings; Checking Drills
2:45 p.m.	Early Slide Drill
3:05 p.m.	Review stall and breaking a stall—practice half-field
3:30 p.m.	Closing remarks; Stretch

Day 15	*1:00–3:30 p.m.*
1:00 p.m.	Conditioning
1:45 p.m.	Partner Passing—spins, turns, drop steps
2:10 p.m.	World Cup Drill at one cage; shooting drill at the other cage (12 minutes each, then switch)
2:35 p.m.	Review Ride—PEARLS
2:50 p.m.	Controlled scrimmage—focus on ride and clears
3:30 p.m.	Closing remarks; Stretch

After Week 3 of practice in the preseason, before designing Week 4, take a moment to assess how far your team has come and what areas need polish—perhaps the ride or settled offense. Don't forget to incorporate situational play into your Week 4 plan: What to do in the last 2 minutes of a game when you're winning . . . when you're losing, etc. If weather is a problem in the preseason, there is nothing like a good game of basketball indoors! Bring your team inside, split them up, and have a round-robin basketball tournament. Focus on footwork, double teams, communication, staying low on defense, and so on.

Having a variety of drills to incorporate into your practices is certainly a bonus, but focus on teaching and mastering several key drills in the pre-season before adding too many others. A common mistake of young coaches is to have so many different drills that their team doesn't get really good at any of them. Nor do they have a chance to become proficient at certain skills, tactics, or strategies. Build off of solid foundation drills like the Pass-Back-Weave Drill, Yale Drill, and the Early Slide Drill. Be sure to incorporate lots of 3 v 2's, 4 v 3's and 5 v 4's. Also, consider adding extra defenders for drills that put more pressure on your offense—like four offensive players versus five defensive players.

Remember, organized and energized practices are effective practices.

Good luck!

14

Off-Season Strategies

Johns Hopkins University's former Professional Strength and Conditioning Coach, Chris Endlich, is the guest contributor to this chapter. Chris has a Master's Degree in Exercise Science and is certified through the National Strength and Conditioning Association and the National Academy of Sports Medicine. In addition to working with the Johns Hopkins Women's Lacrosse Team, Chris works with a number of individual athletes from high school through the professional ranks in many sports.

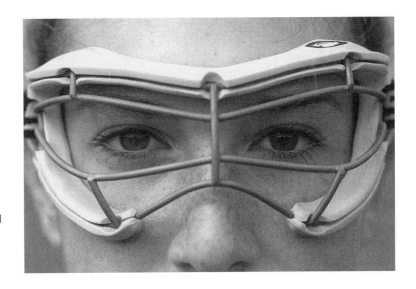

Lacrosse players need to be focused on the field, as well as during their workouts.

Not long ago, football players were among the only athletes consistently lifting weights; they wanted strength and bulk. Many female athletes thought that lifting would tighten their muscles and make them big, limiting their performance. However, a program that's safe and tailored for women's lacrosse players, such as the one outlined here, builds strength, speed, and quickness without sacrificing the ability to move efficiently. In women's lacrosse, it's the strongest, fastest, and quickest players who stand out. An optimal training program will develop each of those facets of your athleticism.

FUNDAMENTALS OF FITNESS

The main focus of this women's lacrosse training program is your core. The core consists of all the muscles between the rib cage and pelvis and is involved in every movement performed on the lacrosse field. This training begins with the core and works outward.

Here's why.

If you were to look at a human anatomy book, you'd see that the only bones between the rib cage and pelvis are vertebrae, the main purpose of which is to protect the spinal cord. For all-important support, the body relies on musculature. Insufficient strength in the core muscles is often the root of many injuries sustained in competition. That's why core comes first in this program.

Traditional floor exercises such as sit-ups and crunches have proven to be inefficient in preparing the body for athletic movements. Instead, this program utilizes a variety of exercises that include movements done on the floor as well as while standing. This way, we can address the various positions a lacrosse player finds herself in while playing.

Next, this program addresses the neglected fact that a lacrosse player spends much of the time during competition with her weight on either one foot or the other. For example, when she runs, she has both feet on the ground only for a split second; the rest of the time she is shifting from one foot to the other. That's why step-downs, lunges, and single leg squats are vital to increasing speed and agility as well as avoiding injury.

Along with single leg exercises, you will also need single arm exercises in order to become a complete player who uses both her left and right hands equally. Balanced strength is extremely important: The muscles that oppose a movement should be comparable in strength to the muscles that produce that movement. For example, when you pass the ball, the muscles of your chest, shoulders, and arms (among others) produce the movement. The opposing muscles—those in the back for example—need to be strong enough to control the forces being produced from the shoulder area. This program trains your muscles equally.

Since our goal isn't bodybuilding or strictly appearance, the focus of this program is on exercises that involve many muscles at the same time. You can always include exercises for individual muscles such as the triceps and biceps, but the bulk of your time should be spent on exercises that work many muscles, such as the chest press or row.

Finally, this program addresses flexibility, one of the most overlooked yet important components of training for lacrosse. You can be strong in the weight room and have great endurance, but if you have tight hips or shoulders, you will most definitely be limited on the field and probably set yourself up for injury. The more flexible you are, the less chance of injury.

THE PROGRAM

This program consists of three main components: warm-up, weight training or conditioning workout, and cool-down. The warm-up prepares muscles for working out; the cool-down adds to muscle efficiency and overall performance through flexibility.

Step 1—The Warm-up

Before you begin any weight lifting or conditioning, you must first warm up the body. Traditionally, athletes jogged around the field and then did some light stretching, but that has proved to be insufficient. Women's lacrosse players must thoroughly prepare their bodies by performing movements that are similar to those they will be using during their practices and games. This program makes use of traditional exercises in addition to various moves from the disciplines of yoga and Pilates.

Jumping Jack Intervals

These are extremely effective variations of the traditional jumping jack that provide a great warm-up and thoroughly prepare your body for any workout you are going to do: the Traditional Jumping Jack, the Staggered-Stance Jumping Jack, and the Twisting Staggered-Stance Jumping Jack.

Traditional Jumping Jack: Start with feet together and arms at the sides. Jump up and move your feet out to the sides while moving your arms out to the side and then over your head. Hands come together just above the head. Immediately jump again and return hands to your sides with feet together. All movements should be to the side and over the head.

Staggered-Stance Jumping Jack: This is the same as the Traditional Jumping Jack but instead of your feet moving out to the side and back in, you move your feet forward and back. Continue the same arm motion as the Traditional Jumping Jack but stagger your feet so that one foot is forward and the other foot is back, and then switch their positions (move the front foot back and the back foot forward). Continue switching your feet while you move your arms out to the side from next to your legs to just above your head.

Twisting Staggered-Stance Jumping Jack: This is similar to the Staggered-Stance Jumping Jack but instead of moving the arms out to the side and over your head, move them side-to-side in a twisting motion. Coordinate the movement so that you turn your upper body in the direction of the leg that is in front. For example, if your left leg is forward and your right leg is back, turn your upper body so that you are facing toward the left.

Continue through the sequence, doing each exercise for about 10 seconds for the prescribed time. For a workout with 2 minutes of Jumping Jack Intervals, you will do each of the three variations in order for 10 seconds, each repeating the sequence 4 times (3 variations at 10 seconds each times 4 circuits equals 2 minutes). Do not rest between variations or between circuits. This should be continuous with smooth, coordinated transitions between movements.

Dynamic Warm-up

After you have started moving your body and increased your heart rate, loosen up your muscles with moves from yoga and Pilates. Perform each of the following moves, in order, for 5–10 seconds; repeat the entire sequence 3 times.

Start in a standing position with your feet spread as far as possible. Next:

1. Twist your upper body left to right
2. Lunge side to side (by bending the knee on that side)
3. Bring your feet together in a squatted position, place your hands on the ground, and push your knees out with your elbows
4. Grab your toes and lift your hips to straighten your legs
5. Keeping your legs straight, walk your hands out until you are in a push-up position
6. Drop your hips to stretch your abdominals
7. Lift your hips and move your weight back to stretch your calves (keep your hands on the ground)
8. Step your right foot forward next to your right hand (in a lunge position) and try to put your right forearm to the ground; your left leg will remain straight
9. Keeping your left leg straight and your hands on the ground, lift your hips up and back to straighten your right leg
10. Drop your right leg back to return to the push-up position; then step your left foot forward next to your left hand (in a lunge position) and try to put your left forearm to the ground; your right leg will remain straight
11. Keeping your right leg straight and your hands on the ground, lift your hips up and back to straighten your left leg

12. Drop your left leg back to return to the push-up position and then walk your hands back toward your feet; keep your legs straight throughout the movement

13. Stand up and stretch your quadriceps by grabbing one foot with the same-side hand behind you

Next, perform each of the following for 5–10 seconds, repeating the entire sequence 2 times.

1. Ankle rocks (rock back and forth from your heels to your toes)
2. Right leg swings (swing your right leg forward and back while balancing on your left leg)
3. Left leg swings (swing your left leg forward and back while balancing on your right leg)
4. Alternating leg lift with a twist (lift and turn your leg so that it is perpendicular to the other leg)
5. Butt kicks (alternate kicking your legs back so that your heel taps your backside)
6. Heel to hamstring run (run in place by lifting your leg so that your heel comes up into your backside and your thigh is parallel to the ground)

Finally, complete one of the following:

1. Sideline to sideline sprints—over and back 2 times
2. Full-court sprints—up and back 4 times
3. Half-court sprints—up and back 5 times
4. Treadmill run—2 minutes, increasing your speed every 20 seconds

Band Work (done only during the weightlifting routine)

A lacrosse player needs strong and balanced hips in order to run fast and change direction quickly. For this part of your workout you will need a fitness band. Fitness bands can be purchased online or at specialty sports and fitness stores. Most fitness centers or schools should carry these as well.

Place the band around your ankles just above the ankle and walk laterally (sideways) to your right for 15 steps, then walk laterally to your left the same distance. The movement should come from your hips; keep your legs straight (don't bend your knees as you walk) and don't bob from side to side with your upper body (keep your upper body straight up and down the entire time). Also, try to keep tension in the band so that you get the full effect of the movement. You should feel a good bit of burn on the outside of your hips as you move. To increase the intensity, shorten the band or take bigger steps. You should move continuously in a controlled and quick manner—but not fast or rushed.

Repeat the movement over and back (15 steps each way) for a total of 3 sets with no rest between sets.

PhysioBall Work (done only during the weightlifting routine)

For your body to move effectively, it must be efficient and balanced. For this, we need a strong core and strong muscles both in the front and the back of the body. You will need a PhysioBall, which you can find at most fitness centers or schools, for the following exercises.

You will complete five different exercises in a circuit; move right from one exercise to the next with no rest in between. You will not be using any weight for these exercises, but it is imperative that you focus on tightening your core the entire time. This is especially true when you are lying facedown with your stomach on the ball. If your core isn't tight, you may begin to feel sick as the ball pushes into you. Pushing your abs into the ball will improve your core strength. The following three exercises are for the back and shoulders. To do them you will lie facedown with your stomach on the ball, back straight, upper body in the air, feet on the ground just outside hip width with legs straight. If someone looked at you from the side, they should be able to draw a straight line through your ears, shoulders, hips, knees, and ankles. Start with your hands hanging straight down below your shoulders but not touching the ground. Perform the following three exercises 10 times each, completing each set before moving to the next. Do not rest between exercises.

"I": With a closed fist and thumbs pointing forward, parallel to each other, raise your arms until they are in line with the rest of your body and then lower them to the starting position. Keep your arms and body straight throughout the entire exercise.

"Y": Perform this exercise just like the "I," but point your thumbs out 45 degrees. Your arms should form a "Y" along with the rest of your body when you are at the top of your movement.

"T": Perform this exercise just like the "I," but point your thumbs out to the side with your palms facing forward. Your arms should form a "T" along with the rest of your body when you are at the top of your movement.

For the next exercise, you will be doing a standard push-up but your hands will be on the PhysioBall while your feet are on the ground. Set up your body so that it is in line through your ears, shoulders, hips, knees, and ankles. Place your hands on the sides of the PhysioBall so that your thumbs are parallel to each other. Lower your body, aiming your chest for just between your hands. Your goal should be to hit the ball with your chest before pushing back up. Don't worry if you cannot do this right away; continue to work on it and eventually you will be strong enough. The first thing you will notice about the push-ups is that you may have trouble stabilizing the ball and your body might shake. Practicing the exercise will allow you to get better at this, but you may need to put the ball against a wall or have someone hold it. Try to improve to the point where you don't need help.

The last exercise for your PhysioBall warm-up is PhysioBall Leg Curls. To perform this exercise, lie on your back on the floor with your feet on the PhysioBall. Specifically, you should have the lower part of your calves and your Achilles tendons resting on the ball.

Begin by lifting your hips so that your upper back, hips, and ankles are in a straight line. Roll the ball back toward your body by pulling your feet in, allowing your knees to bend but keeping your hips straight as you do so. At the top of the exercise, you should have a straight line through your shoulders, hips, and knees. Pause for a second then move the ball back out to the starting position. Be sure to keep your abs tight throughout the entire movement.

Summary: Your PhysioBall work should comprise the following five exercises, done for 10 repetitions each, in order:

1. "I"
2. "Y"
3. "T"
4. Push-ups with hands on the ball
5. Leg curls with a hip lift

Step 2—Weight Training and Conditioning

This is the main part of your workout. Lacrosse is a fast-paced game with little time to rest and lots of change of direction with quick starts. Therefore, you must complete both your conditioning and weight training sessions in a similar fashion. While weight training, you can address this by completing your core work during the "rest times" between sets of an exercise. Or, you can complete a number of exercises in a circuit fashion, performing a set of each in succession with only enough time to move from one exercise to the next.

For your conditioning, you should focus on interval work where you alternate a challenging level with a recovery level. An example of this is sprinting the straight part of a track while jogging the curved part for a set time. This change in speed combined with the continuous movement will help build a great endurance base while improving the ability to accelerate and decelerate. Specific examples of these types of workouts will be discussed after the cool-down.

Step 3—The Cool-down

After every workout, whether lifting or conditioning, you need to perform the following routine. Do not rush through it. A flexible body moves much more efficiently and effectively than a tight body. Hold each stretch for about 20 seconds. The total routine takes about 10 minutes.

From a standing position:

1. Legs out wide, stretch to the middle
2. Move your upper body toward the right foot
3. Move your upper body toward the left foot
4. Stagger your feet so that you are in a lunge with your right foot forward; bend your right knee keeping your left leg straight until you feel a stretch in your left hip flexor
5. With your right hand on your right hip, reach your left hand up as high as you can over your head, then lean toward your right bending at the hip
6. Switch your feet and arms to stretch the other side
7. Grab a pole, tree trunk, or fence with both hands, bend at your waist and stretch the sides of your upper body
8. In a doorway or corner, place your hands on the sides of the doorway or wall and lean forward to stretch the front of your upper body
9. Finally, stretch your calves on a step or slanted board

From a seated position:

1. Legs out wide, stretch to the middle
2. Legs out wide, stretch toward the right foot
3. Legs out wide, stretch toward the left foot

4. Repeat each of the first three stretches
5. Butterfly—bring the bottom of your feet together, keep your back straight, and hold onto the ankles (not the feet); push down on your thighs with your elbows

Lying on your back:

1. Pull right knee into the chest hugging the leg
2. Straighten the right leg for a hamstring stretch
3. Take the right leg across your body for a lower back and glute stretch; make sure to keep both shoulders on the ground
4. Roll onto your left side, pull your right foot toward your back to stretch your quad
5. Repeat for the left leg

Make sure to spend extra time on any areas that feel tight.

WEIGHT TRAINING AND CONDITIONING WORKOUTS

No matter what time of year it is, it's time to train for the next lacrosse season. However, be sure to give yourself enough time before starting training to heal any injuries and address health issues. Also, before starting any training program, make sure you are mentally prepared and have enough energy to focus on your training goals because, as you probably know, a lacrosse season can be taxing. This is your opportunity to lay a solid foundation for your upcoming season. Your focus should be on increasing your overall strength, balance, flexibility, and quickness.

Here are off-season and preseason programs tailored specially for lacrosse players by Trainer Chris. He suggests using the off-season 8-week program for as long as you need, until you are about 4–6 weeks out from the start of your lacrosse season; at that point, he recommends switching to the preseason workout.

Off-Season Weeks 1 through 4

Lift 1—Two days per week (e.g., Monday and Friday)

Squat (Barbell, DB, or Machine) with Leg Raises
Flat DB Press on a PhysioBall with PhysioBall Crunches
Pull-ups/Pull-downs with Cable Twists
Single Leg DB Squats
Single Arm DB Press on a flat bench with feet up
Single Leg Stiff Leg Deadlifts (Windmills)
Single Arm Rows (palm face down)
Conditioning—30 minutes continuous alternating 2-minute intervals

Lift 2—One day per week (e.g., Wednesday)

Squat (Barbell, DB, or Machine) with Plank
Incline DB Press with V-ups
Pull-ups/Pull-downs with Side Hip Lifts
Single Leg DB Step-downs
Alternating DB Press on a PhysioBall
Lying Leg Curl
Single Arm Rows (thumbs up grip)
Conditioning—30 minutes continuous alternating 1-minute intervals

Plyometrics—Complete during each conditioning session after the warm-up but before the agilities

1. Single Leg Hops (side to side)—left foot for 10 secs, then right foot for 10 secs
2. Prison Squat (squat with hands behind head)—hold
3. Double Leg Hops (side to side)
4. Machine Gun
5. Prison Squat—hold
6. Single Leg Hops (forward and back)—left foot for 10 secs, then right foot for 10 secs
7. Prison Squat Jumps—short jumps, work on coming off the ground quickly
8. Double Leg Hops (forward and back)
9. Machine Gun
10. Prison Squat Jumps

Conditioning 1—One day per week

Box and One
Full-field Sprints with rest

Conditioning 2—One day per week

Short Cone Suicide
Sideline to Sideline Sprints with rest

Off-Season Weeks 5 through 8

Lift 1—Two days per week

Leg Press with Sit-ups
Incline DB Press with Kickouts
Pull-ups/Pull-downs with V-ups with a twist
Alternating Lunges
Alternating Flat DB Press on a bench with feet up
Leg Curls
Standing Cable Row
Conditioning—30 minutes continuous alternating 1-minute intervals

Lift 2—One day per week

DB Squat to Curl to DB Squat to Shoulder Press
Sit-ups
Squat Thrust to Push-up to Mountain Climber to Squat Jump
Hanging Leg Raise
DB Forward Lunge to Stiff Leg Deadlift to Row
Lying Leg Raise
Lateral Lunge with a Twist
Alternating Shoulder Press
Russian Twists
Lateral Raise to External Rotation
Lying Reverse DB Flyes
Side Plank Hip Lifts

Plyometrics—Complete during each conditioning session after the warm-up but before the agilities

 1. Single Leg Hops (side to side)—left foot for 10 secs, then right foot for 10 secs
 2. Prison Squat (squat with hands behind head)—hold
 3. Double Leg Hops (side to side)
 4. Machine Gun
 5. Prison Squat—hold
 6. Single Leg Hops (forward and back)—left foot for 10 secs, then right foot for 10 secs
 7. Prison Squat Jumps—short jumps, work on coming off the ground quickly
 8. Double Leg Hops (forward and back)
 9. Machine Gun
10. Prison Squat Jumps

Conditioning 1—One day per week

Box and Two Drill
Full-field Suicide Sprints with rest

Conditioning 2—One day per week

Pro-Agility Extended (5–7 cones, alternating from the middle out)
Increasing Sprints—start from midfield and go 10, then 20 back, then 30 back, etc., until 100-
    yd sprint . . . with rest
Decreasing Sprints—start from goal line and reverse sprints 100 down to 10

Once you have completed the second 4-week program, you can repeat each of the programs again until you are about 4 to 8 weeks from the start of the next season. At that point, you will begin a new group of workouts to get you through the preseason and prepare you for your first game.

Preseason Weeks 1 through 4

Lift 1—Two days per week

Squat into Squat Jumps
Flat DB Press on a PhysioBall into Standing MB Chest Press
Lat Pull-down into Standing MB Shoulder Extension
Interval Sprints (20 on, 10 off)
Leg Press into Box Jumps
Incline DB Press into Standing MB Overhead Press
Standing Cable Row into Bent-Over MB Rows
Interval Sprints (20 on, 10 off)
Leg Extension
Leg Curl
Lateral Raise
Interval Sprints (20 on, 10 off)

Lift 2—One day per week

Alternating Lunges into Lunge Jumps into High Knees
Push-ups into Mountain Climbers
Standing Row
Step-ups with a leg lift (running form) into Step-up Jumps
Alternating Shoulder Press into Mountain Climbers
Pull-down
Lateral Lunges into Lateral Jumps into High Knees
Push-ups into Mountain Climbers
Reverse Flyes

Plyometrics—Complete during each conditioning session after the warm-up but before the agilities

1. Single Leg Hops (side to side)—left foot for 10 secs, then right foot for 10 secs
2. Prison Squat (squat with hands behind head)—hold
3. Double Leg Hops (side to side)

4. Machine Gun

5. Prison Squat—hold

6. Single Leg Hops (forward and back)—left foot for 10 secs, then right foot for 10 secs

7. Prison Squat Jumps—short jumps, work on coming off the ground quickly

8. Double Leg Hops (forward and back)

9. Machine Gun

10. Prison Squat Jumps

Conditioning 1—One day per week

Circle Drill (center cone plus 8 cones in a circle, 5-yd radius)
Suicide Sprints—using goal line to 50-yd line, every 10 yds

Conditioning 2—One day per week

Diagonal Cone Drill
Increasing Sprints/Decreasing Sprints × 2

Conditioning 3—One day per week

5-yd slides for time
Full-field Sprints

WORKOUT DETAILS

Off-Season Weeks 1–4: Lift 1

After the warm-ups, this workout has two parts. In the first part, the exercises are set up in pairs; alternate the two exercises with no rest until you have completed all the sets for that pair (e.g., Squat and Leg Raise). Once you have completed that pair, move on to the next pair of exercises (e.g., Flat DB Press and PhysioBall Crunches) and repeat the process.

The second part is set up as a circuit where you will complete a set of each of the exercises in order with no rest between exercises. After you have completed the first circuit, repeat the sequence an additional time to complete the series.

After you have completed the lifting portion of the workout, you will need to complete 30 minutes of conditioning in 2-minute intervals. This can be done on a cardio machine if you need to be inside or you can run outside on a track, field, or road.

Lift 1 Exercise Explanations

Squat (Barbell, DB, or Machine): If using a barbell, place bar on upper back while holding bar with your hands. If using dumbbells, hold one in each hand. If using a machine, follow the directions written on that machine. No matter which you use, stand with your feet about hip-width apart. Squat down as if you were trying to sit down on a chair. Keep your head and chest facing forward and your abs tight. Try to lower your body until your hips are just higher than your knees and then stand back up by pushing your hips forward.

Lying Leg Raises: Lie flat on a bench or the floor with your feet directly above your hips

TABLE **14.1**
Off-Season Weeks 1–4: Lift 1

Complete 2 Days per Week	Week 1	Week 2	Week 3	Week 4
Warm-up:				
Jumping Jack Intervals—2 minutes				
Dynamic Warm-up				
Band Work				
PhysioBall Work				
Part I: Complete each of the following pairs of exercises, resting only when moving to the next pair				
Squat (Barbell, DB, or Machine)	3×15	3×15	3×10	3×10
Alternate with Leg Raise (15)				
Flat DB Press on a PhysioBall	3×12	3×12	3×10	3×10
Alternate with PhysioBall Crunches (15)				
Pull-ups or Pull-downs	3×12	3×12	3×10	3×10
Alternate with Cable Twists (10 each side)				
Part II: Complete the following as a circuit with no rest until you have completed all the sets				
Single Leg DB Squats	2×10 each	2×10 each	2×15 each	2×15 each
Single Arm DB Press on a flat bench with feet up	2×10 each	2×10 each	2×15 each	2×15 each
Single Leg Stiff Leg Deadlift (Windmills)	2×10 each	2×10 each	2×15 each	2×15 each
Single Arm Cable Rows (palm down)	2×10 each	2×10 each	2×15 each	2×15 each

Conditioning: Either using a cardio machine (such as a treadmill, elliptical, or stair climber) or running outside, alternate 2 minutes of high-intensity work with 2 minutes of moderate-intensity work for 30 minutes

Post-Workout Stretch Routine

and your hands holding onto something behind your head (such as the bench). Pull your abs in tight and lower your legs (keeping them straight) until just before your back arches (an arched back will indicate that you have gone too far). Immediately bring them back up so that they are again just above your hips. Do not allow them to travel any farther back than your hips! Your range of motion will be limited by your flexibility and strength through your core.

Each person will be different, and you should try to challenge yourself to improve the range over time.

Flat DB Press on a PhysioBall: Lying on a PhysioBall with your head and upper back supported by the ball and your hips in line with your shoulders and knees, hold a dumbbell in each hand with your arms fully extended (but not locked) above your shoulders and your hands facing toward your feet. Next, lower the dumbbells by allowing your elbows to bend, making sure to keep your hands directly above your elbows at all times. Once the dumbbells are slightly higher than your chest, press them immediately upward to return to the original position. Make sure to keep your abs tight the entire time.

PhysioBall Crunch: Lie on your back on a PhysioBall with the ball centered on the middle of your back. Start by stretching back to lengthen the front of your body, then crunch your shoulders up toward your hips. Pause in this position for a moment, then return to the stretched position.

Pull-ups (underhand): Stand underneath a pull-up bar and place your hands on the bar about shoulder-width apart with your palms facing you. Pull yourself up until your chin is just above the bar, then lower yourself until your arms are straight.

Pull-down (underhand): Using a lat pull-down machine, grab the bar with the prescribed grip and pull it down to the top of your chest. Make sure to pull your shoulder blades down and back and stick your chest up and forward throughout the exercise.

Cable Twists: Using an adjustable cable column, adjust the column so that the handle is just below shoulder height. Step away from the column about 2–3 feet and line up your body so that your feet are squared (about hip-width apart) and facing perpendicular to the column. Hold the handle with both hands (fingers interlaced) and arms straight just below shoulder height. Pull your abs tight and twist from one side to the other, only moving your upper body. Your hips down should not move and your arms should stay straight. You should feel this through your core, not your arms and shoul-

ders. If you do feel it in your arms and shoulders, check to make sure they are straight and that your hands stay in between your shoulders. Once you have completed the prescribed number of repetitions, turn around so that you can work the other side.

Single Leg DB Squat: Hold a dumbbell in one hand and lift the foot on the same side (if the dumbbell is in your right hand, lift your right foot) so that it is off the ground but still next to the planted foot. Squat down as far as you can while working on your balance. Your goal should be to touch the hand with the dumbbell to the foot that is still on the ground while keeping your back relatively straight and your chest and head up.

Single Arm DB Press on a flat bench with feet up on bench: Lying on a flat bench with feet on the bench, hold a dumbbell in one hand with your arm fully extended (but not locked) above your shoulders and your hand facing toward your feet; the other hand should be placed on your stomach. Lower the dumbbell by allowing your elbow to bend, making sure to keep your hand directly above your elbow at all times. Once the dumbbell is slightly higher than your chest, press it immediately upward to return to the original position. Once you have completed the prescribed number of repetitions for that arm, repeat the movement for the other arm. Make sure to keep your abs tight the entire time. Note that the prescribed number of reps is for each arm, so 10 reps would mean 10 reps for each arm.

Single Leg Stiff Leg Deadlifts (Windmills): From a standing position, bend your knees slightly, lift one foot off the ground, pull your shoulders back, and stick your chest out and up with your arms directly out to the sides at shoulder level. While maintaining the slight bend in your knees, lean forward from the hips until your upper body is parallel to the floor. Keeping your arms to your sides, try to touch the foot that is down with the opposite hand by rotating at your hips, but make sure your legs remain relatively straight (except for a slight bend in the knees to prevent hyperextension). Keep your back straight by looking forward and not down throughout the movement. Tighten your hamstrings and stand back upright. If you feel the movement more in your back than your hamstrings, check to make sure your back is straight and not rounded. Take your time performing this exercise, concentrate on form more than anything else. Complete all repetitions for the first leg before beginning the other leg.

Single Arm Rows (palm face down): Stand in front of a cable machine or cable column while holding the handle with one hand just below shoulder level. Squat down about halfway and then, using only one arm, pull the handle toward your body in a rowing motion. Return your hand to the starting position and repeat. Follow the prescribed grip in the workout and complete all repetitions for that arm before switching arms.

Off-Season Weeks 1–4: Lift 2

After the warm-ups, this workout has two parts. In the first part, the exercises are set up in pairs; alternate the two exercises with no rest until you have completed all the sets for that pair (e.g., Squat and Plank). Once you have completed that pair, move on to the next pair of exercises (e.g., Incline DB Press and V-ups) and repeat the process.

The second part is set up as a circuit where you will complete a set of each of the exercises in order with no rest between exercises. After you have completed the first circuit, repeat the sequence an additional time to complete the series.

After you have completed the lifting portion of the workout, you will need to complete 30 minutes of conditioning in 1-minute intervals. This can be done on a cardio machine if you need to be inside or you can use traditional running on a track, field, or road.

Lift 2 Exercise Explanations

Squat (Barbell, DB, or Machine): If using a barbell, place bar on upper back while holding bar with your hands. If using dumbbells, hold one in each hand. If using a machine, follow the directions written on that machine. No matter which you use, stand with your feet about hip-width apart. Squat down as if you were trying to sit down on a chair. Keep your head and chest facing forward and your abs tight. Try to lower your body until your hips are just higher than your knees and then stand back up by pushing your hips forward.

Plank: This exercise is similar to a push-up position but you are resting on your forearms instead of your hands. Keep your hips slightly above your shoulders and ankles while focusing on keeping your abdominals tight throughout the prescribed time.

Incline DB Press: Using an inclined bench (about 45°), hold a pair of dumbbells with your hands just above your shoulders. Lower the weight to about 3–4 inches above your chest (near chin level) and then press it back up to return to the beginning position. Keep your shoulder blades pulled back and your abdominals tight throughout the movement. Also be sure to not lock your elbows at the top of the movement.

V-up: Lie on your back on the ground. Lift your legs and your torso until your hands touch your feet. At the top of the movement your

TABLE **14.2**
Off-Season Weeks 1–4: Lift 2

Complete 1 Day per Week	Week 1	Week 2	Week 3	Week 4
Warm-up:				
Jumping Jack Intervals—2 minutes				
Dynamic Warm-up Short/Stretch Specific Muscles				
Band Work				
PhysioBall Work				
Part I: Complete each of the following pairs of exercises, resting only when moving to the next pair				
Squat (Barbell, DB, or Machine)	3×15	3×15	3×10	3×10
Alternate with Plank (30 seconds)				
Incline DB Press	3×12	3×12	3×10	3×10
Alternate with V-ups (10)				
Pull-ups or Pull-downs	3×12	3×12	3×10	3×10
Alternate with Side Hip Lifts (10 each side)				
Part II: Complete the following as a circuit with no rest until you have completed all the sets				
Single Leg DB Step-downs	2×10 each	2×10 each	2×15 each	2×15 each
Alternating DB Press on a PhysioBall	2×10 each	2×10 each	2×15 each	2×15 each
Lying Leg Curl	2×10	2×10	2×15	2×15
Single Arm Cable Rows (thumbs up grip)	2×10 each	2×10 each	2×15 each	2×15 each

Conditioning: Either using a cardio machine (such as a treadmill, elliptical, or stair climber) or running outside, alternate 1 minute of high-intensity work with 1 minute of moderate-intensity work for 30 minutes

Post-Workout Stretch Routine

body should form a "V." Return to the starting position with your legs and your torso on the ground and repeat.

Pull-ups (underhand): Stand underneath a pull-up bar and place your hands on the bar about shoulder-width apart with your palms facing you. Pull yourself up until your chin is just above the bar, then lower yourself until your arms are straight.

Pull-down (underhand): Using a lat pull-down machine, grab the bar with the prescribed grip and pull it down to the top of your chest. Make sure to pull your shoulder blades down and back and stick your chest up and forward throughout the exercise.

Side Hip Lifts: This exercise is similar to the Plank Position, but instead you are on your side with your forearm perpendicular to your body.

Keeping your body in line (you should be able to draw a straight line through your ears, shoulders, hips, knees, and ankles), allow your hips to lower toward the ground. Just before your hip touches the ground, lift up to return to the starting position. This would count as one repetition.

Single Leg DB Step-downs: Start by standing on a bench with one foot on the bench and the other hanging off. While holding a dumbbell in each hand, squat down on the leg whose foot is on the bench until the toes on the opposite foot just barely touch the floor. Do not put any weight on the foot closest to the ground but stand back up using the leg whose foot is on the bench. Maintain a relatively straight back and keep your chest and head up. Without putting the hanging foot on the bench, repeat the step-down for the prescribed number of repetitions before switching legs.

Alternating DB Press on a PhysioBall: Lying on a PhysioBall with your head and upper back supported by the ball and your hips in line with your shoulders and knees, hold a dumbbell in each hand with your arms fully extended (but not locked) above your shoulders and your hands facing toward your feet. While keeping one arm straight, lower the other dumbbell by allowing your elbow to bend, making sure to keep your hands directly above your elbow at all times. Once the dumbbell is slightly higher than your chest, press it immediately upward to return to the original position. When that arm is straight, repeat the movement for the other arm. Make sure to keep your abdominals tight the entire time. Note that the prescribed number of reps is for each arm, so 10 reps would mean 10 reps for each arm.

Lying Leg Curls: Using a leg curl machine (I prefer lying, but you can use the seated if it is the only one available), line your knees up with the axis of rotation (there should be a hinge joint at the edge of the pad and it should be marked). Raise the weight until your heels are as close to the back of your upper legs as possible, pause for a moment then return the weight to the original position. Be sure to keep your feet straight and your abs tight throughout the entire movement.

Single Arm Rows (thumbs-up grip): Stand in front of a cable machine or cable column while holding the handle with one hand just below shoulder level. Squat down about halfway, and then, using only one arm, pull the handle toward your body in a rowing motion. Return your hand to the starting position and repeat. Follow the prescribed grip in the workout and complete all repetitions for that arm before switching arms.

Off-Season Weeks 1 through 4: Conditioning 1

Conditioning 1—One day per week

Jumping Jack Intervals—2 minutes
Dynamic Warm-up

Plyometrics
    Do each of the following for 10 seconds in order with no rest unless noted. Rest for 1 minute, then repeat for a total of two circuits.

   1. Single Leg Hops (side to side)—left foot for 10 secs, then right foot for 10 secs
   2. Prison Squat (squat with hands behind head)—hold

3. Double Leg Hops (side to side)
4. Machine Gun
5. Prison Squat—hold
6. Single Leg Hops (forward and back)—left foot for 10 secs, then right foot for 10 secs
7. Prison Squat Jumps—short jumps, work on coming off the ground quickly
8. Double Leg Hops (forward and back)
9. Machine Gun
10. Prison Squat Jumps

Box and One

Set up four cones in a square with approximately 5 yards between each, then place a fifth cone in the middle, as demonstrated here. You may also use the painted area on a basketball court.

```
        B     C
           E
        A     D
```

Perform each of the following patterns, resting 10 seconds between each repetition of a pattern and 1 minute before moving to the next pattern.

1. Starting from A, sprint to B, slide to C, backpedal to D, sprint forward 15 yards—repeat this for a total of four repetitions.
2. Starting from D, sprint to C, slide to B, backpedal to A, sprint forward 15 yards—repeat this for a total of four repetitions.
3. Starting from A, sprint to B, backpedal to A, sprint diagonally to and around C (inside-out), then sprint through D—repeat this for a total of four repetitions.
4. Starting from D, sprint to C, backpedal to D, sprint diagonally to and around B (inside-out), then sprint through A—repeat this for a total of four repetitions.
5. Starting from A, sprint to and around E, sprint to and around B, sprint to and around C, sprint to and around E, then sprint through D—repeat for a total of four repetitions.
6. Starting from D, sprint to and around E, sprint to and around C, sprint to and around B, sprint to and around E, then sprint through A—repeat for a total of four repetitions.

Full-Field Sprints with Rest

Sprint the length of a field (120 yards) as fast as you can. Staying on that end of the field, rest for 40 seconds (continue to walk around, don't stand still). At the end of the 40 seconds, sprint back to the end of the field you started from, again resting for 40 seconds. Repeat this sequence for a total of five repetitions; this will count as one set. You will be completing two total sets with 4–5 minutes of rest between sets (you will end up running a total of 10 full-field sprints). Only take as much rest as you need between sets. Don't take 5 minutes simply because it is the maximum amount of rest you are allowed. Your goal is to make each sprint in 16 seconds or less. If you don't make the time for any of the sprints in a set, take a longer rest between sets (but no more than 5 minutes).

Post-Workout Stretch Routine

Off-Season Weeks 1 through 4: Conditioning 2

Conditioning 2—One day per week

Jumping Jack Intervals—2 minutes
Dynamic Warm-up

Plyometrics
	Do each of the following for 10 seconds in order with no rest unless noted. Rest for 1 minute, then repeat for a total of two circuits.

1. Single Leg Hops (side to side)—left foot for 10 secs, then right foot for 10 secs
2. Prison Squat (squat with hands behind head)—hold
3. Double Leg Hops (side to side)
4. Machine Gun
5. Prison Squat—hold
6. Single Leg Hops (forward and back)—left foot for 10 secs, then right foot for 10 secs
7. Prison Squat Jumps—short jumps, work on coming off the ground quickly
8. Double Leg Hops (forward and back)
9. Machine Gun
10. Prison Squat Jumps

Short Cone Suicide
	Place six cones in a straight line each 1 yard apart as follows:

A   B   C   D   E   F

Using A as your starting point, move from A to B and back to A. Next, move from A to C and back to A. Continue this until you have moved to each of the cones and back to A, then sprint 20 yards forward. This would count as one repetition. Complete each of the following movements, resting 30 seconds between each repetition for that particular movement and 2 minutes before starting the next movement.

1. Sprint-backpedal × 6
2. Slide-slide × 3 (your left foot should be at A, begin by sliding to your right)
3. Slide-slide × 3 (your right foot should be at A, begin by sliding to your left)
4. Backpedal-sprint × 6
5. Sprint-sprint × 6

Sideline-to-Sideline Sprints with Rest
	Sprint the width of a field and back (about 60 yards each way, so a total of 120 yards) as fast as you can. Immediately turn around and jog to the opposite sideline (should be within 30 seconds). Wait an additional 30 seconds and then repeat the sprint. Continue repeating this sequence for a total of 10 sprints.

Post-Workout Stretch Routine

Off-Season Weeks 5 through 8: Lift 1

After the warm-ups, this workout has two parts. In the first part, the exercises are set up in pairs; alternate the two exercises with no rest until you have completed all the sets for that pair (e.g., Leg Press and Sit-ups). Once you have completed that pair, move on to the next pair of exercises (e.g., Incline DB Press and Kickouts) and repeat the process.

The second part is set up as a circuit where you will complete a set of each of the exercises in order with no rest between exercises. After you have completed the first circuit, repeat the sequence an additional time to complete the series.

After you have completed the lifting portion of the workout, you will need to complete 30 minutes of conditioning in 1-minute intervals. This can be done on a cardio machine if you need to be inside or you can use traditional running on a track, field, or road.

TABLE 14.3
Off-Season Weeks 5–8: Lift 1

Complete 2 Days per Week	Week 5	Week 6	Week 7	Week 8
Warm-up:				
Jumping Jack Intervals—2 minutes				
Dynamic Warm-up				
Band Work				
PhysioBall Work				
Part I: Complete each of the following pairs of exercises, resting only when moving to the next pair				
Leg Press	3 × 15	3 × 15	3 × 10	3 × 10
Alternate with Sit-ups (15)				
Incline DB Press	3 × 12	3 × 12	3 × 10	3 × 10
Alternate with Kickouts (10)				
Pull-ups or Pull-downs	3 × 12	3 × 12	3 × 10	3 × 10
Alternate with V-ups with a twist (20 total)				
Part II: Complete the following as a circuit with no rest until you have completed all the sets				
Alternating Lunges	2 × 10 each	2 × 10 each	2 × 15 each	2 × 15 each
Alternating Flat DB Press on a bench with feet up	2 × 10 each	2 × 10 each	2 × 15 each	2 × 15 each
Leg Curl	2 × 10	2 × 10	2 × 15	2 × 15
Standing Cable Row	2 × 10	2 × 10	2 × 15	2 × 15

Conditioning: Either using a cardio machine (such as a treadmill, elliptical, or stair climber) or running outside, alternate 1 minute of high-intensity work with 1 minute of moderate-intensity work for 30 minutes

Post-Workout Stretch Routine

Lift 1 Exercise Explanations

Leg Press: Using a leg press machine, place your feet about shoulder-width apart on the platform. Bend your hips, knees, and ankles to allow the weight to descend. Once your hips and knees are at about 90°, press the weight back up to return to the original position, but do not allow the knees to hyperextend (lock out). Make sure to keep your back straight, your abs tight, and your hips down (do not allow your hips to roll up) throughout the entire movement.

Sit-ups: Lie on your back on the floor with your knees bent at about 45° and feet on the floor. Pull your abdominals in tight, push your feet into the ground, and lift your upper body off the floor toward your knees. Make sure you keep your feet on the ground and do not pull on your neck with your hands. Return to the floor under control and repeat for the prescribed number of repetitions. Do not anchor your feet under anything and do not have anyone hold them. Your feet should be free to move, forcing you to really work your core to complete the movement.

Incline DB Press: Using an inclined bench (about 45°), hold a pair of dumbbells with your hands just above your shoulders. Lower the weights to about 3–4 inches above your chest (near chin level) and then press them back up to return to the beginning position. Keep your shoulder blades pulled back and your abdominals tight throughout the movement. Also be sure to not lock your elbows at the top of the movement.

Kickouts: Sitting up on the ground or a bench, place your hands behind you and lean back slightly. Keep your legs slightly bent and lift your feet off of the ground. Next, roll your legs up and move the upper body forward as well, coming into a "V" position. Return to the start-ing position and repeat for the prescribed number of repetitions.

Pull-ups (underhand): Stand underneath a pull-up bar and place your hands on the bar about shoulder-width apart with your palms facing you. Pull yourself up until your chin is just above the bar, then lower yourself until your arms are straight.

Pull-down (underhand): Using a lat pull-down machine, grab the bar with the prescribed grip and pull it down to the top of your chest. Make sure to pull your shoulder blades down and back and stick your chest up and forward throughout the exercise.

V-up with a twist: This is similar to the V-up but instead of finishing at the top in a "V," you bend one leg and rotate your torso toward that leg. The other leg should also be off the ground but straight out. Return to the ground and repeat for the other leg.

Alternating Forward Lunges: Holding a medicine ball with both hands or dumbbell in each hand, step forward and lunge down until both knees and the front hip are at approximately 90°. Immediately push off the front foot to return to the starting position, making sure to use the glutes and quadriceps of that leg and not the lower back. Repeat for the other leg.

Alternating Flat DB Press on a bench with feet up: Lying on a flat bench with feet on the bench, hold a dumbbell in each hand with your arms fully extended (but not locked) above your shoulders and your hands facing toward your feet. While keeping one arm straight, lower the other dumbbell by allowing your elbow to bend, making sure to keep your hands directly above your elbow at all times. Once the dumbbell is slightly higher than your chest, press it immediately upward to return to the original position. When that arm is straight, repeat the movement for the other arm. Make sure to keep your abdominals tight the entire time. Note that the prescribed number of reps is for each arm, so 10 reps would mean 10 reps for each arm.

Leg Curls: Using a leg curl machine, line your knees up with the axis of rotation (there should be a hinge joint at the edge of the pad and should be marked). Raise the weight until your heels are as close to the back of your upper legs

as possible, pause for a moment, then return the weight to the original position. Be sure to keep your feet straight and your abdominals tight throughout the entire movement.

Standing Cable Row: Stand in front of a cable machine or cable column while holding the handle (a "V-grip" with your hands facing each other). Squat down about halfway and then pull the handle toward your body in a rowing motion. Maintain the squat position, making sure not to go up and down with your body.

Off-Season Weeks 5 through 8: Lift 2

After the warm-ups, this workout is set up in groups of exercises. Each group has a series of exercises which should be done in order. Complete a set of each exercise in the group, then rest about 30 seconds before beginning the next set of the group. Complete all sets of the group, then rest about 1 minute before starting the next group. Repeat the process for all of the groups.

Lift 2 Exercise Explanations

DB Squat to Curl to DB Squat to Shoulder Press: Stand holding a dumbbell in each hand. Squat down as low as you can. As you stand up, curl the weights up toward your shoulders. With the weights still at your shoulders, squat down again. This time, as you stand up, press the dumbbells straight up above your shoulders. Once you are in the standing position, lower the dumbbells back to the starting position (hanging down by your sides). This would count as one repetition.

Sit-ups: Lie on your back on the floor with your knees bent at about 45° and feet on the floor. Pull your abdominals in tight, push your feet into the ground and lift your upper body off the floor toward your knees. Make sure you keep your feet on the ground and do not pull on your

neck with your hands. Return to the floor under control and repeat for the prescribed number of repetitions. Do not anchor your feet under anything and do not have anyone hold them. Your feet should be free to move, forcing you to really work your core to complete the movement.

Squat Thrust to Push-up to Mountain Climber (10) to Squat Jump: Begin this exercise from a standing position. Squat down, place your hands on the ground, and kick your legs back to land in a push-up position. Next, complete a push-up followed by 10 mountain climbers (5 each leg). Next, jump your feet forward to return to the squatted position and jump straight up. Land with your knees bent and repeat for the prescribed number of repetitions.

Hanging Leg Raise: Hang from a pull-up bar with either an overhand or parallel grip. Raise

TABLE 14.4
Off-Season Weeks 5–8: Lift 2

Complete 1 Day per Week		Week 5	Week 6	Week 7	Week 8
Warm-up:					
Jumping Jack Intervals—3 minutes					
Dynamic Warm-up					
Band Work					
PhysioBall Work					

Complete each of the following groups of exercises, resting only when moving to the next group

		Week 5	Week 6	Week 7	Week 8
Group 1	DB Squat to Curl to DB Squat to Shoulder Press	3 × 10 each	3 × 10 each	3 × 10 each	3 × 10 each
	Sit-ups	10	10	10	10
Group 2	Squat Thrust to Push-up to Mountain Climbers (10) to Squat Jump	3 × 10 each	3 × 10 each	3 × 10 each	3 × 10 each
	Hanging Leg Raise	10	10	10	10
Group 3	DB Forward Lunge to Stiff Leg Deadlift to Row	3 × 10 each	3 × 10 each	3 × 10 each	3 × 10 each
	Lying Leg Raise	10	10	10	10
Group 4	Lateral Lunge with a Twist	2 × 10 each	2 × 10 each	2 × 10 each	2 × 10 each
	Alternating Shoulder Press	2 × 10 each	2 × 10 each	2 × 10 each	2 × 10 each
	Russian Twist	20	20	20	20
Group 5	Lateral Raise to External Rotation	2 × 15	2 × 15	2 × 15	2 × 15
	Lying Reverse DB Flyes	2 × 15	2 × 15	2 × 15	2 × 15
	Side Hip Lifts	15 each	15 each	15 each	15 each

Post-Workout Stretch Routine

your knees up toward your shoulders as high as you can go, then slowly lower them back to the starting position. To make this more challenging, keep your legs straight instead of bending them.

DB Forward Lunge to Stiff Leg Deadlift to Row: Stand holding a dumbbell in each hand. Per-form a forward lunge with each leg. Once you have done a single lunge for each leg and you are standing with your feet together, bend at your waist to perform a stiff leg deadlift. Instead of coming right back up, stay in this bent position and row the weights up toward your chest. Let the weights go back down and stand up. This would count as one repetition.

Lying Leg Raises: Lie flat on a bench or the floor with your feet directly above your hips and your hands holding onto something behind your head (such as the bench). Pull your abdominals in tight and lower your legs (keeping them straight) until just before your back arches (an arched back will indicate that you have gone too far). Immediately bring them back up so that they are again just above your hips. Do not allow them to travel any farther back than your hips! Your range of motion will be limited by your flexibility and strength through your core. Each person will be different and you should try to challenge yourself to improve the range over time.

Lateral Lunge with a Twist: From a standing position, step directly out to one side, keeping your feet facing forward. The leg you just stepped with should be bent in a similar fashion to a squat and the other leg should be fairly straight. While lunging, twist your upper body toward the lunging side. Push with the bent leg to return to the starting position and immediately step toward the other leg.

Alternating Shoulder Press: From a standing position, hold a dumbbell in each hand at about ear level. Press one dumbbell upward until your arm is relatively straight (but not locked). Lower the weight back to its starting position, then repeat for the other arm. Pull your abdominals tight to help avoid overarching your back.

Russian Twists: Lying on the floor, sit up so that your upper body is off the floor, your knees are bent and your feet are on the floor. Keeping your core tight, twist side to side for the prescribed number of repetitions. To make the exercise more challenging, hold a weight in your hands near your chest and/or lift your feet off the ground.

Lateral Raise to External Rotation: From a seated position on a chair or PhysioBall, hold a dumbbell in each hand. With your elbows directly at your side and elbows at 90°, raise your elbows and hands together to the sides in an arc. Making sure to keep your hand directly in line with your elbow, raise your arm until everything is in line with your shoulder. At no time should you be able to see your forearm and be sure not to shrug. From the top position, keep your shoulder and elbow in line but raise the dumbbell until your hands are directly over your elbows. Then lower the weight back to the starting position by first returning the hands to directly in front of the elbows, then the arms back to your sides.

Lying Reverse DB Flyes: Lying face-down on an inclined bench (about 30°), hold a dumbbell in each hand with the prescribed grip. Keeping your arms straight throughout the movement, raise the dumbbells out to your sides so that from behind you appear to make a "T." Pause for a moment, and then return the dumbbells to the starting position.

Side Hip Lifts: This exercise is similar to the Plank Position, but instead you are on your side with your forearm perpendicular to your body. Keeping your body in line (you should be able to draw a straight line through your ears, shoulders, hips, knees, and ankles), allow your hips to lower toward the ground. Just before your hip touches the ground, lift up to return to the starting position. This would count as one repetition.

Off-Season Weeks 5 through 8: Conditioning 1

Conditioning 1—One day per week

Jumping Jack Intervals—2 minutes
Dynamic Warm-up

Plyometrics

Do each of the following for 10 seconds in order with no rest unless noted. Rest for 1 minute, then repeat for a total of two circuits.

1. Single Leg Hops (side to side)—left foot for 10 secs, then right foot for 10 secs
2. Prison Squat (squat with hands behind head)—hold
3. Double Leg Hops (side to side)
4. Machine Gun
5. Prison Squat—hold
6. Single Leg Hops (forward and back)—left foot for 10 secs, then right foot for 10 secs
7. Prison Squat Jumps—short jumps, work on coming off the ground quickly
8. Double Leg Hops (forward and back)
9. Machine Gun
10. Prison Squat Jumps

Box and Two

Set up four cones in a square with approximately 5 yards between each, then place two more cones out to the sides as demonstrated here. You may also use the painted area on a basketball court along with the sidelines.

```
          C   D
     A    B   E    F
```

Perform each of the following patterns, resting 10 seconds between each repetition of a pattern and 1 minute before moving to the next pattern.

1. Starting from A, sprint to B, slide to C, sprint to D, slide to E, sprint through F—repeat this for a total of four repetitions.
2. Starting from F, sprint to E, slide to D, sprint to C, slide to B, sprint through A—repeat this for a total of four repetitions.
3. Starting from A, sprint to E, backpedal to B, sprint diagonally to and around D, then sprint through F—repeat this for a total of four repetitions.

4. Starting from F, sprint to B, backpedal to E, sprint diagonally to and around B, then sprint through A—repeat this for a total of four repetitions.

5. Starting from A, sprint to and around E, sprint diagonally to and around C, sprint to and around B, sprint diagonally to and around D, then sprint through F—repeat for a total of four repetitions.

6. Starting from F, sprint to and around B, sprint diagonally to and around D, sprint to and around E, sprint diagonally to and around C, then sprint through A—repeat for a total of four repetitions.

Full-Field Suicide Sprints with Rest

For this drill, you will be using the end lines, restraining line, and midfield as your markers. Complete the following sprints:

1. End line to opposite end line and back × 4 with 1 minute rest between each
2. End line to opposite restraining line and back × 4 with 45 seconds rest between each
3. End line to midfield and back × 4 with 30 seconds rest between each
4. End line to near restraining line and back × 4 with 15 seconds rest between each

Post-Workout Stretch Routine

Off-Season Weeks 5 through 8: Conditioning 2

Conditioning 2—One day per week

Jumping Jack Intervals—2 minutes
Dynamic Warm-up

Plyometrics

Do each of the following for 10 seconds in order with no rest unless noted. Rest for 1 minute, then repeat for a total of 2 circuits.

1. Single Leg Hops (side to side)—left foot for 10 secs, then right foot for 10 secs
2. Prison Squat (squat with hands behind head)—hold
3. Double Leg Hops (side to side)
4. Machine Gun
5. Prison Squat—hold
6. Single Leg Hops (forward and back)—left foot for 10 secs, then right foot for 10 secs
7. Prison Squat Jumps—short jumps, work on coming off the ground quickly
8. Double Leg Hops (forward and back)
9. Machine Gun
10. Prison Squat Jumps

Pro-Agility Extended

For this drill, place 5–7 cones in a straight line with each cone 5 yards away from the one next to it. Starting from the middle cone, slide to the next cone, then slide back past the starting cone to the cone next to it on the other side. Continue alternating slides until you have gone to all the cones (each slide should be longer than the previous one). The drill should look like this:

$$7 \quad 5 \quad 3 \quad 1 \quad 2 \quad 4 \quad 6$$

The cones have been numbered so you can see which cone to slide to next (i.e., start from 1, slide to 2, then to 3, 4, 5, 6, and 7). Complete 10 repetitions with about 1 minute rest after each.

Increasing/Decreasing Sprints

For this drill, use a football field that has lines every 5 yards. Starting at midfield (the 50-yard line), sprint 10 yards to the 40-yard line, then rest for about 20 seconds. Next, sprint 20 yards to the opposite 40-yard-line and rest for about 20 seconds. You will continue increasing the distance you sprint until your last sprint, which will be 100 yards, each time resting 20 seconds. Once you have completed all the sprints, rest about 2 minutes and then reverse the sequence so that your sprints go from 100 yards to 90 yards to 80 yards, etc., again resting 20 seconds between sprints.

Post-Workout Stretch Routine

Preseason Weeks 1 through 4: Lift 1

After the warm-ups, this workout is set up in groups of exercises. Each group has a series of exercises that should be done in order. Complete a set of each exercise in the group, then rest about 30 seconds before beginning the next set of the group. Complete all sets of the group before starting your sprints. For the sprints, use a treadmill. While standing on the outside of the treadmill, input a fairly high speed and hold on to the rails; the tread will be moving between your feet but you will not step on it yet. Once the treadmill has reached the speed you put in, support your weight with your arms and start sprinting. When you feel you are ready, let go of the rails and sprint for 20 seconds. At the end of the 20 seconds, place your hands on the rails again and jump off so that you are straddling the moving tread again. Rest for 10 seconds and repeat the 20-second sprint for the prescribed number of repetitions. If you are on a track, sprint as hard as you can for 20 seconds and then rest for 10 seconds before repeating the process. Once you are done with the sprints, rest for about 2 minutes, then move to the next group. Repeat the process for all of the groups.

T<small>ABLE</small> **14.5**
Preseason Weeks 1–4: Lift 1

Complete 2 Days per Week		Week 1	Week 2	Week 3	Week 4
Warm-up:					
Jumping Jack Intervals—3 minutes					
Dynamic Warm-up					
Band Work					
PhysioBall Work					
Complete each of the following groups, resting only after you have finished the entire group					
Group 1	Squat into Squat Jumps (15)	3 × 10	3 × 10	3 × 8	3 × 8
	Flat DB Press on a PhysioBall into Standing MB Chest Press (20)	3 × 10	3 × 10	3 × 8	3 × 8
	Lat Pull-down into Standing MB Shoulder Extension (20)	3 × 10	3 × 10	3 × 8	3 × 8
Sprints (20 seconds on, 10 seconds off)		4	4	6	6
Group 2	Leg Press into Box Jumps (10)	3 × 10	3 × 10	3 × 10	3 × 10
	Incline DB Press into Standing MB Overhead Press (20)	3 × 10	3 × 10	3 × 8	3 × 8
	Standing Cable Row into Bent-over MB Rows (20)	3 × 10	3 × 10	3 × 8	3 × 8
Sprints (20 seconds on, 10 seconds off)		4	4	6	6
Group 3	Leg Extension	2 × 15	2 × 15	2 × 10	2 × 10
	Leg Curl	2 × 15	2 × 15	2 × 10	2 × 10
	Lateral Raise	2 × 15	2 × 15	2 × 15	2 × 15
Sprints (20 seconds on, 10 seconds off)		4	4	6	6
Post-Workout Stretch Routine					

Lift 1 Exercise Explanations

Squat into Squat Jumps: If using a barbell, place bar on upper back while holding bar with your hands. If using dumbbells, hold one in each hand. If using a machine, follow the directions written on that machine. No matter which you use, stand with your feet about hip-width apart.

Squat down as if you were trying to sit down on a chair. Keep your head and chest facing forward and your abs tight. Try to lower your body until your hips are just higher than your knees and then stand back up by pushing your hips forward. Once you have finished the set of squats with weight, immediately complete a set of squat jumps (do not use weight for the jumps). Stand with your feet about shoulder-width apart. Squat down as low as you can while maintaining a straight back and keeping your chest facing forward (not down). Jump as high as you can, throwing your arms directly over your head. When you land, be sure to bend your knees and squat as low as you can. Minimize your time in this squatted position and jump up again. Continue this for the prescribed number of repetitions, making sure to land in a squat every time, including the last jump.

Flat DB Press on a PhysioBall into Standing MB Chest Press: Lying on a PhysioBall with your head and upper back supported by the ball and your hips in line with your shoulders and knees, hold a dumbbell in each hand with your arms fully extended (but not locked) above your shoulders and your hands facing toward your feet. Next, lower the dumbbells by allowing your elbows to bend, making sure to keep your hands directly above your elbows at all times. Once the dumbbells are slightly higher than your chest, press them immediately upward to return to the original position. Make sure to keep your abdominals tight the entire time. Once you have completed the prescribed number of repetitions, put the weights down and grab a medicine ball. Standing in a slightly squatted position, hold the medicine ball between your hands at chest level. Quickly press the ball directly in front of you as if you were passing it to a partner. This exercise is meant to be explosive, so try to go as fast as you can.

Lat Pull-down into Standing MB Shoulder Extension: Using a lat pull-down machine, grab the bar with an overhand grip and pull it down to the top of your chest. Make sure to pull your shoulder blades down and back and stick your chest up and forward throughout the exercise. Once you have completed the prescribed number of repetitions, grab a medicine ball. Standing in a

slightly squatted position, hold the medicine ball between your hands with your arms hanging down. Keeping your arms straight, quickly lift the ball out in front of you and then over your head. The movement should be from the shoulders only and should be in an arcing motion. Reverse the movement to return the ball to the starting position and repeat. This exercise is meant to be explosive, so try to go as fast as you can.

Leg Press into Box Jumps: Using a leg press machine, place your feet about shoulder-width apart on the platform. Bend your hips, knees, and ankles to allow the weight to descend. Once your hips and knees are at about 90°, press the weight back up to return to the original position, but do not allow the knees to hyperextend (lock out). Make sure to keep your back straight, your abdominals tight, and your hips down (do not allow your hips to roll up) throughout the entire movement. Once you have completed the prescribed number of repetitions, stand in front of a box or bench that is 12–24 inches high. Squat down and jump as high as you can, landing softly in a squat on top of the bench. Immediately step back down and repeat. Do not step forward or jump off the bench—simply step backward.

Incline DB Press into Standing MB Overhead Press: Using an inclined bench (about 45°), hold a pair of dumbbells with your hands just above your shoulders. Lower the weight to about 3–4 inches above your chest (near chin level) and then press it back up to return to the beginning position. Keep your shoulder blades pulled back and your abdominals tight throughout the movement. Also be sure to not lock your elbows at the top of the movement. Once you have completed all of the repetitions, place the dumbbells on the ground and grab a medicine ball. Standing in a slightly squatted position, hold the medicine ball between your hands in front of your chin with your elbows directly below your hands. Quickly press the ball directly above then back down to the starting position. This exercise is meant to be explosive, so try to go as fast as you can.

Standing Cable Row into Bent-Over MB Rows: Stand in front of a cable machine or cable column while holding the handle (a "V-grip" with your hands facing each other). Squat down about halfway and then, pull the handle toward your body in a rowing motion. Maintain the squat position, making sure not to go up and down with your body. Once you have finished your set of Cable Rows, immediately grab a medicine ball and complete a set of Bent-Over Medicine Ball Rows. Holding the medicine ball in your hands, bend forward at your waist with your back straight, a slight bend in your knees and your arms hanging below your shoulders. Pull the ball up toward your chest then lower it to the starting position. This is an explosive exercise so it should be done as fast as possible.

Leg Extension: Using a leg extension machine, line your knees up with the axis of rotation (there should be a hinge joint at the edge of the

pad and should be marked). Raise the weight until your legs are fully extended (it is ok to lock out on this exercise). Pause for a moment then return the weight to the original position. Be sure to keep your feet straight and your abdominals tight throughout the entire movement.

Leg Curl: Using a leg curl machine, line your knees up with the axis of rotation (there should be a hinge joint at the edge of the pad and it should be marked). Raise the weight until your heels are as close to the back of your upper legs as possible, pause for a moment, then return the weight to the original position. Be sure to keep your feet straight and your abdominals tight throughout the entire movement.

Lateral Raise: From a standing position, hold a dumbbell in each hand. With your elbows directly at your side and elbows at 90°, raise your elbows and hands together to the sides in an arc. Making sure to keep your hand directly in line with your elbow, raise your arm until everything is in line with your shoulder. At no time should you be able to see your forearm and be sure not to shrug. Pause for a second or two, and then return the dumbbell to the starting position.

Preseason Weeks 1 through 4: Lift 2

After the warm-ups, this workout is set up in groups of exercises. Each group has a series of exercises that should be done in order. Complete a set of each exercise in the group, then rest about 30 seconds before beginning the next set of the group. Complete all sets of the group, then rest about 1 minute before starting the next group. Repeat the process for all of the groups.

TABLE 14.6
Preseason Weeks 1–4: Lift 2

Complete 1 Day per Week		Week 1	Week 2	Week 3	Week 4
Warm-up:					
Jumping Jack Intervals—3 minutes					
Dynamic Warm-up					
Band Work					
PhysioBall Work					

Complete each of the following groups, resting only after you have finished the entire group

		Week 1	Week 2	Week 3	Week 4

Group 1	Alternating Lunges—20 total
	  into Lunge Jumps—20 total
	  into High Knees—20 total
	Push-ups—15
	  into Mountain Climbers—40
	Standing Row—10
		2 sets	2 sets	3 sets	3 sets

Group 2	Step-ups with a leg lift (running form)—15
	  each leg into Step-up Jumps—15 each leg
	Alternating Shoulder Press—10 each arm
	  into Mountain Climbers—40
	Pull-down—10
		2 sets	2 sets	3 sets	3 sets

Group 3	Lateral Lunges—20 total
	  into Lateral Jumps—20 total
	  into High Knees—20 total
	Push-ups—15
	  into Mountain Climbers—40
	Reverse Flyes—15
		2 sets	2 sets	3 sets	3 sets

Post-Workout Stretch Routine

Lift 2 Exercise Explanations

Alternating Lunges into Lunge Jumps into High Knees: From a standing position (do not use any weights), step forward and lunge down until both knees and the front hip are at approximately 90°. Immediately push off the front foot to return to the starting position, making sure to use the glutes and quadriceps of that leg and not the lower back. Continue alternating legs until you have completed the prescribed number of repetitions and then move immediately into Lunge Jumps. Stand with your feet about shoulder-width apart. Step forward with one foot so that you are now standing in a staggered stance. Next, squat down so that both of your knees are bent and your upper body is vertical; this is your starting position. From this position, jump straight up as high as you can and switch your feet landing in a similar position to where you started but with your feet switched (make sure you land with both knees bent). Without resting, immediately jump up again switching your feet and landing in the starting position. Try to jump as high as you can each time and minimize the time spent on the ground. Do not just simply move your feet back and forth; make sure you squat as low as you can each time. Each jump counts as one and the prescribed number is for total jumps. As soon as you have finished the set of Lunge Jumps, perform a set of High Knees, where you are running in place working on your running form.

Push-ups into Mountain Climbers: Lie face-down on the floor with your hands on the ground underneath your shoulders. Your hands should be near your armpits but about 1–2 inches below (toward your hips). Keeping your body as straight as possible, draw in your abdominals and push upward, extending your arms until they are straight but not locked out. Pause for a moment, and then lower yourself by bending your elbows until your shoulders are just below your elbows. Continue the sequence for the prescribed number of repetitions. After you finish the last push-up, immediately complete a set of Mountain Climbers. From your push-up position, bring one foot forward toward your chest and touch the ground next to the opposite knee. With a slight jump, switch your feet; the jump should be very small and quick and should not really be noticeable. The movement itself should be quick and should appear as if you are running but with your hands on the ground. Make sure you keep your abdominals tight throughout the movement.

Standing Row: From a standing position, bend forward at your waist with your back straight, a slight bend in your knees and your arms hanging below your shoulders. Pull the dumbbells up toward your chest, then lower them to the starting position.

Step-ups with a Leg Lift (running form) into Step-up Jumps: Start by standing next to a bench with one foot on the bench and the other on the floor. Stand up on the foot that is on the bench and immediately lift the knee of the leg that was touching the ground. Return the leg that you lifted to the floor under control and repeat. Once you finish the prescribed number of repetitions for that leg, immediately complete a set of Step-up Jumps before switching legs. The jumps are the same as the actual Step-ups but should be done explosively so that the knee lift forces you to jump so that you are just slightly off the bench in the air. Land under control and repeat.

Alternating Shoulder Press into Mountain Climbers: From a standing position, hold a dumbbell in each hand at about ear level. Press one dumbbell upward until your arm is relatively straight (but not locked). Lower the weight back to its starting position, then repeat for the other arm. Pull your abdominals tight to help avoid overarching your back. As soon as you have finished the prescribed number of repetitions, put the dumbbells down and go into a push-up position. Bring one foot forward toward your chest and touch the ground next to the opposite knee. With a slight jump, switch your feet; the jump should be very small and quick and should not really be noticeable. The movement itself should be quick and should appear as if you are running but with your hands on the ground. Make sure you keep your abdominals tight throughout the movement. Note that the prescribed number of repetitions is for the total number of steps, not per leg.

Pull-down: Using a lat pull-down machine, grab the bar with an overhand grip and pull it down to the top of your chest. Make sure to pull your shoulder blades down and back and stick your chest up and forward throughout the exercise.

Lateral Lunges into Lateral Jumps into High Knees: You will need an open space to perform this series of exercises, preferably a full basketball court. From a standing position, step directly out to one side, keeping your feet facing forward. The leg you just stepped with should be bent in a similar fashion to a squat, and the other leg should be fairly straight. Push with the bent leg to return to the starting position and immediately step toward the other leg. Once you have finished the prescribed number of repetitions, start performing Lateral Jumps. Jump side to side from one leg to the other, making sure you bend the leg you land on. This should be done explosively and as quickly as possible. After you have completed all of the prescribed number of Lateral Jumps, perform a set of High Knees, where you run in place, working on your running form.

Reverse Flyes: From a standing position and with a dumbbell in each hand, start by bending over from your hips but with a slight bend in your knees. Your arms should be hanging straight down and you should have your chest up and your back arched. Keeping your arms straight throughout the movement, raise the dumbbells out to your sides so that from behind you appear to make a "T." Pause for a moment and then return the dumbbells to the starting position.

Preseason Weeks 1 through 4: Conditioning 1

Conditioning 1—One day per week

Jumping Jack Intervals—2 minutes
Dynamic Warm-up

Plyometrics

Do each of the following for 10 seconds in order with no rest unless noted. Rest for 1 minute, then repeat for a total of two circuits.

1. Single Leg Hops (side to side)—left foot for 10 secs, then right foot for 10 secs
2. Prison Squat (squat with hands behind head)—hold
3. Double Leg Hops (side to side)
4. Machine Gun
5. Prison Squat—hold
6. Single Leg Hops (forward and back)—left foot for 10 secs, then right foot for 10 secs
7. Prison Squat Jumps—short jumps, work on coming off the ground quickly
8. Double Leg Hops (forward and back)
9. Machine Gun
10. Prison Squat Jumps

Circle Drill

Start by placing a cone on the field. Next, place eight cones around that cone each 5 yards from the first cone. Starting from the middle cone, move to each of the outside cones and back to the middle, working around the circle until you have moved to each of the cones. Complete the following patterns:

1. With your left foot closest to the middle cone, slide out to each cone and then back in moving clockwise, repeat this for a total of two times through resting 30 seconds between repetitions.
2. With your left foot still closest to the middle cone, again slide out to each cone and then back in but move counterclockwise, repeat this for a total of two times through resting 30 seconds between repetitions.
3. With your right foot closest to the middle cone, slide out to each cone and then back in moving clockwise, repeat this for a total of two times through resting 30 seconds between repetitions.
4. With your right foot still closest to the middle cone, again slide out to each cone and then back in but move counterclockwise, repeat this for a total of two times through resting 30 seconds between repetitions.
5. From the middle cone, sprint to each of the outside cones, then backpedal back to the middle cone, working clockwise and completing two times through resting 30 seconds between repetitions.
6. From the middle cone, sprint to each of the outside cones, then backpedal back to the middle cone, working counterclockwise and completing two times through resting 30 seconds between repetitions.
7. Sprint from the middle cone to each of the outside cones and back, moving clockwise and completing two times through resting 30 seconds between repetitions.
8. Sprint from the middle cone to each of the outside cones and back, moving counterclockwise and completing two times through resting 30 seconds between repetitions.

Suicide Sprints

Using the goal line to the 50-yard line, every 10 yards, starting from the end line, sprint to each line and back from the 10-, 20-, 30-, 40-, and 50-yard lines continuously. Repeat for a total of five repetitions, resting 2 minutes between repetitions.

Post-Workout Stretch Routine

Preseason Weeks 1 through 4: Conditioning 2

Conditioning 2—One day per week

Jumping Jack Intervals—2 minutes
Dynamic Warm-up

Plyometrics

Do each of the following for 10 seconds in order with no rest unless noted. Rest for 1 minute, then repeat for a total of two circuits.

 1. Single Leg Hops (side to side)—left foot for 10 secs, then right foot for 10 secs
 2. Prison Squat (squat with hands behind head)—hold
 3. Double Leg Hops (side to side)
 4. Machine Gun
 5. Prison Squat—hold
 6. Single Leg Hops (forward and back)—left foot for 10 secs, then right foot for 10 secs
 7. Prison Squat Jumps—short jumps, work on coming off the ground quickly
 8. Double Leg Hops (forward and back)
 9. Machine Gun
10. Prison Squat Jumps

Diagonal Cone Drill

Set up two parallel lines, one with five cones and the other with four cones; the two lines should be about 5 yards apart. Within each line, the cones should be about 10 yards apart. The easiest way to do this is to use the lines of a football field. Put one cone on the goal line, the 10-, 20-, 30-, and 40-yard lines all in one straight line. Next, make another line of cones using the 5-, 15-, 25-, 35-, and 45-yard lines. This second line should run parallel to and be about 5 yards away from the first line. It should look like the following:

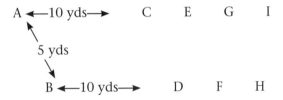

Perform each of the following patterns, resting 20 seconds between each repetition of a pattern and 1 minute before moving to the next pattern.

 1. Starting at A with your back to C, slide to each cone in order (A to B to C to D, etc.). When you reach I, sprint through A. Repeat this for a total of two repetitions.
 2. Starting at I with your back to G, slide to each cone in order (I to H to G to F, etc.). When you reach A, sprint through I. Repeat this for a total of two repetitions.
 3. Starting at A with your back to B, backpedal to B, sprint to C, backpedal to D, sprint to E, backpedal to F, sprint to G, backpedal to H, sprint to I, plant your right foot, turn to your left, and sprint through A. Repeat this for a total of two repetitions.
 4. Starting at I with your back to H, backpedal to H, sprint to G, backpedal to F, sprint to E, backpedal to D, sprint to C, backpedal to B, sprint to A, plant your left foot, turn to your right, and sprint through I. Repeat this for a total of two repetitions.

5. Starting at A, sprint diagonally to each cone (e.g., A to B to C, etc.). When you reach I, sprint through A. Repeat this for a total of two repetitions.

6. Starting at I, sprint diagonally to each cone (e.g., I to H to G, etc.). When you reach A, sprint through I. Repeat this for a total of two repetitions.

Make sure you focus on your change of direction at each cone. Strive to be as efficient as possible in your movements and minimize unnecessary steps.

Increasing/Decreasing Sprints

For this drill you will want to use a football field that has lines every 5 yards. Starting at midfield (the 50-yard line), sprint 10 yards to the 40-yard line then rest for about 20 seconds. Next, sprint 20 yards to the opposite 40-yard line and rest for about 20 seconds. You will continue increasing the distance you sprint until your last sprint, which will be 100 yards, each time resting 20 seconds. Once you have completed all the sprints, rest about 2 minutes and then reverse the sequence so that your sprints go from 100 yards to 90 yards to 80 yards, etc., again resting 20 seconds between sprints. Repeat both the increasing and decreasing sprints one more time to complete the drill, resting 2 minutes between each.

Post-Workout Stretch Routine

Preseason Weeks 1 through 4: Conditioning 3

Conditioning 3—One day per week

Jumping Jack Intervals—2 minutes
Dynamic Warm-up

Plyometrics

Do each of the following for 10 seconds in order with no rest unless noted. Rest for 1 minute, then repeat for a total of two circuits.

1. Single Leg Hops (side to side)—left foot for 10 secs, then right foot for 10 secs
2. Prison Squat (squat with hands behind head)—hold
3. Double Leg Hops (side to side)
4. Machine Gun
5. Prison Squat—hold
6. Single Leg Hops (forward and back)—left foot for 10 secs, then right foot for 10 secs
7. Prison Squat Jumps—short jumps, work on coming off the ground quickly
8. Double Leg Hops (forward and back)
9. Machine Gun
10. Prison Squat Jumps

5-yard Slides (for time)

This is a relatively simple (but not easy) drill. Place two cones five yards apart or use the lines of a football field. Starting from one cone (or line), slide to the other cone (or line) and back. Continue doing this for 20 seconds, trying to see how many total slides you can get (every time you return to the starting line counts as one slide). Rest for 1 minute then repeat for a total of five sets (each set is 20 seconds followed by a 1-minute rest). Work on your form (staying as low as you can) and your change of direction. Try to beat your highest number each time.

Full-Field Sprints

Sprint the length of a field (120 yards) as fast as you can. Immediately turn around and jog back to the beginning (should be within 45 seconds). As soon as you are at the beginning, turn and sprint the length of the field again. Repeat this for a total of four reps. Those four reps make up one set and you will do three total sets with 4 minutes of rest in between each set.

Post-Workout Stretch Routine

Good luck! Remember, you'll get out of your workouts what you put into your workouts.

15

Recruiting

Players from all over the country dream of being recruited and playing lacrosse in college. Courtesy US Lacrosse.

So, you want to play lacrosse in college . . . Whether you're a novice to the sport or you've been playing since you could walk, listen up. This chapter will introduce you—and your parents and coaches—to the athletic recruiting process for women's lacrosse players. We're going to take you through the roles of all the key people involved: college coaches, student athletes, parents, high-school coaches, club coaches, and guidance counselors.

You might want to contact college players you know to pick their brains about specific programs' atmospheres, policies, and idiosyncrasies. Other resources for student-athletes include US Lacrosse (www.uslacrosse.org) and the Intercollegiate Women's Lacrosse Coaches Association (www.iwlca.org).

It is also worth visiting the NCAA web site (www.ncaa.org) to obtain a copy of the "NCAA Guide for the College-Bound Student-Athlete." There's more information at the NCAA Clearinghouse web site (www.ncaaclearinghouse.net).

There's no one "right" way to get recruited; there's not a single scientific surefire method to getting yourself a position on the collegiate lacrosse team of your choice. The bottom line is this: Student-athletes need to take action, and take it early. Sitting back and waiting until your senior year for college coaches to court you is foolish. Even if you're one of a handful of elite players who has achieved a high level of recognition, there is a laundry list of things to do before choosing a collegiate program. All recruits need to be savvy to the process. The time to start is now.

Note: Sometimes, athletes and their parents get sucked into the hype of club lacrosse programs that "guarantee" college scholarships (for the mere price of the hundreds or thousands of dollars it costs to be involved in them). The old adage holds: If it sounds too good to be true, it is. Far too many factors are involved in the recruiting process for any club program to guarantee anything. The main determining factors when it comes to scholarship awards are a girl's academic talent and athleticism, her opportunity to be exposed to college coaches, and the changing needs of a particular collegiate lax program in any given year. What a good club program can do for an athlete is give her quality instruction in the game; provide ample opportunities to participate in tournaments, clinics, and play days where college coaches can evaluate her play; and contact college coaches on the player's behalf, putting her in touch with appropriate college programs.

GETTING EXPOSURE

It's becoming more important for high-school players to be seen early and often so they can vie for a growing but finite number of spots on college lacrosse teams. Those student-athletes who sit back and wait for schools to find them are at a real disadvantage. Basically, athletes need to be as aggressive about the recruiting process as they are when chasing down ground balls.

Most players harbor gross misconceptions about the amount of scholarship dollars available to be spent by women's lacrosse programs. There are very few "full rides" out there. A full ride is limited, by NCAA rules, to tuition, room, board, and books. It's the brass ring of scholarships. Unless you excel at a specialty position—goalie, for instance—or, unless you're a superstar complete player—keep in perspective that if you're fortunate enough to receive a three-quarter tuition scholarship, you're a big winner.

The fundamental truth is that the number of talented scholarship-level players out there is far greater than the number of scholarships available. It is extremely competitive for lacrosse players to earn scholarship dollars. Players often get caught up in the myth being proliferated by any number of misinformed parents and high school/club coaches that full rides are plentiful and that good players are entitled to them. Good is a relative term that depends on lots of things: It's simply not up to parents or high-school or club coaches whether a player is scholarship material. The decision is ultimately up to a college coach, period.

That said, it's the athlete's responsibility to get herself on college coaches' radar screens. It is not presumptuous for a student-athlete to e-mail a coach and introduce herself. It's smart. It's necessary. It's exposure.

How does a student athlete go about getting exposure? When does she start? A women's lacrosse player entering her freshman year of high school is a recruitable athlete, according to the NCAA. Nowadays, freshmen and sophomores in high school often give college coaches a head's-up about not only their playing schedules, club programs, camps, and tournaments but also their academic backgrounds. Coach Tucker says: "I think college coaches like to hear directly from the student-athletes if they're interested in a particular school. No matter who they hear from, and how many times, ultimately, a college coach needs to evaluate players in person in order to make decisions about their levels of play."

Pick a Division, Any Division

If you're a student-athlete who wants to play lacrosse in college, there's homework to be done. However, the timetables of your assignments will vary, depending on the division of the school that you're investigating. No athletic scholarship dollars are involved in the Division III recruiting process; there's need-based financial aid only. Need-based financial aid is also available from Division I and II schools, as well as athletic scholarship dollars. This section compares and contrasts the recruiting procedures of each of the various divisions.

DIVISION I

Duke, Maryland, Northwestern, and Virginia are lacrosse powerhouses among the 100-plus Division I schools that sponsor women's lacrosse. Fully funded Division I women's lacrosse programs have a total of 12 scholarships to offer over four years. Generally, this works out to offering about three per year.

Within Division I are the Ivy League Schools, eight unique institutions including Dartmouth, Yale, Harvard, and Princeton. The Ivys don't offer athletic scholarships but do offer need-based financial aid. Aid packages are supplemented by endowments.

DIVISION II

These schools are of various sizes, some fairly large and some slightly smaller. Limestone College in South Carolina, Stonehill College in Massachusetts, and West Chester University in Pennsylvania are well-known programs in this division. These may offer athletic scholarships, but many are not fully funded by the university or the college and therefore don't offer the maximum of 12 scholarships allowed by the NCAA.

DIVISION III

Middlebury, Gettysburg, College of New Jersey, Ursinus—Division III encompasses the vast majority of NCAA collegiate lacrosse programs, 241-plus and growing. These are usually smaller colleges and universities than Division I schools and offer need-based financial aid only. These institutions place an emphasis on academics and the well-rounded student-athlete.

A TO-DO LIST/TIME LINE FOR HIGH-SCHOOL STUDENT-ATHLETES

Freshman Year—Laying the Groundwork

A college-bound lacrosse player in her FRESHMAN year of high school needs to:

- Realize she's now a recruitable student athlete
- Focus on her academics—take challenging classes. Admissions directors like to see Honors and AP level classes.
- Improve her game while playing on her high-school team, playing club lacrosse, and attending camps and clinics
- Start to gather information on each of the various divisions of collegiate play: I, II, and III
- Contact college coaches by e-mail, mail, or phone and introduce herself. Let them know what high school/club she plays for and that she is interested in their school and lacrosse team.

Sophomore Year—Getting More Active

Especially if you want to play for a highly competitive program, you need to get moving during your sophomore year of high school. First, continue to focus on your academics—work hard in school. Next, write to coaches. Introduce yourself by sending your academic/athletic resume (see the sample resume at the end of the chapter). Make sure you have the coaches' names and the names of the colleges spelled correctly.

College web sites have contact information for athletic teams and coaches. US Lacrosse is another resource (www.uslacrosse.org). It never hurts to cover all the bases by phoning or e-mailing the college athletic department to confirm that the coach you're writing to is still there and to double-check proper titles and the spellings of names.

A few weeks after contacting coaches, follow up with e-mail. In the winter of sophomore year, follow up your e-mails with phone calls. Don't sit by the phone expecting a reply. Even though you're technically recruitable, a college coach cannot, according to NCAA rules, write or e-mail you until September 1 at the start of your junior year and cannot call you until July 1 following your junior year. The NCAA limits coaches' calls to one per athlete per week. However, you can call a college coach as often as you want—as long as the coach picks up the phone, you are all set!

During your preseason, invite coaches to come see you play. Send your lacrosse schedule and be up-front about your goals: Is your aim to play at the Division I level? To be a star at the Division III level? To earn a college scholarship? To be a collegiate All-American?

During the spring season, keep college coaches aware of your team's progress as well as your academic status. Let them know what classes you are taking and what summer camps and tournaments you'll be playing in. If you're starting to think that all of this one-way contact is paramount to pestering, rest assured that a few thoughtful notes, e-mails, and carefully timed calls are appropriate. Coach Tucker says: "It all boils down to the student-athlete taking responsibility for her own recruitment. Don't wait for anyone else to notice you; insist that you be noticed. If you sit back, 15 other players will get noticed before you. College coaches want evidence of self-confidence, and of the organizational skills it takes to get on their radar screens."

During the spring season and summer club season of this year, begin videotaping your play. Start collecting footage of game and tournament play. Organize these clips before you start your junior year and send highlights to college coaches.

During the summer following both freshmen and sophomore years, make unofficial visits.

Unofficial Visits

What's an unofficial visit? An unofficial visit is when a student-athlete travels on her own terms via her own means. She's permitted to contact the coach and request to meet, but she and her parents must make all the arrangements and no money can be spent on that player by the coach. The best timing of unofficial visits is during sophomore and junior years.

Unofficial visits allow you to make your own arrangements to spend time touring the campus, soaking up the atmosphere, inquiring about academic programs, and observing a lacrosse practice or game. Don't expect the coach to buy you so much as a bottle of water; NCAA rules prohibit it. (It becomes an "official" visit whenever any expense, however minor, is involved.)

It is important to have the courtesy and foresight to call ahead and let the coach know when you are visiting. That way, you'll have a better chance of actually meeting with a member of the coaching staff and watching a practice in the fall or in the spring. Observe the mannerisms, the energy, the style of play, and the types of interactions between the players and coaches. Can you picture yourself on this team?

Unofficial visits enable you to narrow down your list of schools by helping you to figure out where you'd be most comfortable fitting in, academically and athletically. *Tip:* Take a notebook on unofficial (and official) visits. Write down your personal impressions, thoughts, questions, etc. If you don't keep a record of your experiences, you'll face a hair-tearing-out time at the end of the process when everything starts running together. What did you like about the team? What are your concerns? What majors are you interested in?

Junior Year—Crunch Time

This is the busiest year, academically and recruiting-wise. It's critical exposure time and potentially, decision-making time. Continue to maintain strong academic performance. Keep in mind that a college coach is permitted by the NCAA to write to you after September 1.

If this date comes and goes without much fanfare, it is not the end of the world. If 40 envelopes

---

SO YOU WANT TO BE IN MOVIES?

Coaches won't recruit players whom they haven't seen in action, either in person or on a video. Most coaches don't expect no-holds-barred $1,500 videos with stretches of slow-mo and rock music. If you're a media savvy parent, coach, friend, or sibling of a player and can double as videographer (translation: you can stand reasonably still to catch a player in action), this usually suffices.

Some college coaches like to watch entire games on video. Most, however, prefer 10- to 12-minute clips shot during games, practices, or tournaments. The video should highlight a player's stick skills and show her scoring, picking up ground balls, and playing defense. *Important*: Make sure your name, address, and phone number are on the video. Also, identify the team you're playing for and your jersey number (or give some identifying feature, such as a red pinney, or screaming yellow socks, or pink bow).

When is it appropriate to send a video? Following sophomore spring season or summer tournament/camp seasons, or during junior season, or immediately following junior year.

are not waiting for you from an array of coaches, don't panic. Stick with your plan of action; continue to keep in touch with college coaches by writing letters and e-mails and expressing your interest during friendly phone calls.

Let's say that on September 30, you're still letter-less. Here's why: Either you haven't had the opportunity to be seen or noticed by the collegiate coaches you may be interested in, or you may not be at the level of play the college coaches are looking for. If you are shooting for a top-10 Division I program and you haven't heard from a soul, you may need to reevaluate the colleges and universities you are looking at. There are excellent programs at every level; with time and effort, you will find a good fit.

It's time for a Junior Year Reality Check. By now, college coaches have compiled solid recruiting lists. If a coach hasn't responded to you in any way, shape, or form, it's probably safe to assume you're not on his or her list. What to do? Forgive, forget, and move on. Period. Direct your energy elsewhere. Step up the communication with coaches who *are* talking to you and bring a new institution into the mix, in place of the one now in the discard pile. Coach Tucker says: "Ask someone—other than your mom—who has seen you play at club games and tourneys to be brutally candid about your potential to play at the collegiate level . . . preferably, a knowledgeable lacrosse coach. The reality is that you need to match your level of play to an appropriate program. There is a college or university lacrosse program out there for everyone. Absolutely there is. From the highest level of Division I play to a fun collegiate club team, there's something for everyone who wants to continue playing lacrosse. Your job—and it's no easy feat—is to figure out where you best fit."

During your junior year reality check, here's how to figure out where you fit, if you haven't already:

- Face the facts: If you're getting blown by regularly while you're out on the field, or your stick skills and game sense are lacking, you need to realize that all those players who dodged by you were on their way not only to goal, but perhaps to spots on college teams at higher levels, where you might aspire to play.
- Watch college lacrosse games. Pick out players and compare yourself to them. Are you as athletic? Do you think you can keep up? Can you do what she's doing on a consistent basis? Assess the level of speed, strength, and stick skills. Be honest with yourself.
- Ask your high school and club coaches for their opinions about your strength, speed, stick skills, and game sense. Where do they see you playing after high school? Brace yourself for their answers; process the information you receive and refocus your selection process.

Sophomore and Junior Days

More and more colleges and universities are holding Sophomore and Junior Days and Sophomore and Junior Weekends when they invite top sophomore and junior recruits and their families to spend the day (or weekend) on campus getting to know the school, team, and coaching staff. Sometimes, the Junior Days and Weekends are taking the place of the official visit because recruits are making decisions to commit earlier and earlier. If there is an event planned, or an overnight stay, you will be asked to pay for any meals and housing, since these are still considered "unofficial" visits. Try to attend as many Junior Days as possible to get the best handle on the schools you are interested in—remember, you need to be invited!

IMPORTANT: where some recruits might be prepared to make an early decision to attend the college of their choice, do not allow yourself to feel pressured into making a decision before you are truly sure of which college or university is the best fit for you. Recruits and their parents must spend time researching schools, doing their homework, visiting and asking lots of questions before verbally committing to a school. If you are fortunate enough to receive a scholarship offer, ask the college coach to give you and your family the time you need to make your decision. Keep in mind that once coaches fill their classes, they are finished, but if you have done your homework, and researched the schools you are interested in, you'll be just fine.

Time to Be Up-front

Here's a problem anyone would enjoy having: A highly talented student-athlete is not interested in 13 of the 20 schools whose coaches have written to her. How to handle all the unwanted attention? Coaches would prefer that she let them down sooner rather than later, either by e-mail, letter, or phone call: "Thank you so much for your interest in me; however, I am choosing to pursue other colleges." Enough said. Better to be taken off the recruiting list so the coach can focus on players who are interested in that particular institution. (*Tip:* College coaches inhabit a small, specialized world; they meet, they talk. They have numerous occasions to interact. They would much prefer to hear directly from student-athletes about their intentions rather than through the grapevine.)

How does a student-athlete know where she falls in the recruiting spectrum? Sometimes, it's not so clear-cut. Try to identify yourself using one of the three descriptions below:

Highly Recruited: You've received numerous letters and e-mails on September 1 and phone calls on July 1 from established and highly ranked lacrosse programs such as Johns Hopkins, Duke, Princeton, Virginia, Dartmouth, Maryland, Northwestern, North Carolina, etc. Coaches

have made it a point to travel to watch you play.

What to do: It can be overwhelming and exhausting to correspond with a dozen colleges and universities. Narrow down your list, graciously thanking the coaches of the schools you are not pursuing, while asking them to remove you from their lists. If your dream school is not in the mix, contact the coach there.

You have the luxury of asking sooner rather than later where you sit on a coach's list of recruits, whether or not you're a scholarship candidate, if you'll earn playing time immediately, and the probability of gaining admission into the institution. But on the other hand, be prepared for some college coaches to pressure you to make an early decision; if you don't, you might lose the scholarship opportunity or the spot on their roster. Consider this: Do you really want to spend four years playing for a coach who pushes you to make a decision before you're ready? This is why it's important to have researched all the schools on your list. On the flip side, if a coach wants to bring in only eight players, once those eight spots are gone, they are gone. So you can't help but feel that pressure—it is unavoidable.

Let the coach know if you're still doing research; ask for time if you need it. Be mindful of the number of recruits the coach wants to bring in, because when that number's met, recruiting stops for that program.

Moderately Recruited: You receive a handful of letters from various colleges—Division I, II, and III—maybe even a couple from Top 10 colleges in each division, but the majority coming from colleges and universities ranked 11 to 20 or lower. The coaches' correspondence is not as consistent as with a higher-level recruit. You receive a couple phone calls on July 1 from these same programs.

What to do: Narrow down your list to the schools you're interested in; if you're excited about a particular school that hasn't contacted you, establish a relationship, but be ready to hear, "We're sorry, but you're not on the top of our list at this time." Stay involved, however. Coaches' recruiting lists are ever-changing; as they find out which top players are not interested in their program, you may bump up closer to the top.

Minimally Recruited: You receive very little if any written correspondence on September 1 and few phone calls on July 1 despite the fact that you have established contact with colleges. You're not on the radar screen for the top I, II, or III programs.

What to do: Continue to take the initiative to promote yourself to programs at all levels—Divisions I, II, and III—where you feel you can contribute. Make sure you have a highlight video or DVD available to either resend to schools or send to new schools in order to match yourself to a program. Coaches need to see you play. If you're not able to perform at this time for top schools, be assured that there are programs that do fit your level of play. Be proactive about hunting them down. The key is to be honest with yourself about your level of play and stay motivated by the love of the game.

The chances for an athletic scholarship, in this case, may be slim, so look into other avenues for financing your education. Be open-minded about the amount of playing time you will receive. It can't hurt to ask whether or not the coach can help you in the admissions process or whether that will be left entirely to you.

Remember to mind your Ps and Qs during visits. Manners are essential, and not just as far as the head coach is concerned. Don't backtalk your mother, or disrespect your father in front of the coach or players. Behave on your unofficial and official visits. Think about it this way: Essentially, college coaches are deciding whether or not to invite you into their families. Coaches spend way too much time with student-athletes and their parents not to surround themselves with good people, rational people, kind people. Coaches recruit players who are a reflection of them and their program. Coaches have crossed recruits off of their list for bad attitudes, poor decision-making, and inappropriate behavior. Similarly, coaches have shifted their recruiting tactics if they know that parents are raving maniacs on the sidelines, berating coaches and officials, screaming at players, arguing every call and questioning decisions by the coach. None of these behaviors goes unnoticed.

Deadlines

Recruits are committing earlier and earlier. It used to be that players would wait until the beginning of their senior year, when they could make official visits, to make decisions about where they wanted to play. Now, many top high-school lacrosse players are signing as early as the spring of their junior year. If a student-athlete and her family have researched several schools, visited campuses, attended several Junior Days/Weekends, assessed the academic and athletic opportunities at these schools and come away with "the warm-and-fuzzies" from one of them, and is ready to sign, then that's great. However, if you haven't done your research and don't feel strongly about a place, don't be pressured to commit.

Do You Mind If I Ask?

If a student-athlete is being actively recruited—meaning she's getting letters, phone calls, and e-mails and the coach has made an effort to watch her play—then she is in a position to ask the following questions of coaches and expect up-front answers:

- Can I get into your school on my own? If not, can you help me gain admission to your school?

- If you can help me to gain admission, exactly what do I have to do to make this happen? (for example, score at least 1300 on the SAT or 24 on the ACT; achieve at least a 3.0 in academic subjects; send two solid letters of recommendation from academic teachers; etc.)
- Where am I on your recruiting list? I understand that you are recruiting a goalie, two defenders, and two attack players this year. Please tell me where I rank on your list.
- Why do you think your lax program would be a good fit for me? (Some areas that can be covered are coaching style, physical demands, offensive/defensive philosophy, opportunities to play.)
- Would I want to attend your school if I was not a lacrosse player? Why?

Senior Year

By this time, you will have narrowed down your list of college choices and may already have verbally committed to a college or university. Request applications for admission to those institutions and start filling them out; it's a time-consuming process that needs to be done neatly and accurately. Now, it's official visit time.

Official Visit

Following the start of classes in a student-athlete's senior year, she can make one expense-paid ("official") visit per campus, not to exceed five total official visits. Before making an official visit, the student-athlete needs to send the college coach her high-school academic transcript and a score from a PSAT, SAT, or ACT. She should inform her high school coach, club coach, and guidance counselor of her plans for official visits.

An official visit, according to the NCAA, may not exceed 48 hours. What may be covered: round-trip transportation between home or high school and campus, meals, lodging,

and complimentary admission to campus athletic events. The official visit ideally allows a student-athlete the opportunity to sit in on a class or two, watch a team practice or game, and attend a campus social event. It's also important to meet informally with the coaching staff. An overnight stay with players in campus housing should give the recruit a good picture of what it would be like to attend the institution.

Tip: Don't spend all your time with the senior student-athletes. They're not who you'll be playing with. Align yourself with freshmen and sophomores and ask lots of questions about what they like and don't like about classes, coaches, programs. Talk to someone who's in your major. Taste-test the food on campus. Write down all your impressions. *Important*: Behave yourself on your official visit; players will report back to their coaches about you.

When you have an opportunity to spend time with the coach, you might ask:

What are the practice sessions like? How many hours a day in-season?
What are the off-season requirements?
What are some of the majors of the team members?
Do athletes get preferential scheduling?
How much traveling does the team do and how often do players miss classes?
Do athletes have special housing or meals?
Do lacrosse players room together?
How many athletes travel to away games?
Which teams compete in your conference?

Be sure to take notes, because you're facing a big decision.

It's Time to Commit

When you call the coach at the school of your choice to let him or her know you'd like to commit to that program, this is known as a verbal commitment. It is essentially a verbal contract. Your next calls need to be to the other coaches who are recruiting you to thank them for all of their effort and to tell them that you have verbally committed to another program. Coaches like to hear from the student-athlete directly—not from the rumor mill. At this point, those coaches are expected to stop recruiting you.

If you've been offered a scholarship, the verbal contract is followed up by a letter of intent. Once a standard NCAA National Letter of Intent is signed, prospective student-athletes are no longer subject to further recruiting contacts and calls. Student-athletes are assured of an athletic scholarship for one full academic year. (If not for the National Letter of Intent program, a student could find her scholarship taken by a more highly recruited student only weeks or days before classes begin.) Institutions can be certain that once the student-athlete has signed a Letter of Intent, there is no need to continue recruiting for that position. (Without the program, last-minute changes by student-athletes could open up scholarships and positions on teams.) For more information about letters of intent, visit www.national-letter.org.

Coach Tucker says: "The recruiting process isn't always smooth and easy. Say a recruit commits to University X and verbally accepts a half-tuition scholarship. Two days before she is to sign the NCAA National Letter of Intent, she calls University X and says 'Oops, I've changed my mind. I'm going to University Y.' So the coach at University X has a half-tuition scholarship drop in her lap late in the recruiting game after the top recruits have committed to other schools. The coach has to wonder whether or not University Y was tampering with the recruit the entire time, and this leaves a bad taste in everyone's mouth. Then there's the flip side. A student-athlete verbally commits to College A. Trusting that she will be accepted into that university, she stops pursuing other schools and takes herself off the market. She takes for granted that she will be admitted into College A. At the 11th hour, she finds out that she didn't get accepted. Recruiting is over for the year and here's a student-athlete without a college and without a team. The coach perhaps didn't have as much influence in the admissions office as everyone assumed; something fell through the cracks. Now the recruit needs to scramble."

SOME SUGGESTIONS

For Guidance Counselors Only:

- Ask your high-school varsity coaches to identify prospective college recruits.
- Invite college coaches to visit your school.
- Meet with students collectively and individually to explain what they might do to promote themselves in athletics and academics.
- Provide to parents of all varsity athletes in the sophomore and junior class a handout of procedures and strategies that might improve student-athletes' admission to the colleges of their choice.

It's Good to Be Gracious

Drop your stick and pick up a pen. Write notes to those college coaches who recruited you. Thank the people who were involved in helping you make one of the most important decisions of your life, including the college coaches who you visited officially and players who may have hosted you on campus. Wish them luck in their seasons.

- Register Division I prospects with the NCAA Clearinghouse and distribute copies of the *NCAA Guide for the College-Bound Student-Athlete.*
- Order copies of *The National Directory of College Athletics*, men's and women's editions.
- Help student-athletes to develop lists of colleges that offer the sport they'd like to play, sorting the list according to categories of likelihood of admission: Reach, Possible, or Likely.
- Contact athletic liaison officers in the admissions offices and/or the varsity coaches of recruited student-athletes to check on the athletes' status.
- Write comprehensive letters of recommendation to be mailed with students' official transcripts.

For Parents Only:

- Encourage your daughter to assume most of the responsibility during the recruiting process; college coaches prefer to deal directly with the student-athletes themselves.
- Help your daughter to research schools by discussing the pros and cons of various choices.
- Stay informed throughout the recruiting process, as your daughter makes contacts, writes letters, arranges visits, etc.
- Be aware of NCAA rules regarding eligibility and the implications of those rules.
- Keep priorities straight and don't believe everything you hear; what is good for a coach and her team might not be what is best for your daughter.
- Determine what sacrifices, if any, you are willing to make financially and research all implications of being a scholarship athlete.
- Help your daughter to prepare for interviews with coaches, but allow her to ask the questions.

- Remember that your key roles are to support and follow-up with your daughter.
- Be aware that being recruited is not synonymous with being offered a scholarship.
- Know that scholarships can range from $1000 to a full ride—and anything in between, such as quarter- or half-tuition. A coach might choose to pay $600 a year for someone's books, if she so desires.

Coach Tucker says: "Here's a likely scenario: I tell the players I'm recruiting that I want to bring in a class of eight, ideally. I'm going to focus on recruiting 30 players in order to get eight. Of these 30, they probably all are worthy of being offered an athletic scholarship; they all could go play at a top collegiate program. However, as a coach and as a business person, I have to start with a mere handful of those student-athletes. Let's say that I offer scholarships to the top six, making this offer in July following their junior year of high school. If one turns down my offer, I'm going to go back to my list of 30 kids, a list that is organized by position and skill level. That whole group of 30 is extremely important to me. In my class of eight, I want no more than two attack players. One is going to be a goalie. Coaches are selective not only of individuals based on talent but of positions based on the needs of their programs in any given recruiting year.

"Parents and student-athletes need to keep in mind that every year, college coaches have different needs and may be looking to bring in class sizes of a very specific makeup. One particular year, we recruited only midfielders and defenders; there were a number of super-star attack players out there that year, but that's not what my program needed. So I had to turn away highly talented attack players.

"I strongly encourage our recruits never ever to put all their eggs in one basket; meaning, they shouldn't blow off eight colleges and universities and focus on only one. Everyone needs a backup school or two; at least one program to fall back on if your dream school doesn't work out for whatever reason. You can have a dream college, but do your homework with your other ones, too.

"There's a stigma attached to not being awarded a scholarship. The priority of parents needs to be: Is my daughter going to be fulfilled at this institution, academically and athletically? Is it a place my family can afford?

"What has caused the scholarship feeding frenzy? More scholarships are available than ever before because there's a new parity in the collegiate women's game: It's not the traditional powerhouse institutions in the East always dominating the game anymore—just look at the fact that Northwestern University (Chicago) won the 2005, 2006, and 2007 NCAA Division I championships. A lot more teams are having success on the field because increasing numbers of schools are offering women's lacrosse at all three levels: Divisions I, II, and III. As a result, the recruiting process is increasingly competitive. It is a business. People are working harder to offer more scholarships and develop more programs across the country—in the far north, for instance, and southwestern United States. In colleges and universities with big football traditions and basketball reputations, the focus is now on women's lacrosse—Florida, South Carolina, and Oregon, for instance.

"All this money that's up for grabs has led some to insist, and others to believe, that there exists a 'scholarship track,' a defined path for student-athletes to follow, at the end of which is a pot-o-gold: the full-ride. Even with the growth of the women's game at the collegiate level, there are more talented high-school players out there than there are excess scholarship dollars."

Multisport Athletes

Coach Tucker says: "As a lacrosse coach, I love to hear that one of my recruits plays multiple sports. In basketball, she's learning how to play defense—which translates to quick feet and good positioning on the lacrosse field. Basketball players understand our rides, because they might be used to doing full-court presses. Track and field events can help a girl develop speed and stamina. Lots of skills from a variety of sports are transferable to the lacrosse field. Solid athletes are solid athletes, no matter where and when they pick up the game of lacrosse. It's never too late to pick up the sport."

Important Factors in the College Selection Process

Location—Closer to home, farther away from home? Can I get there by car, or do I have to get on a plane? Can my family get to see me play? How far do they have to travel to do so?

Size—Do I want a school with 30,000 students, or a school with 3,000 students? Do I want to be in classes of 500, or classes of 15?

Affordability—Am I a scholarship candidate? Can my family afford to send me to the school of my choice? Is financial aid an option to help me afford college?

Surroundings—Do I like a more urban campus? Am I attracted to a more rural campus? Will I enjoy a west coast school, or a school on the east coast, or something in between?

Academics—Does the school have the major I am interested in? Will I have access to tutors if needed? Is there an academic advisor I can talk to? Are study halls offered?

Campus Life—What activities, clubs, events does the school offer their students? What do students do for fun?

Final Thoughts

The recruiting process can be exciting, stressful, fun, frustrating, enjoyable, and nerve-racking all at the same time. To effectively maneuver through this important process student-athletes want to be proactive, organized, and prepared. Utilize the resources around you: the Internet, guidance counselors, club coaches, high-school coaches, your parents, friends currently on college teams, unofficial visits, official visits, camps, clinics, US Lacrosse, the IWLCA (Intercollegiate Women's Lacrosse Coaches Association), and the NCAA.

Best of luck!

SAMPLE ATHLETIC RESUME

Sally M. Williams
122 Sunset Drive
Liverpool, New York 13090
555-612-8876 (phone)
555-612-6487 (fax)
555-365-8493 (cell)
swilliams@yahoo.com

2008 VARSITY LACROSSE SEASON—Lexington High School, Lexington, NY

Varsity starter (sophomore)—48 goals/16 assists
Ranked 5th in scoring in Class A, Section III for the season
First Team All League
Second Team All CNY (Central New York)
New York State Scholar Athlete Award

National Tournament—New York Team #1
Empire State Games—2008
Northwestern Elite 7 v 7 Tournament All-Star Team
Boston College 3 v 3 Tournament Champions

Will be attending the following tournaments/camps this summer:
Champions Challenge—Superstars Club Team Red Jersey #19
Star Spangled Banner—Superstars Club Team
XYZ Elite Camp—Liverpool, NY
Empire State Games—Central Team

2007 VARSITY LACROSSE SEASON

Varsity starter (freshman)—16 goals/26 assists
League Champions—Sectional Semifinals
First Team All League
New York State Scholar Athlete Award

Attended the following tournaments/camps:
National Tournament—New York Team #1
Empire State Games—Bronze Medal
ABC Elite camp
XYZ Winter Camp

ACADEMIC ACHIEVEMENTS

Sophomore Year—   ranked #1 in class of 750 students
                       GPA of 99 (Honors and AP courses)
                       National Junior Honor Society
                       High Academic Awards in French, English, Chemistry
                       NYS Scholar Athlete Award in Lacrosse, Field Hockey,
                           Indoor Track
                       All Honors, AP courses

Freshman Year—   ranked #2 in class of 750 students
                       GPA of 98 (Honors courses including a sophomore-year course of
                           Math A Honors)
                       High Academic Awards in French, Earth Science, Global
                           Studies, Math, and the Top 4 in Class Awards
                       NYS Scholar Athlete in Lacrosse, Field Hockey, Indoor Track
                       Earth Science Symposium Award

Other Varsity Sports

Varsity Field Hockey— Varsity starter freshman and sophomore years
                       First Team All League (Sectional Title game)
                       NYS Scholar Athlete
                       Second Team All League (Sectional Title game)
                       NYS Scholar Athlete

Varsity Indoor Track— Varsity runner freshman/sophomore year
                       Triple Jumper/Long Jumper/4×400 relay/4×800 relay
                       Second Team All League in 4×400
                       Sectional Meet—2nd place 1600 meter relay (64 sec)
                       State Qualifiers—3rd place 1600 meter relay (65 sec)

PERSONAL INFORMATION

Parents—Mike and Lucy Williams
Cell: 555-297-1497 / 555-967-0705
Williamsfamily@yahoo.com

Graduation—2009
Height—5′9½″
Weight—130 lbs
Midfielder—dominant lefty but shoots comfortably with right hand, too

High-School Coach—Eva Smith   555-413-1801 (school), 555-615-4008 (home)
Superstars Club Coach—Dennis Martin 555-386-0083

Highlight Video to follow

Thanks for your consideration!

Index